Renegotiating
Secondary School Mathematics

To Kate

Renegotiating Secondary School Mathematics

A Study of Curriculum Change and Stability

Barry Cooper

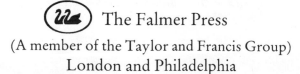 The Falmer Press

(A member of the Taylor and Francis Group)
London and Philadelphia

UK   The Falmer Press, Falmer House, Barcombe, Lewes, East Sussex, BN8 5DL

USA   The Falmer Press, Taylor & Francis Inc., 242 Cherry Street, Philadelphia, PA 19106-1906

First published 1985

Library of Congress Cataloging in Publication Data

Cooper, Barry, fl. 1975–
  Renegotiating secondary school mathematics.

  (Studies in curriculum history; 2)
  Bibliography: p.
  Includes index.
  1. Mathematics—Study and teaching (Secondary)—
Great Britain—History. I. Title. II. Series.
QA14.G7C66 1984 510'.7'12 84-18671
ISBN 1-85000-014-X
ISBN 1-85000-013-1 (pbk.)

Jacket design by Leonard Williams

Typeset in 11/13 Garamond by
Imago Publishing Ltd, Thame, Oxon

Printed in Great Britain by Taylor & Francis (Printers) Ltd, Basingstoke

Contents

		Page
Acknowledgements		vi
Foreword		vii
1	Introduction	1
2	A Framework for Understanding Subject Redefinition	5
3	The Secondary Mathematics Curriculum before Reform	35
4	The Association for Teaching Aids in Mathematics	69
5	Movements for Change: the Oxford Conference	91
6	Movements for Change: the Liverpool Conference	127
7	Developments: the OEEC, The Times and Mathematics	157
8	The Conferences of April 1961 and 'Modern Mathematics'	173
9	The Search for Resources	209
10	The School Mathematics Project and the Midlands Mathematical Experiment	235
11	Conclusion	271
Bibliography		285
Author Index		295
Subject Index		299

Acknowledgements

This book is based upon my DPhil thesis. I am especially grateful for the advice and encouragement of my supervisor, Colin Lacey, over a period of several years. I have also received helpful comments on earlier drafts of this work from Ivor Goodson, Trevor Pateman, Stephen Ball and Stephanie Cant. I would also like to acknowledge the seemingly tireless support of Maisie Carter and her colleagues in the School of Education Library at the University of Sussex. Last, but not least, I must thank all those involved with the reform of school mathematics who allowed me to interview them.

Foreword

In the late 1950s and early 1960s a major reform of the content of selective secondary school mathematics was carried out throughout Europe and the USA. In the climate of crisis which was believed to exist within the subject elements of 'modern mathematics' were introduced into new textbooks and syllabuses and much of the content of existing mathematics seemed destined to disappear. Recently, a similar perception of crisis has developed and various individuals and groups have again successfully argued that another phase of redefinition of mathematics is necessary. In particular in England the Cockcroft Report has given legitimacy to this viewpoint.

Each new wave of redefinition of mathematics has failed to adequately recognize the importance of previous reconstructions and struggles over the definition of the subject. In such a situation it is vitally important that the history of these subject events is recovered so that new initiatives can be viewed in the light of previous experience. For this reason alone it is important that the work of Barry Cooper should form a part of the newly launched series *Studies in Curriculum History*.

Cooper's work focuses on some of the key aspects of the historical reconstruction of school mathematics in the postwar period. It should be noted though that the criteria for selectivity in the account are primarily sociological and the concern above all theoretical. Hence the account does not set out to be a detailed history of school mathematics and should not be judged as such. However, we have taken the view that such work is important to a broadly conceived notion of curriculum history. At its currently pre-paradigmatic stage curriculum history needs to involve a coalition of specialist scholars. In this sense it may be worth reiterating the points made in the initial volume in the series. This argued that as well as 'primary' curriculum histories largely derived from original sources it was also important initially to develop historical sociology or 'secondary' histories, employing historical data to examine or exemplify sociological curriculum themes. At this point we added:

> the disadvantage of blurring 'curriculum history' should be more than compensated for by the potential for cross reference and dialogue between a range of curriculum scholars. At the present stage this would seem a necessary prerequisite to any attempts to formally define the 'field' of curriculum history. Territorial dialogue should precede territorial definition.

It is above all for these reasons that the series will contain books representing a range of approaches relevant to the construction of curriculum histories.

Ivor Goodson
Series Editor
University of Sussex

December 1984

1   *Introduction*

The study presented below is the outcome of only one part of my
original plan of research for a doctoral degree.[1] I came to that project as
an ex-teacher of SMP mathematics who had turned to the study of
sociology. Not surprisingly, given the experience of teaching, I was
curious about how and why the 'traditional' version of school
mathematics that I had studied as a pupil had been partially transformed
to become the 'modern maths' that I had recently taught in a comprehensive school. Furthermore, as I was becoming increasingly convinced
of the value of sociological approaches in the study of educational
change, it was perhaps inevitable that I should apply such an approach,
with its tendency to use theoretical concerns in selecting areas of
empirical investigation, in my attempt to understand some aspects of the
historical reconstruction of school mathematics. Specifically, I had
originally intended, in focusing on the School Mathematics Project
(SMP) — the most 'successful' of the mathematics curriculum projects
of the 1960s, to examine sociologically the origins and sources of a
curriculum innovation, its patterns of diffusion and its situated use in a
variety of schools. I intended to attempt to account theoretically for the
relationships between these aspects of its life by reference to the
stratified nature of our educational system.

With this aim, I started my research in these three areas. In relation
to the original innovation, I began, in 1976, to collect documentary and
interview-based data. In relation to its diffusion, I carried out, also in
1976, a questionnaire survey of the mathematics departments in the
secondary schools of two local education authorities. Finally, in 1977, I
carried out two small-scale case studies of mathematics departments in
comprehensive schools.

I had originally planned my research on the basis of having two
years as a fulltime research student but, in early 1977, after only four

terms, I was appointed to a lectureship. The limitations this imposed, coupled with my changing concerns as I came across new sources of data and realised just how little sociological attention had been paid to the sources of curriculum innovation, led me to change my plans. I decided that, in the thesis itself, I would only want — and certainly only be able — to encompass the first of my original three aims. I also developed, for comparative reasons, an interest in the Midlands Mathematical Experiment (MME), a rival to SMP in the early 1960s.

For these reasons, the following study primarily develops an account, in terms drawn from the sociologies of science, the professions and education, of the initial processes of the redefinition of English secondary school mathematics that occurred during the late 1950s and early 1960s, with particular reference to SMP and MME. Some material on the diffusion of the products of these projects and the use of those of SMP in schools is, however, presented in chapter 10.

Nevertheless, notwithstanding the analysis presented in chapter 10, the curtailment of my original plans inevitably places one major limitation on my account. In my original proposal, I had drawn on Raynor's model of the curriculum in which he distinguished 'intended' from 'transactional' curricula.[2] This study is now primarily concerned with the former and has little to say about the latter. I shall, that is, focus my attention on the processes leading up to the initial proposals, by such groups as SMP and MME, for redefinition of secondary school mathematics. While, as I have said, a gesture is made in chapter 10 towards the 'transactional' dimension of curriculum analysis, a detailed study of the situated implementation of 'modern mathematics' is beyond the scope of this book.

Taken as a study of the origins of an innovation, this work has a number of other limitations. In particular, I have had no access to the files of key individuals, as Goodson had in his study of the transformation of rural studies.[3] Mathematics is, of course, a higher status subject area than the latter. My problems of access may, therefore, have been those of any researcher studying the 'powerful'.[4] Not only this, but the particular individuals involved with SMP, the project I had originally intended to focus upon, were, by the time I began, in influential and busy positions. Thwaites — a key figure — originally declined to be interviewed; the results of a previous survey did not, as I had hoped they would, become available; individuals had been both geographically and socially mobile. My resources were limited. I had, therefore, to rely less on inside informants than I should have originally preferred, and more on records of meetings and various secondary sources. Against this, however, must be set the problem of memory over such long periods as fifteen to twenty years. One interviewee, for example, even failed to recall accurately the year of conferences he had attended.

The major consequence of these problems has been that I have had to rely on inference from limited data more often than I should have ideally liked. In chapter 10, in particular, I believe I have produced a plausible account of why SMP became the 'new orthodoxy' but, because I have had no direct access to the individuals who originally adopted SMP in their schools, it can be no more than plausible. To adequately research such an issue would, I now believe, ideally require participant observational research in schools over a longish period of time in order that the contextualized nature of such decisions and their relationship to teachers' construction of career could be better grasped. Such an approach is not, of course, available in historical work. In spite, however, of these problems, which also apply to some of my claims concerning the motives of members of the Association for Teaching Aids in Mathematics (ATAM), I believe that, by drawing on a range of sources, including some originally involved informants, I have been able to delineate some essential features of the process of redefinition.

Outline of the Book

The order of the following chapters, of which I shall provide only the briefest sketch here, is partly, though not entirely, chronological. In chapter 2, I discuss previous sociological work relevant to my research. In particular, I develop a theoretical model which is used to analyze the subsequent empirical material. In chapter 3, in order to provide a basis to which to relate the activities and results of subject redefinition to be analyzed later, I describe the highly-stratified secondary school mathematics curriculum of the mid-1950s, paying some attention to the perspectives that legitimated its differentiation. The following six chapters then provide an account of the activities of various groups of actors who began to work to redefine aspects of this version of school mathematics. In chapter 4, the contribution of the Association for Teaching Aids In Mathematics, a 'radical' rival to the much older Mathematical Association, to de-legitimating the postwar curriculum is considered. In chapters 5 and 6, the simultaneous and corresponding activities, after 1957, of an alliance of university applied mathematicians and employers of mathematics and science graduates are focused upon. In chapters 7, 8 and 9, the further activities, after 1959, of both of these groupings are analyzed, together with the increasing intervention in the social processes of redefinition of university pure mathematicians. An account is also provided of the sequence of events initiated by Thwaites, the founder of SMP, which finally ensured the at least temporary legitimacy, in the minds of many actors in educational, industrial, media and political arenas, of the 'need' for some major redefinition of selective school mathematics. In chapter 10, a comparative account is given of the early redefining proposals and activities of two projects, SMP and MME, whose members utilized the climate of opinion constructed by 1961 to promote similar new syllabuses, textbooks and recommendations for the reform of examinations.[5] In chapter 11, there follows a conclusion in which I attempt to draw out some implications of the study for the sociological analysis of curriculum change.

Notes

1 See COOPER (1982).
2 RAYNOR (1973), p. 78.
3 GOODSON (1983).
4 See BELL (1978).
5 For outlines of other projects begun in the early 1960s and which I shall be unable, for lack of space, to discuss here, see the relevant publication of the Mathematical Association (1968).

2　A Framework for Understanding Subject Redefinition

Bernstein, discussing the sociology of education in 1974, wrote:

> ... the news of much contemporary sociology appears to be news about the conditions necessary for creating acceptable news. Theories are less to be examined and explored at conceptual and empirical levels, but are to be assessed in terms of their underlying models of man and society ... We are told and socialised into what to reject, but rarely told how to create.[1]

This seemed to me, at the time, to have much truth in it — although it perhaps underestimated the extent to which most of those rejecting approaches also, in fact, offered alternative research programmes. While I was perhaps less convinced than Bernstein of the unimportance of meta-theoretical discussion, I certainly shared his concern to produce substantive sociological news. I was also convinced that the production of such news would involve the application of existing theory, which might well be modified in the process, to the area of social activity I wished to examine and understand.

For this reason I began my work on two fronts. I began collecting relevant documentary material and carrying out interviews with those who had participated in the events leading to those changes in what counted as school mathematics that I wished to explain. At the same time, I began to study sociological work in a number of related areas in order that I would be able to draw on previous work in producing a theoretical model with which to commence analysis of the data I was collecting. In practice, of course, the two activities interrelated, affecting one another in various ways.[2] My developing theoretical understanding began to suggest that some empirical work would be more fruitful, with respect to explanation, than other possible alternatives. Similarly, as data were collected, sujected to preliminary analysis, and leads followed

5

up, I realized the possible fruitfulness of new areas of theoretical work.

For these reasons, many published accounts of sociological research, in so far as their form suggests that a model or theory was developed and then independently used and/or tested in the investigation of separately collected data, are inevitably somewhat misleading. The practice is usually much less tidy. This book, however, follows this common presentational practice. A working model is apparently derived from a review of relevant literature, applied in the analysis of empirical material, and then discussed again in a conclusion. This presentational device, as I have noted, tends to underplay the ways in which the nature of the empirical material itself affected the choice of literature, my reading of it and the development of the model. It also underplays the extent to which a model is developed during the writing-up of a piece of research, having often remained partially implicit during the period of data collection and initial analysis. It can also mislead by apparently setting 'neutral' theory-free data against theory. I certainly do not wish to appear to claim that either my selection of data or its forms of analysis were unaffected by my developing theoretical concerns. They were and, in my opinion, always will be. Such is the nature, in the opinion of many philosophers, of both the natural and the social sciences.[3] Those seeking explanations inevitably search where they expect to find. It is the role of criticism to alleviate the possible negative consequences of this intimate relationship between theory and description.

Below, therefore, after critically discussing a range of relevant literature, I present my working theoretical model. I term it model to stress that it makes general claims about what type of explanation we should seek for changes in what counts as school mathematics. In presenting such a model, rather than providing a list of hypothetical empirical generalizations of the type a hypothetico-deductive philosopher of science might demand, I am following a view of explanation which is gaining increasing support within both philosophy and sociology. Here the belief is that observed events and their correlations are the superficial consequence of underlying social structures and relationships. The goal of the social scientist is to provide an increasingly adequate account of these underlying levels of social reality and, in doing so, to explain the events under examination.[4] Hence my model attempts to set out the social relationships and interests whose interaction produced change in what counted as school mathematics. It will be seen that its nature has also been partly motivated by my concern, shared with Bernstein and many others,[5] to transcend the limitations of the structure/action dichotomy in social theory.

I draw on three main areas of previous sociological work: the sociologies of science, the professions and education. As I have stressed, my ongoing analyses of empirical material directed my interpretation and use of this resource in a number of ways. To this extent, therefore, the model is grounded in both an examination of previous substantive theory and my own empirical work.

Perspectives from the Sociology of Science

Since the late nineteenth century, the nature of the mathematics practised in universities has undergone many changes. There has not been any simple paradigm shift. Rather 'mathematics', by 1960, consisted of various subgroups working, to some extent, within different 'cognitive and technical norms',[6] on different orders of phenomena and different types of problems. What had changed, with some exceptions — such as computing — was the relative numerical strength and status within the overall discipline of groups carrying particular norms.[7] The main purpose of this section is to discuss a set of concepts capable of capturing this complexity. Or, to put it differently, I shall attempt to outline some features of the academic subject considered as a social phenomenon.

The two major perspectives available in the literature respectively emphasize either distinctive conceptual frameworks (for example, Hirst, Kuhn in his early work[8]) or relatively boundaried social and communicational networks (for example, Mullins, Mulkay, Kuhn in his later work[9]). These are often confused. As an example of this within the sociology of education, we can examine Bernstein's article on the 'classification and framing' of educational knowledge.[10] He begins, referring implicitly to Hirst's claim[11] that there exist logically distinct forms of knowledge:

> Irrespective of the question of the intrinsic logic of the various forms of public thought, the *forms* of their transmission, that is their classification and framing, are social facts.[12]

Here, he leaves open his own position on Hirst's views. Later in the article, however, we find him distinguishing 'pure' and 'impure' versions of his specialized collection code in terms of whether GCE 'A' level subjects are drawn or not from 'a common universe of knowledge'.[13] Nowhere is it made clear whether this commonness derives from distinctive intrinsic logics or varying densities of social interaction between subject practitioners.

A similar ambiguity has been a feature of Kuhn's work on science.[14] It is possible, by concentrating attention on Kuhn's concept of a paradigm, to interpret his work on revolutions in science as being primarily concerned with ideas rather than the social structure of science. This concept of a paradigm has been usefully summarized by Esland:

> It contains the prior knowledge, the projected problems, the frameworks of meaning, criteria of truth and validity; it has assumptions 'as to how entities of the universe interact with each other and with the senses'; and it has a system of methodological rules which can be legitimately employed to find solutions.[15]

A non-structural reading of Kuhn would see mature subjects as definable in terms of members' adherence to such shared ideas. Such an emphasis on the ideational may represent an adequate reading of the original edition of Kuhn's major work, but he made important modifications to his position in the second edition. These served to add a more explicitly sociological dimension to his work. In the postscript to this edition he wrote:

> The term 'paradigm' enters the proceeding pages early, and its manner of entry is intrinsically circular. A paradigm is what the members of a scientific community share, *and*, conversely, a scientific community consists of men who share a paradigm. Not all circularities are vicious ... but this one is a source of real difficulties. Scientific communities can and should be isolated without recourse to paradigms; the latter can then be discovered by scrutinizing the behaviour of a given community's members. If this book were being rewritten it would therefore open with a discussion of the community structure of science....[16]

However, while this helps to clarify this important issue it raises the further problem of how to conceptualize the broad outlines of this structure. Esland has pointed to the usefulness, in this respect, of the work of symbolic interactionists on the professions. He recommends Bucher and Strauss' model of the profession as:

> loose amalgamations of segments pursuing different objectives in different manners, and more-or-less delicately held together under a common name at a particular period of history.[17]

He goes on to argue that the process of integration of school subjects might also be helpfully conceptualized in these terms if we equate subjects and their associations with segments. More recently, Goodson has developed this suggestion and considered the consequences for the fate of a particular Environmental Studies 'A' level proposal of there being competing segments *within* the subjects of geography and biology.[18]

A major problem, however, in a study of the kind presented here, is that without carrying out a major and expensive sociometric study of the subject of mathematics in advance, it is difficult to develop very clear ideas on the likely nature of interested and effective segments within the subject. It is possible, however, to obtain some help of a general nature from recent empirical studies in the sociology of science.

Crane, for example, in her *Invisible Colleges*, having discussed the many studies utilizing a 'citation' method for identifying scientific communities, concluded:

> Science as a whole appears to consist of hundreds of research areas that are constantly being formed and progressing through ... stages of growth before tapering off.[19]

It must be stressed, however, that this conclusion is largely based on analyses of the communication and use of research findings. An obvious difficulty therefore arises in attempting to utilize such conclusions in the analysis of particular events in the history of a subject, where both the communication patterns and the boundaries of effective networks are likely to change through time in relation to the nature of these events.

This is brought out clearly in work on innovation in science. Griffith and Mullins, reviewing work on innovations in physics, biology, mathematics, psychology and sociology, show how, from within the relatively loose network of 'normal science', well-defined and more structured 'coherent activist groups' — each a carrier of a 'distinctive approach with broad theoretical implications' — form to act as the promoters of major conceptual reorientations.[20] Another important issue therefore arises for research into school subjects. As Goodson's work also shows, it is not possible to assume, as some writers have done within the sociology of education,[21] that within a subject there exists a consensus on cognitive norms. But neither, of course, should we assume that subgroups within a subject necessarily differ in this respect. Some subgroups will presumably be distinguishable not by disagreement on theoretical approaches but rather in terms of the object of their study. The 'political arithmetic' tradition, for example, exists within both the sociology of education and the sociology of health and illness. Furthermore, as I indicated earlier, one might expect various clusters of normally competing subgroups to come together, at least temporarily, to resist a threat to their general interest — as 'mathematicians' for example.

I have now outlined the general approach I wish to operate with in relation to academic subjects and, by extension, subject associations. Subjects will be regarded not as monoliths, that is as groups of individuals sharing a consensus both on cognitive norms and on perceived interests, but rather as constantly shifting coalitions of individuals and variously sized groups whose members may have, at any specific moment, different and possibly conflicting missions and interests. These groups may, nevertheless, in some arenas, all successfully claim allegiance to a common name, such as 'mathematics'.

It still remains to relate the above discussion of mainly university subjects and research to the problem of scientific education, particularly at school level. I want to argue its relevance to the latter on two grounds. First, it is difficult to imagine the possibility of understanding major reform in a school subject such as mathematics, which is very much alive in university and other settings, without a consideration of the values, interests and actions of non-school-based practitioners. As Musgrove, one of the first British sociologists to urge study of the school curriculum, wrote:

> [Sociology] will illuminate our understanding of the curriculum by revealing school subjects not simply as intellectual, but as social systems ... [The sociologist] will examine subjects both within the school and within the nation at large as social systems sustained by communication networks, material endowments and ideologies. Within a school and within the wider society subjects are communities of people, competing and collaborating with one another, defining and defending their boundaries, demanding allegiance from their members and conferring a sense of identity upon them.[22]

Secondly, and more specifically, the nature and purpose of scientific and mathematical education make it almost inevitable that any attempt to account for the transformation of the secondary mathematics curriculum will centrally involve reference to university mathematicians' practices and interests. This is simply because of the nature of the feeder relation between selective school and university science and mathematics. Kuhn's work is again relevant here. He has argued that initial education in science is primarily socialization into a paradigm.[23] More specifically, discussing this in the American context, he stressed that such education is carried on through the device of the textbook:

The single most striking feature of this education is that, to an extent totally unknown in other creative fields, it is conducted entirely through textbooks. Typically the undergraduate and graduate student of chemistry, physics ... acquires the substance of his field from books especially written for students. Until he is ready, or very nearly ready, to commence work on his own dissertation, he is neither asked to attempt trial research projects nor exposed to the immediate products of research done by others, that is to the professional communications that scientists write for each other. There are no collections of 'Readings' in the natural sciences. Nor is the science student encouraged to read the historical classics of his field — works in which he might discover other ways of regarding the problems discussed in his textbook, but in which he would also meet problems, concepts and standards of solution that his future profession has long since discarded and replaced.[24]

He goes on to note that, in periods of 'normal science', that is, when any particular community shares a set of cognitive and technical norms, while competing textbooks may differ in respect of level of difficulty and pedagogic emphasis, they do 'not in substance or conceptual structure'.[25] Neither do they describe the sorts of problems that a professional scientist may be expected to solve and offer a variety of techniques available for this work. Rather:

these books exhibit concrete problem solutions that the professional has come to accept as paradigms, and they then ask the student, either with a pencil and paper or in the laboratory, to solve for himself problems very closely related in both method and substance to those through which the textbook or the accompanying lecture has led him. Nothing could be better calculated to produce 'mental sets'.[26]

Textbooks, however, do change. As is well-known, Kuhn sees scientific advance as punctuated by periods of 'scientific revolution' in which paradigms displace one another. And, since he sees textbooks as the major educational device for socializing 'successors' into the consensus that, in his terms, comprises a paradigm during periods of normal science, it follows that 'one characteristic of scientific revolutions is that they call for the rewriting of science textbooks'.[27] This statement, which appears as an aside, does not even hint at the possible conflict this might be expected to produce within a subject consisting of groups carrying different paradigms. In relation to selective school textbooks in particular, the additional complication arises that the scientists (or mathematicians) practising within any new paradigm or set of norms may have few immediate allies amongst the school-based scientists (or mathematicians) teaching their successors and, possibly, writing textbooks. The extent of this problem will, presumably, be largely a function of the age structure and educational experiences of the latter professional group.

Furthermore, and perhaps more importantly, specific occupational interests may be involved. Hagstrom and others have argued that contributions to science should be seen as gifts in exchange for recognition.[28] While this functionalist version of exchange theory has been rightly criticized,[29] we might at least hypothesize that many subject practitioners who owe their prominence and positions to contributions made within previously dominant paradigms will resist new ideas which threaten to undermine their work. While there is evidence that prominent scientists do sometimes successfully move from one research area to another,[30] this is likely to be much more difficult in the case of any major paradigmatic change (involving, as it would, something akin to 'conversion'). As the physicist Planck, perhaps with some exaggeration, wrote:

> A new scientific truth does not triumph by convincing its opponents and making them see the light, but rather because its opponents eventually die, and a new generation grows up that is familiar with it.[31]

Or, following Kuhn, it might be more accurate to write is *made* familiar with it.

As well as professional status, other more specifically material interests are at stake in these disputes. In the English university system, resources, to a certain extent, become available as a function not merely of prominence but also of student numbers (the two are not, of course, unrelated). Academics might well be seen, therefore, as having a material interest in their version of their subject being on the school curriculum in order that the school generates sufficient and, preferably, well-socialized potential students. (They may also be genuinely concerned to advance intellectual work in their subject. There is no necessary contradiction here.) Presumably, therefore, subgroups working within different norms can be expected to make different claims on the school curriculum. The extent and nature of this intra-subject conflict are, of course, empirical questions but what would seem to follow from these theoretical considerations is that both the possible rewriting of a school textbook for potential university students and its insertion into school practice are likely to be issues that arouse considerable conflict within a subject community (and, in so far as its socialisées work outside of the educational system, also outside of it). That this is the case empirically for mathematics will become clear in the course of this study.

To summarize, I am arguing that, given the above features of the scientific community, scientific change and scientific education, any textbook or syllabus of the sort produced by such projects as SMP and MME — to be used in schools supplying a large proportion of potential university students — is likely to be best understood as the result of a process of political conflict and negotiation both within the subject and between groups within the subject and external interest groups. The latter, particularly industrial and commercial employers of graduate labour, will, in fact, be seen to have played an important role in relation to the transformation of the secondary mathematics curriculum. The related issue of 'resources', which is central to understanding the limits of industrial and commercial influence on curriculum change, will be considered towards the end of this chapter. I want now to move on to discuss some sociological writing which concerns itself specifically with the school curriculum.

The Sociology of the Curriculum: the Work of Young, Bernstein and Esland

In an article published in 1973 Davies noted that much sociological work on educational innovations had involved no element of study of the sources of innovation:

> There are . . . two problems at the level of innovation which are rarely examined; the sources of the innovations, and the higher institutional decision-making processes which determine which innovations should be filtered through to schools and other educational institutions.[32]

It is with these related problems, though mainly the first, that I am concerned here. Roughly contemporaneously with Davies' paper, a number of more-or-less theoretical papers appeared having as a major focus the understanding of these and related problems. I shall concentrate here on the seminal work of Young, Bernstein and Esland which appeared, in 1971, in the collection *Knowledge And Control*.[33] In particular, I shall focus on the relevance of their analyses to my project here, that is to the understanding of change within one subject over a period of a few years.

M.F.D. Young

Young was particularly concerned that sociologists were too willing to take educators' problems for research topics and not ready enough to make sociological problems.[34] Specifically, he argued that the school curriculum, previously relatively neglected, and implicitly therefore, regarded as worthwhile, should become a focus of sociological attention:

> ... education ... is a selection and organization from the available knowledge at a particular time which involves conscious or unconscious choices. It would seem that it is or should be the central task of the sociology of education to relate these principles of selection and organization that underly curricula to their institutional and interactional settings in schools and classrooms and to the wider social structure.[35]

This programmatic statement led to much debate in the early 1970s[36] but, by 1975 — when I conceived this study — there were still few empirical studies available that had been informed by such a position. Young himself had noted the need for such work, and implicitly recommended it:

> We have had virtually no theoretical perspectives or research to suggest explanations of how curricula, which are no less social inventions than political parties or new towns, arise, persist and change, and what the social interests and values involved might be.[37]

In relation to the possibility of such studies, one major problem with Young's contribution is that he did not develop, in spite of his central concern with the stratification of knowledge, a clear theoretical position with respect to 'the wider social structure' and the 'social interests and values involved'. Rather, he operated with a somewhat sketchy model of 'interest groups' and 'dominant groups' and an implied class structure. He wrote, for example:

> Those in positions of power will attempt to define what is to be taken as knowledge, how accessible to different groups any knowledge is, and what are the accepted relationships between different knowledge areas, and between those who have access to them and make them available.[38]

The problem here, however, is that most sociologists, whether Marxist, Weberian or even functionalist, would be willing to accept that such a relationship between 'positions of power' and knowledge definition exists. The important questions, though, are concerned with different views of who is in positions of power, what the bases of the latter are, and the degree of success of attempts at control. I want to argue that, until we have available more empirically-based studies of curriculum change orientated to examining these particular issues, we will be unable to develop adequate answers to these questions. In the absence of such evidence for particular claims, for example, Young moved about during his essay from an emphasis on society-wide dominant groups, such as social classes, as the final arbiters of knowledge definition to an emphasis on the universities. Such questions — basically concerning the degree of relative autonomy of the educational system — cannot be settled by theoretical work alone. Neither should we assume that any final answers will be available. Rather, the extent of educational autonomy is likely to be some function of the socio-historical context, if that is not self contradictory.[39] Sociologists needed to move, therefore, in the early 1970s, away from general theoretical concerns towards the analysis of specific examples of curriculum change.

Several of the problems arising from Young's emphasis on a very general level of analysis can be illustrated by a consideration of his following remarks:

> Further, that as we assume some pattern of social relations associated with any curriculum, ... changes will be resisted in so far as they are perceived to undermine the values, relative power and privileges of the dominant groups involved.[40]

While this suggests some useful avenues for research, a number of points must be raised which may serve to indicate that, as formulated, and because of its generality, it provides only blunt instruments for this purpose. First, although the statement clearly does allow for the possibility, its emphasis on resistance to change does tend to deflect our concern away from the possibility of changes originating within the 'dominant groups' (however defined). Secondly, it perhaps seems to suggest that, within any particular dominant group (for example, the universities), there will be agreement on values and perceived interests. This, as I argued in the last section, should not be assumed even in the case of 'subjects' and is unlikely, therefore, to be the case for more broadly defined groups of actors.

One reason for these forms of weakness appearing in Young's analysis may have been his deliberate concentration on rather gross formal characteristics of knowledge rather than on curriculum 'content'. His claim that high status knowledge (in England) is characterizable in terms of certain formal criteria brings this out clearly. He described the 'dominant characteristics of high status knowledge', which he hypothesized are the 'organizing principles underlying academic curricula' thus:

> These are literacy, or an emphasis on written as opposed to oral presentation; individualism (or avoidance of group work or cooperativeness) which focuses on how academic work is assessed and is a characteristic of both the 'process' of learning and the way the 'product' is presented; abstractness of the knowledge and its structuring and compartmentalising independently of the knowledge of the learner; finally and linked to the former is what I have called the unrelatedness of academic curricula, which refers to the extent to which they are 'at odds' with daily life and common experience.[41]

This quote, and the emphasis it represents, tend to deny the possible importance of research which concentrates equally or alternatively on the non-formal, or substantive, characteristics of school knowledge, such as syllabus or textbook content. If we assume too readily, as Young seemed to, that only those changes in the 'organizing principles' of curricula that seem to reflect major changes in the structure of social domination should be studied, we shall have unnecessarily restricted the scope of the sociology of the curriculum before we have any clear idea of what its explanatory potential might be. This is, of course, a matter of emphasis. As Davies noted, changes in 'content' are usually associated with changes in pedagogy, views of the child and of the purposes of education.[42] But if, as is likely, SMP, MME, and similar projects have led to substantial changes in the content of secondary school mathematics for some pupils but to relatively little pedagogic change, then it is presumably as important to account for the former as the latter. Young's ideas may be useful here in accounting for the lack of major pedagogic change, as well as possibly for SMP's eventual success — in terms of its relative lack of challenge to basic 'organizing principles'. But, as formulated, that is, very generally, and especially because of his somewhat undifferentiated view of subjects and the universities, his ideas are likely to be of much less help in accounting for the specifics of syllabus change. It is, of course, possible to argue from the remarks quoted earlier that any changes in content must be acceptable to 'dominant groups' to succeed. But this is only a very general statement which, while it may lead to more useful specific hypotheses, in itself accounts for little. Furthermore, in the absence of some well-grounded definition of dominance, a severe danger of producing merely tautologous statements exists. Besides which, some 'dominant groups' may approve, while others do not.

The major point here is that Young, in his concern not to take academic knowledge as given, underemphasized the importance of attempting explanations of change in the particulars of academic knowledge as well as in its 'organizing principles'. That such a study, given the stratified nature of our educational system, and the way in which any major proposal for change tends to open up a general discussion in which all those concerned with differing aspects of it become involved, is also likely to concern itself with more formal aspects of knowledge I take as given. For example, a possible shift in content from 'quadratic equations' to 'linear programming' is more than just a change in content. For some pupils, it is also a shift from 'pure' to 'applied' mathematics and, hence, represents a possible move away from 'unrelatedness' to one (very restricted) version of 'daily life' in Young's terms. But Young's programme, which was drawn up without the benefit of much relevant empirical work being available, failed to take account of the complexity of this. Furthermore, in relation to the question of the criteria for the status of knowledge, and perhaps again partly because of his lack of empirical material, Young, although he made some relevant remarks,[43] also failed to consider adequately the possibility of there being major between-subject (for example, classics versus engineering) and within-subject (for example, pure versus applied mathematics) differences.

A final reason why I find Young's formulation of his analysis too general for my purpose relates to the periods of time considered. His concerns were, to some extent, with change over much longer periods of time than were mine and, hence, many things that he wanted to explain, such as actors' constructs of 'ability', I wanted rather to take as unexplained givens in order to utilize them as elements of the explanation of the transformation of the mathematics curriculum over a period of a few years. Young's relativizing does not only lead to an 'infinite regress' problem with respect to questions of validity but also, more mundanely, with respect to explanation. The time periods involved in changes in 'dominant' constructs of 'ability' are much longer than those involved in changes in the content, at least, of mathematics and science curricula. To explain, we have to take some beliefs and values as given even while assuming that, given another study with different organizing concerns, they might themselves be explained in terms of another level of reality and thus, in this sense, be relativized.

Some of the problems associated with Young's programme were demonstrated in his nevertheless useful paper on the Schools Council.[44]

Discussing what he termed 'academic expertise' projects, distinguishable from 'good practice' projects, he wrote:

> the 'academic expertise' style characterizes those projects, particularly in the sciences and mathematics, which draw on university 'subject experts', who start with a fairly explicit idea of 'what ought to be learnt'. In these projects the fundamental 'structure' of 'what is to learnt' is not in question, because the academic experts involved in the project are also in a position to be the definers of this 'structure'.[45]

Here we can see the working out of his assumption, in the absence of detailed empirical work, of there being a substantial degree of consensus within the subject. In the case of mathematics, where eventually one of the original university-based organizers of the conferences which culminated in the production of SMP could later attack the project in an article entitled 'On the enfeeblement of mathematical skills by "modern maths" and by similar soft intellectual trash in schools and universities', this would seem to have been a dubious assumption.[46] Had Young been working with a more adequate notion of mathematical and scientific subjects, he might not have made it. But there are other weaknesses in the article. He wrote, for example, of the Schools Council:

> it is an agency which has spent £4.3 million since its inception in 1964, at present spends on both 'projects' and administration £1 million a year, and increasingly as the Nuffield Foundation has withdrawn from research in education has become the *only* source of funds for curriculum development projects in primary and secondary schools.[47]

This was written in 1972, and SMP gained its industrial support in the early 1960s, but, nevertheless, in an article concerned with 'the politics of educational knowledge' and specifically referring to subject definition in mathematics and science, it is strange to find only a passing reference to this possible source of funds and control.[48] It is perhaps his overemphasis on theory and lack of attention to evidence that accounts for this omission. Empirical studies are needed to establish possible sources of funds and their consequences. The Schools Council is (or rather was) not the only possible source and, given this, an examination of the relationships of projects to other sources is presumably a necessary part of any attempt to increase our understanding of the ways in which 'dominant groups' in an 'institutional order' negotiate preferred changes.

Notwithstanding these criticisms, Young did make a number of useful suggestions in the article as to how to go about such research. For example, and this is a suggestion I shall follow in this study:

> Clearly one would need to know something of the educational background and ideas of participants in various conferences and working parties — as well as the characteristics of the Council as a particular institutional context ... in order to begin an explanation of what is debated and what is not, and the possible meaning of such debates in terms of maintaining academic legitimacies.[49]

Although I would prefer 'cognitive and technical norms' to the looser 'legitimacies', this is the approach I shall take here in mainly focusing my research around those conferences during the late 1950s and early 1960s in which the ground rules for the reform of school mathematics, by SMP and others, were partially negotiated. In so doing I am accepting Young's claim, drawn from Bourdieu's work, that one major concern of the sociology of the curriculum must be a study of how 'various kinds of intellectual activity gain and maintain intellectual support'.[50] A study of conferences, and their articulation with the press, Parliament, and so on, will hopefully enable some light to be thrown on these issues.

Finally, it can be agreed that Young's stress in this article on the importance of studying the relationship of 'types of child and types of knowledge' is, in the context of our stratified social and educational system, well-chosen if we wish to advance the traditional concern of the sociology of education with social class.[51] It remains his major contribution to have made explicit the long-standing implicit concern of the sociology of education with the relation of social class to the curriculum.

It has been my main criticism of Young's work that, while seminal in doing much to open up the possibility of a conflict-orientated sociology of the curriculum, he has not adequately developed his concepts of the 'subject', 'dominant groups', the 'institutional order', and so on. Below I shall argue that similar criticisms can be developed of Bernstein's writings on the curriculum.

Bernstein on the Curriculum

I shall discuss, as an example of Bernstein's work on the curriculum on which subsequent papers build, the paper on the classification and framing of educational knowledge.[52] Consider this opening quote from the article:

> How a society selects, classifies, distributes, transmits and evaluates the educational knowledge it considers to be public, reflects both the distribution of power and the principles of social control.[53]

This reified usage might be considered useful as shorthand in an introductory remark. Unfortunately, however, the argument of the paper as a whole is constructed in such a way that it never moves beyond this inadequate conceptualization of curriculum determination. As Gibson, and earlier Pring, have both noted, it is not clear that Bernstein is not merely redescribing rather than explaining aspects of curriculum and schooling.[54] Gibson shows, in particular, that Bernstein's uses of his central concepts of classification and framing, especially of the latter, are often merely tautologous and that, perhaps more importantly, he allows causal efficacy to concepts which are arguably no more than ideal-typical redescriptions of what they are intended to explain. I would argue that these problems, and others in the work, result fairly directly from Bernstein's adherence to a paradigm (derived from Durkheim's *The Division of Labour in Society*[55]) that includes no adequate theorization of social conflict and structure and which, in fact, emphasizes social consensus.

Particular problems arise from Bernstein's reliance on Durkheim's typology of mechanical and organic solidarity.[56] First, Durkheim was concerned with intra-societal differences of the order traditional versus modern through time, and one would not therefore expect that the same conceptual scheme would be useful for analyzing changes within one of Durkheim's societal types. Secondly, like Young's, the work becomes rather formal in orientation. While major changes in curriculum structure are treated, however inadequately, changes in content and pedagogy within subjects are relatively neglected. Both these features render the model developed of little help in the type of study of curriculum change intended here.

Possibly related to the above is Bernstein's somewhat monolithic view of subjects, something he shares with Young. His discussion of socialization into subject loyalty fails to raise the possibility of within-subject debates and differences.[57] The latter are ignored in the article.

To summarize the argument so far, it is precisely Bernstein's concern with 'underlying principles which shape curriculum, pedagogy and evaluation'[58] which renders his model not especially helpful here. The treatment of curriculum only in terms of its structure (that is relations between contents) leads to a neglect of the 'principles' underlying the reproduction and/or transformation of content and pedagogy within subjects. For example, while it might be useful to demonstrate that the relative status of mathematics has increased over the past 150 years (as we probably could in terms of his simple but useful indicators[59]), we would also need to examine what the various versions of mathematics over this period comprised, especially as therein might lie a part of any explanation of the changes identified. Similarly, strong classification may produce, or at least be associated with, 'specific identities' for learners but, unless we know more of the nature of these (possibly multiple) identities within subjects, we will remain in no position to be able to understand the relationships between subject communities and external interest groups (a concern both of Bernstein in ensuing papers[60] and of mine here). For such purposes, his concepts are of little use. He might reply, of course, that he sees the 'structure of educational knowledge' as the distinctive focus of the sociological study of the curriculum[61] and, indeed, his work has initiated much debate in that area.[62] But this emphasis, quite arbitrarily, ignores much else that might be sociologically accounted for — not just the within-subject changes I have referred to above — but also the ways in which subjects are removed from, and added to, the school timetable. To study these issues we shall need to focus on the relationships between groups of actors with various perceived interests; this aspect of subjects Bernstein's work tends to ignore. He may be correct in claiming that his paper attempts to show 'the relationships between a particular symbolic order and the structuring of experience'[63] but it certainly does not, as it stands, take much further our understanding of the full range of meanings of 'how a society selects ... educational knowledge'. The 'distribution of power and the principles of social control' would have had to have received more, and different, analysis to have provided this.

Similar weaknesses, which I have no space to detail here, characterize his subsequent papers on the curriculum.[64] My position on Bernstein's work will be, therefore, that while some of his insights may prove of value in this study, his overall stress on free-floating 'principles' and his tendency to present tautologies as causal propositions make it unlikely that I shall be able to draw on his theoretical work in developing my working model. These problems are compounded by his neglect of within-subject changes.

Esland on the Curriculum

Esland's contribution to *Knowledge And Control*, already referred to, is based around the insight that subjects have careers.[65] Because of this, it is probably the most useful piece in that collection for my purposes. Although it is primarily concerned with developing a programme for researching the legitimation of integrated studies, the operational model developed, drawing on the interpretive sociologies of knowledge of Schutz, Berger and Luckmann,[66] on Kuhn's analysis of science,[67] on Bourdieu's work on cultural legitimation,[68] and on the symbolic interactionist work on the professions,[69] focuses on issues that will be central in this study of subject redefinition. One central assumption is simply that subjects must not be regarded as 'givens':

> It is ... necessary not to consider subjects as givens, but to analyse what a teacher thinks a subject is. The knowledge which a teacher thinks 'fills up' his subject is held in common with members of a supporting community who collectively approve its paradigms and utility criteria, as they are legitimated in training courses and 'official' statements. It would seem that teachers, because of the dispersed nature of their epistemic communities, experience the conceptual precariousness which comes from the lack of significant others who can confirm plausibility. They are, therefore, heavily dependent on journals, and, to a lesser extent, conferences, for their reality confirmation. The content and ideologies of these would be important data.[70]

That Esland developed a more adequate model of the subject than either Young or Bernstein becomes clearer still in his development of his research programme, in which he stresses the differentiated nature of subjects. He pursued this through the concept of the actor's perspective, maintained by 'plausibility structures'.[71] Because of the usefulness of the former concept here, I shall reproduce in full his development of it:

> It is assumed that all teachers have a 'subject' and a pedagogical perspective of varying degrees of theoretical consistency and clarity.... [These] perspectives are meant to represent the *constitutive categories of thought* through which a teacher understands his occupational world ... [and] ... can be represented in the following way:
> A *Pedagogical Perspective*
>   1 *Assumptions About Learning*

a) Which psychological theories — explicit or implicit — are dominant?

b) What assumptions are held about the qualities of responses from pupils which indicate whether learning is taking place?

c) How does the teacher define favourable outcomes — the 'good pupil'?

d) What is the definition of unfavourable outcomes — the 'bad pupil'?

e) How does the teacher explain the distribution of good and bad pupils?

f) What are the intentions, embedded in teaching procedures, for favourable outcomes?

2 *Assumptions About The Child's Intellectual Status*

a) What is the teacher's implicit model of the child's thinking — psychometric or epistemological? Is the child reified?

b) Assumptions about age and learning. What are the constraints which chronological age is thought to place on learning?

c) Assumptions about social class and its relation to thinking.

3 *Assumptions About Teaching Style*

a) Is a didactic or problem-setting technique thought to be most effective in the production of desired outcomes?

b) Degree of control over communication thought to be necessary.

c) Degree of legitimation and public emphasis given to pupil-initiated cognitive structures.

d) Degree of reification of knowledge.

B *Subject Perspective*

a) Which paradigm is defined as crucial, and what is the degree of integration between paradigms? What is the teacher's world view of the subject?

b) Which problems are defined as important for the subject?

c) How strongly articulated is the utility dimension of the knowledge — for example 'pure' versus 'applied'; the subject content or its technology?

d) What are the criteria of utility — *extrinsic*: economic, humanitarian, world-improving, social integration; or

> *intrinsic*: developing particular qualities of awareness?
e) Assumptions about inferential progression from commonsense to theoretical knowledge.

C *Career Perspective*
Assumptions About Career Location And Relations With Epistemic Communities
a) Degree of public legitimacy for his definition of subject and its methodology.
b) Perception of crucial diffusion centres of legitimate ideas and degree of access to them.
c) Significant others who reinforce his reality.
d) Ethnocentrism of social organization — nature of budgetary and departmental separation within institutions.[72]

Here a number of questions for research are suggested, many of which will be important in this study. While the use of the term assumptions under C is questionable (since the entries here seem to raise issues of structural location as much as of consciousness), this scheme does have the merit of explicitly recognizing the possibility of intra-subject conflict under B and also allows the importance of researching change in subject content. Esland's stress on ideas and their social location, and in particular his recommending of Bucher and Strauss' analysis of professional conflict,[73] will be followed here in an attempt to account for the complex process of change — in which, in practice, issues of content and pedagogy are interwoven in various ways. I shall, in particular, try to examine the relations between the aims of various actors in the debate on mathematics reform and their occupational locations.

Esland's article also had the merit, like those of Young and Bernstein, of pointing beyond the merely educational contexts of subjects. He recognized that various social changes had resulted in a situation where:

> [There exists] an open market situation where the members of subject communities are induced to appeal in competition with others for public support and scarce resources, in order to justify their existence and desired expansion.[74]

Such processes of competition will be one concern of this study. The relations between mathematics and industrially-based actors will be of particular concern. As Esland suggested, though without providing any evidence:

> Schools and universities do not have a monopoly over the

generation and transmission of theoretical knowledge. In a society characterized by a pluralism of 'knowledge producing' and knowledge validating agencies, critical problems of choice and accommodation arise for educational institutions. Industrial organizations are powerfully able to affirm or deny the validity of an epistemology and are, therefore, particularly important as plausibility structures. This is maintained through the problem orientation of industry which ideologizes knowledge as technology.[75]

Unfortunately, however, the basis of this power, and its limits, were not examined by Esland, and neither was the possibility of conflict within 'industry' explicitly raised.

Of the many other potentially important issues raised by Esland I shall only mention two here. First, he makes a useful reference to image-manipulation. He noted, of teachers, that, in relation to different publics such as parents, colleagues, pupils and headmaster, different elements of an actor's perspective will be expressed.[76] This is important here in that it moves away from the possible determinism implicit in his use of the term 'constitutive categories of thought' and, in fact, allows for the possibility of strategic and/or manipulative communication, which is so often a feature of curriculum movements.[77] The second is his stress on the role of 'critical reality definers' and 'charismatic individuals' in processes of knowledge redefinition, drawn from his reading of Ben-David and Collins, and Davie.[78]

The list of publics quoted above, however, does point to one major difference between his project and the study reported here. He intended to focus on the level of the school, and move out from there. I shall focus on the sources of innovation *per se* rather than on any particular institutional location. This will lead me to focus on conferences and, to a lesser extent, journals. But it would, nevertheless, seem appropriate and useful to ask many of the questions listed under A, B and C in his scheme of actors other than teachers in schools. In this sense, many of his suggestions will be seen to orientate my collection and analysis of data.

Towards a Working Analytic Model

Up to this point, in a fairly discursive manner, I have concentrated on assessing the potential usefulness of a range of ideas for this study of knowledge redefinition. I have argued that a variety of concepts and insights drawn from the sociologies of science and education may be of value and that others, for a number of reasons, are of less potential usefulness. It remains to bring this discussion together, drawing in more detail on Bucher and Strauss' work, to establish analytic guidelines for this study. In doing so, I shall briefly discuss the related issues of power and resources, the stratified nature of the educational system, the roles of individuals and segments within the subject, and the relationship between the subject and other arenas and communities.

Bucher and Strauss' model of the professions as loose amalgamations of segments with distinctive 'missions' and interests is intended to be one of process, capable of capturing processes of change.[79] They attempt this by relating the model to the concept of a social movement:

> Segments are not fixed, perpetually defined parts of the body politic. They tend to be more or less continually undergoing change. They take form and develop, they are modified, and they disappear. Movement is forced upon them by changes in their conceptual and technical apparatus, in the institutional conditions of work, and in their relationship to other segments and occupations. Each generation engages in spelling out, again, what it is about and where it is going. In this process, boundaries become diffuse as generations overlap, and different loci of professional activity articulate somewhat different definitions of the work situation. Out of this fluidity new groupings may emerge ... [The] movement of segments can fruitfully be analysed as analogous to social movements.[80]

Professions and, by analogy, subjects are, on this view, a 'number of social movements in various kinds of relationship to each other'.[81] Bucher and Strauss suggest, by analogy with the study of political movements, that such movements within professions should be analyzed in terms of their conditions of origin, recruitment, leadership, the development of organizational apparatus, ideologies and tactics.[82]

Such a conflict approach to the study of professions (or subjects) raises the question of how to understand the relative power of segments and their constituent individual members. I intend here to follow Archer's suggestion in her *Social Origin of Educational Systems*[83] that power must be conceptualized in terms of the availability of various kinds of resources to actors. Furthermore, as, for example, Bhaskar has stressed, some part of these resources must be seen as being non-randomly distributed to actors by virtue of their location in various sets of structured social relationships.[84] To illustrate this approach, before moving on to discuss the role of individuals and relations across the boundary of the subject in change, I shall digress slightly to discuss the distribution of relevant resources within the secondary educational system.

It is well-established that within the secondary sector, as one moved from secondary modern through grammar to independent schools, that is from low to high status schools in terms of social prestige, the occupationally-defined class origins of both teachers and pupils shifted upwards.[85] This structural feature was, presumably, a major cause of the relative differences in status. Apart from status, however, many other features, such as expenditure per pupil and the qualifications of teachers, varied in parallel.[86] Especially important in relation to a study of subject redefinition, the type of post-school education which teachers had received and its institutional location, varied systematically across these school types. Teachers in the selective schools tended to have been prepared by one professional route — the high status graduate route; those in the non-selective schools by the lower status training college route.[87] Not only were these two routes of different educational and social status but also the respective supplying institutions and the schools they supplied embodied, ideationally, different traditions: according to Lawton, the 'nineteenth century public school tradition, and the curriculum ideas inherited from the elementary schools' respectively.[88] In Esland's terms, subject practitioners, both as students and teachers, were, to an extent, being socialized into differentiated subject and pedagogic perspectives of differing value as negotiable resources in various social arenas. Simplifying, teachers in secondary schools at this time can be seen as having been members of one of two distinctive educational subcultures of different social status. These two broad groups will have differed in their potential access to many kinds of resource. Alongside that of status, both general and academic, some of the most salient were financial, temporal, degree of professional self-confidence (reflecting status to some extent) and 'social' — in the sense of which institutions and organizations actors had privileged access to. The nature of their broadly distinctive perspectives, or missions, would also have constrained their opportunities for convincing groups in other arenas of the value of their professional activities. Lesser differences, but of a comparable kind, also, of course, existed within these groups, between, for example, teachers in independent and grammar schools.

Other constraints and opportunities arose from the typically different origins and destinations of their pupils.[89] In Merton's terms, the role sets of practitioners working in the typical locations of the two subcultures will have been quite different.[90] Again, however, there was much variation in this respect within the subcultures.

Within the secondary sector, then, actors and segments will have had differential access to various resources with which to engage in conflict over professional issues. Similar differences existed between the universities and the selective schools, with the universities' control over entrance requirements being a particularly important source of power.

It is important to stress, however, that the structured distribution of resources described above represented no more than a set of constraints and possibilities — however influential — for individuals and segments. Resources could always be utilized, more or less success-fully, to generate more resources from, for example, outside of the educational system. Mathematics teachers could, for example, and did, cooperate and compete in attempts to gain extra resources from industry to realize their missions. As I implied in my critical discussion of Young's work, such relations between educationally-based segments of a subject and interest groups in industry, and the exchange of resources and/or control over subject redefinition across such bound-aries, merit careful study in the case of 'applicable' subjects like mathematics.

There is still one sense, however, in which the above discussion presents a somewhat static, and hence partial, account of these proces-ses. It implicitly assumes fixed missions. Clearly though, as Esland and others have noted, segments and individuals, in competing for resources and legitimacy, might be expected to at least modify their missions.[91] The development of missions over time may well have to be under-stood, therefore, not only in terms of apparently intrinsic conceptual developments within the subject itself, but also in terms of the politics of inter-segmental conflict in changing political and economic contexts.

This leads me to the related issue of the careers of individuals within segments. Bucher and Strauss see 'career' as a central concept in their model:

> The kinds of stages and the locales through which a man's career moves must be considered in terms of the segment to which he 'belongs'. Further, the investigator must be prepared to see changes not only in stages of career but in the ladder itself. The system that the career is moving through can change along the way and take on entirely new directions. The fate of individual careers is closely tied up with the fate of segments, and careers that were possible for one generation rarely are repeatable for the next generation.[92]

This suggests that any analysis of subject redefinition must involve some concern with the construction of careers in changing contexts. Ben-David and others have already successfully used such an approach to explain the emergence of new specialities in science.[93] Holt, who used this approach in studying the rise of chemistry in Britain, summarizes its concerns and insights thus:

> What happened in a particular time and place that caused the communication of ideas in a particular discipline to become significantly effective? It is assumed that (i) ideas necessary for the emergence of a new discipline are usually available over a comparatively long period of time and in various places; (ii) only some of these embryos continue in further growth; (iii) such growth occurs in time and place because some individuals become interested in the new idea, not only for its intellectual content but also as a means to the end of a new intellectual identity and, even more importantly, a new occupational role; (iv) the conditions under which such interest emerges can be identified and form the basis for building a predictive theory.[94]

Leaving aside the question of whether social science can hope to produce predictive theory, we can note that it may be useful to consider the role of individuals within the subject in these terms. In particular, the relative success of entrepreneurs in creatively utilizing their available resources to convince groups outside of the educational arena of the value of their missions, and the relationship of this to their careers, merits some analysis in studies of subject change.

In this respect, it is necessary to briefly discuss the professional or, in this case, subject association. According to Bucher and Strauss, in a 'process' model:

> associations must be regarded in terms of just whose fateful interests within the profession are served. Associations are not everybody's association but represent one segment or a particular alliance of segments.... Established associations become battlegrounds as differing emerging segments compete for control.[95]

Further, in relation to alliances with external groups:

> Those who control the professional associations also control the organs of public relations. They take on the role of spokesmen to the public, interpreting the position of the profession as they see it. They also negotiate with relevant special publics.[96]

Bucher and Strauss, in discussing medicine, were, of course, describing associations with substantial control over recruitment to the profession — a major resource in any intra-professional conflict. Most subject associations, and certainly the two discussed in this study, lack such a basis for power over their members. It might therefore be expected that individual subject practitioners, especially if they have substantial resources by virtue of their location, would be more easily able than professionals such as doctors and lawyers to bypass such associations in their negotiations with potential resource holders outside of the subject.

Bringing these various considerations together then, in this study, which will be broadly concerned with the relationships existing between school mathematics and that used and practised in higher education and industry, and hence mainly with school teachers, university mathematicians and some representatives of industrial employers, the following will represent the central assumptions of my working model (whose usefulness will be partially tested in analyzing the evidence available to me).

A Working Model

1 By analogy with Bucher and Strauss' account of a profession in conflict terms, and following the suggestions of Esland and Musgrove, the subject of mathematics will be seen as a set of segments, or social movements, with distinctive missions, or perspectives, and material interests.

2 The relations of conflict and cooperation between these segments, and their alliances with groups inside and outside the subject, will be seen as major explanatory factors in the account of changes in what counts as school mathematics.

3 The relative power of these segments, and of individuals, will be analyzed in terms of the resources available to them. This availability will be seen partly as a reflection of the segment's (or individual's) position in a set of structured relationships and associated subcultures constituting a stratified educational (and social) system but also, again partly, as a reflection of the segment's (or individual's) success in forging alliances with other powerful, that is resource-controlling, groups.

4 Particular attention will be paid to understanding changes in the conditions for action for subject members, especially changes in the distribution of resources and in climates of opinion over time. This will require some analysis of changes in extra-subject

arenas (such as the industrial, commercial and political) which motivated changing degrees of involvement of extra-subject personnel in processes of subject redefinition.

5 Accepting the central thrust of Kuhn's analysis of the function of the textbook as being to initiate students into a paradigm, but placing it in the context of Bucher and Strauss' analysis of intra-professional conflict over recruitment and the accounts of the sociologists of science of the differentiated nature of sub-jects, segments within the university mathematics community (and industry and commerce) will be expected to compete for control and/or influence over the redefinition of mathematics in feeder secondary schools and especially over the nature of syllabuses and textbooks.

6 Missions will be seen as partially negotiable in the interests of the careers of segments and individuals. Furthermore, following Ben-David's analysis of scientific change, the perceived career consequences of various proposals for redefinition will be considered to be possibly important factors in accounting for the responses of interested actors to these proposals.

7 Similarly, the relative diffusion rates of textbooks, materials and proposed changes in practice might be partially understood, in terms of this approach, by examining whose interests and missions are represented therein, and the relationship of these missions and interests to those of potential adopters. Reactions to the materials and proposals, and the nature of their realiza-tion in classrooms, might similarly be partially accounted for as consequences of subcultural conflict of perspective and interest.

8 Finally, since any redefinition of a school subject is characteris-tically a compromise between the different demands of various powerful groups, we should expect its legitimacy to be con-tinuously subject to attack as changes occur in the distributions of resources and climates of opinion in various arenas.

Notes

1 BERNSTEIN (1974), p. 145.
2 See, for example, LACEY (1976).
3 See, for example, BHASKAR (1979a) and BARNES (1982).
4 Again, see BHASKAR (1979a).
5 See BERNSTEIN (1974) and, for example, ARCHER (1979).
6 MULKAY (1972), pp. 16–17.
7 See DAVIS and HERSH (1983).

8 HIRST (1974) and KUHN (1962).
9 See, for example, GRIFFITH and MULLINS (1972). See also MULLINS (1972), MULLINS (1973), MULKAY (1972) and the postscript to the second edition (1970) of KUHN (1962).
10 BERNSTEIN (1971).
11 HIRST (1974).
12 BERNSTEIN (1971), p. 49.
13 *Ibid.*, p. 51.
14 KUHN (1962).
15 ESLAND (1971), p. 81.
16 KUHN (1970), p. 176.
17 BUCHER and STRAUSS (1961), p. 326, and ESLAND (1971), p. 107.
18 GOODSON (1983).
19 CRANE (1972).
20 GRIFFITH and MULLINS (1972), pp. 959–60.
21 See the discussion below of the work of Young and Bernstein.
22 MUSGROVE (1968).
23 KUHN (1963).
24 *Ibid.*, pp. 345–6.
25 *Ibid.*, p. 346.
26 *Ibid.*, p. 346.
27 *Ibid.*, p. 347.
28 HAGSTROM (1965), pp. 12–22.
29 See, for example, FISHER (1973), p. 1108, and GUSTIN (1973), p. 1122.
30 See, for example, MULLINS (1972) and MULKAY (1972), pp. 36–45.
31 PLANCK (1950), quoted in MULKAY (1972), p. 32.
32 DAVIES (1973), p. 322.
33 YOUNG (Ed.) (1971).
34 *Ibid.*, p. 1.
35 YOUNG (1971), p. 24.
36 See, for example, BANKS (1974), GORBUTT (1972), PRING (1972), YOUNG (1973) and WILLIAMSON (1974).
37 YOUNG (1971), p. 24.
38 *Ibid.*, p. 32.
39 See BHASKAR (1979b), pp. 137–8, commenting on Althusser's ideas.
40 YOUNG (1971), p. 34.
41 *Ibid.*, p. 38.
42 DAVIES (1973), p. 324.
43 YOUNG (1971), p. 35.
44 YOUNG (1972).
45 *Ibid.*, p. 77.
46 HAMMERSLEY (1968).
47 YOUNG (1972), p. 71.
48 *Ibid.*, p. 71.
49 *Ibid.*, p. 76.
50 *Ibid.*, p. 76–7.
51 See, for example, the comments on class and the curriculum in SMITH (1971).
52 BERNSTEIN (1971).

32

53 *Ibid.*, p. 47.
54 See Pring (1975) and Gibson (1977).
55 Durkheim (1964).
56 *Ibid.*, especially chapters two and three.
57 Bernstein (1971), pp. 54–63.
58 *Ibid.*, p. 47.
59 *Ibid.*, p. 48.
60 Bernstein (1975) and Bernstein (1977).
61 Bernstein (1971), p. 68.
62 See, for example, Gibson (1977) and Cherkaoui (1977).
63 Bernstein (1971), p. 68.
64 See Bernstein (1975) and Bernstein (1977).
65 Esland (1971).
66 See, for example, Schutz (1967) and Berger and Luckmann (1967).
67 Kuhn (1962).
68 See Bourdieu and Passeron (1977).
69 See, for example, Bucher and Strauss (1961).
70 Esland (1971), p. 99.
71 On 'plausibility structures', see Berger (1970).
72 Esland (1971), pp. 85–6.
73 Bucher and Strauss (1961).
74 Esland (1971), p. 103.
75 *Ibid.*, pp. 99–100.
76 *Ibid.*, p. 85.
77 See Walker and MacDonald (1976), chapter three.
78 Ben-David and Collins (1966) and Davie (1961).
79 Bucher and Strauss (1961).
80 *Ibid.*, p. 332.
81 *Ibid.*, p. 333.
82 *Ibid.*, p. 332.
83 Archer (1979).
84 Bhaskar (1979a) and (1979b).
85 On teachers, see, for example, Floud and Scott (1961).
86 On 'quality', as measured by graduate status, see, for example, Central Advisory Council for Education (1959), p. 432. On expenditure, see, for example, Midwinter (1977).
87 See footnote 86 on 'quality'.
88 See Lawton (1973), p. 79.
89 See Halsey et al (1980).
90 Merton (1957).
91 Esland (1971), p. 85, and Walker and MacDonald (1976), chapter three.
92 Bucher and Strauss (1961), p. 334.
93 Ben-David and Collins (1966).
94 Holt (1970), p. 181.
95 Bucher and Strauss (1961), p. 331.
96 *Ibid.*, p. 332.

3   The Secondary Mathematics Curriculum Before Reform

In this chapter I shall describe the differentiated secondary mathematics curriculum of the 1950s and some of its supporting 'plausibility structures'. I shall also outline some central features of the university mathematics of the period. The origins of these curricula will only be briefly described and certainly not adequately explained. As Archer has written in her recent sociological history of educational change:

> ... we open up with the results of *prior* interaction. Here, for the purposes of analysis, such phenomena have been treated as elemental — that is, no attempt is made to account for how the structure we take as our starting point had developed from previous interaction between groups and individuals in the context of antecedent structures even further back in history. The decision to do this was governed by the need to avoid ultimate regress to historically distant and sociologically complex inter-relationships. Quite simply, one has to break into the historical sequence at some point, and that point was chosen with reference to the problems in hand. Some things always have to be taken as given ... [1]

This principle has governed my work but, here too, the selection of what is to be taken as given has not been entirely arbitrary. As many commentators have noted, secondary school mathematics curricula had remained relatively unchanged in respect of content and pedagogy from the first world war to the late 1950s. [2]

There were two distinct curricular traditions within secondary school mathematics during this period. These can be seen as two special cases of what Lawton has termed the public school and elementary traditions within English education. [3] The origins of this differentiation can be discerned in the educational arrangements of the Victorian period. The Taunton Report of 1868 illustrates this clearly.[4]

This Report carefully classified education into three 'grades', each appropriate for the children of a particular social grouping. The first, continuing to eighteen or nineteen years of age, was for the sons of 'men with considerable incomes independent of their own exertions, or professional men, and men in business, whose profits put them on the same level' plus 'the great majority of professional men, especially the clergy, medical men and lawyers; the poorer gentry; all in fact, who, having received a cultivated education themselves, are very anxious that their sons should not fall below them'.[5] These two subgroups were both seen as wanting more mathematics in their sons' mainly classical curriculum.[6] The second grade, continuing to about sixteen, was seen as fit for the children of the 'mercantile classes'.[7] Generally, for these, a curriculum less classical in orientation and with more stress on the practical was both seen as wanted and was recommended. Here, rather than mathematics, we find a reference to 'arithmetic, [and] the rudiments of mathematics beyond arithmetic'.[8] The third grade, appropriate for those staying at school until about fourteen and being the sons of 'the smaller tenant farmers, the small tradesmen, [and] the superior artisans' should include 'very good arithmetic' as part of a curriculum based on the three Rs.[9] For the remainder of the working classes, the Revised Code of 1862 had specified elementary arithmetic.[10]

That similar forms of differentiation existed in the 1950s will be shown to have been the case below. By then, however, with various changes having occurred in the structure of post-primary education, there were, in relation to secondary mathematics, the two broad traditions, or subcultures, of selective and non-selective school mathematics. It is these, each of which was also internally differentiated in various ways, that I shall describe below.

The Selective School Mathematics Curriculum

The main school course in mathematics in the 1950s in the selective schools, that is the independent, direct grant and grammar schools, was a transformed version of the curriculum of the independent schools of the 1860s and 1870s that had been described as 'mathematics' in the Taunton Report. At that time, mathematics, a subject whose position in the curriculum was only then becoming secure, had consisted mainly of the study of Euclid's geometry (perhaps reflecting the classical orientation of the curriculum in general in these schools). The Clarendon

Report of 1864, for example, noted that at Harrow in 1861, amongst sixth form leavers, about half had studied six books of Euclid, about a third some trigonometry, and about two-thirds algebra to quadratic equations. The few who had gone further had studied the geometry of conic sections, mechanics and analytical geometry. Those who had studied the calculus had relied upon additional private tuition.[11] I shall sketch the history of the transformation of this curricular selection up to the 1950s, concentrating on the eleven to sixteen course.[12]

By the 1870s the reliance on the rote-learning of Euclid's 2,200 year-old geometry was under considerable organized attack. In 1871 the Association for the Improvement of Geometrical Teaching had been formed by some independent school masters and university dons specifically to argue that proofs other than Euclid's should be allowed in examinations. More generally, they wanted school geometry moved away from its reliance on Euclid's texts. By 1888, after a campaign involving the production of pamphlets, reports and a new textbook, Oxford and Cambridge were persuaded to allow such proofs — with some provisos — in school examinations. In the early 1900s, further progress was made in achieving their mission by the association (renamed the Mathematical Association in 1897). Godfrey and Siddons, of Harrow, and other members had argued, in *Nature* in 1902, for a more general reform of school mathematics. In conjunction with members of the British Association, a decision was made by the Mathematical Association to set up its Teaching Committee, and in 1902–1903 various examination boards finally agreed to accept non-Euclidean proofs. Many new textbooks were immediately written. The curriculum content was now — in these schools — arithmetic plus pre-1800 algebra, geometry and trigonometry, these all being taught and examined separately. It was also during this period, as a result of activities within the Association of Public School Science Masters as well as the Mathematical Association and the British Association, that elements of what became the 'applied mathematics' of the 1950s 'A' level course became established in the curriculum.

After the First World War, the string of reports on mathematics teaching by the Mathematical Association had begun to be produced. An analysis of the membership of the Teaching Committees which produced these demonstrates very clearly the public school and university domination of the association's policy-making (see Table 1).[13]

These reports were, until the late 1950s, to largely legitimate the content and implicitly criticize the pedagogical practice of contemporary secondary school mathematics. In them, the broad outlines of the content of the school course were taken as given and an emphasis was

Table 1: Membership of the Teaching Committee and various sub-committees of the Mathematical Association for selected reports

	Member's Location								
Report	University	Training college	HMI	Independent school	Direct grant school	Grammar school	Technical college	Elementary or central school	Uncoded
Arithmetic (1932)	—	—	2	9	—	2	—	2	2
Algebra (1934/57)	—	—	2	8	—	2	—	2	2
Geometry (1938)	—	—	1	7	1	2	—	1	1
Trigonometry (1950)	2	—	—	8	1	1	2	—	2
Calculus (1951)	2	—	—	4	—	2	—	—	1
Higher Geometry (1953)	4	—	—	5	—	—	—	—	—
Sixth Form Algebra (1957)	2	—	—	3	2	1	—	—	—
Analysis I (1957)	3	—	—	2	—	2	—	—	—

placed, by reporting 'good practice,' on improving its teaching. In the reports on geometry in particular, an argument was developed against 'premature' rigour and formalism in the teaching of mathematics to children.[14] Rather, pupils should approach any branch of the subject through a series of stages, of which three were especially relevant to school mathematics. In stage A, the emphasis should be on experiment, for example, geometrical drawing. In stage B, there should be more emphasis on deduction. An attempt should be made to organize material but not in an axiomatic way. The idea of proof should be introduced. Stage C should take this further, with more rigour being introduced into the teaching.[15]

A potentially significant change in the content and organization of this curriculum occurred towards the end of the Second World War. In the autumn of 1943, partially in response to criticisms of mathematics teaching made in the Spens (1938) and Norwood (1943) reports of the Consultative Committee of the Board of Education and the Secondary Schools Examination Council respectively,[16] the Mathematical Association, the Joint Four group of unions and the examination boards held a conference, on the initiative of the Cambridge Board and chaired by Professor G.B. Jeffery of the Mathematical Association, to prepare proposals for a new syllabus for the School Certificate.[17] Their report of 1944 argued for further moves away from a formal approach to geometry, an increased stress on the integration of the then separate branches of school mathematics, especially geometry and trigonometry, and for some study of the calculus. It also recommended that less emphasis be put on difficult manipulation in arithmetic and algebra.[18] As a result of the acceptance of these recommendations by most of the examination boards, selective schools were soon able to choose between two alternative syllabuses for the School Certificate and, later, GCE examinations.

As far as the pedagogical practice of the 1950s is concerned, it appears, from evidence available from contemporary sources, that the Mathematical Association's A-B-C recommendations were not widely heeded in the selective schools. Rather, an emphasis on rote-learning and the routine practice of examination questions seems to have prevailed. This situation had been criticized by Spens in 1938:

> No school subject, except perhaps classics, has suffered more than mathematics from the tendency to stress secondary rather than primary aims, and to emphasize extraneous rather than intrinsic values. As taught in the past, it has been informed too little by general ideas, and instead of giving broad views has concentrated too much upon the kinds of methods and problems that have been sometimes stigmatized as 'low cunning'.[19]

Many comments in the Inspectorate's publication of 1958 on mathematics teaching suggest that this situation had not changed appreciably by the mid-1950s.[20] In Bernstein's terms, standardized, context-tied operations were probably being stressed in most classrooms.[21] Popular textbooks of the time, full of drill exercises, paralleled this practice.[22]

Two further aspects of this curriculum will be briefly mentioned here. The first relates to the perceived function of the mathematics course. As will become clear in later chapters, the primary function of this was seen by many, though not all, interested parties as that of preparing pupils for further study of mathematics and science. Indeed, the Ministry's 1951 pamphlet on the eleven to sixteen 'grammar-type' curriculum, entitled *The Road to the Sixth Form*, described mathematics as a subject in which 'progress is along a straight line' and argued that 'there is no reason why mathematics should not be dropped by some pupils as early as the end of the third year'.[23] The concern of the 1960s, exemplified by the Dainton Report's recommendation that all sixth form leavers should be mathematically 'literate', was not widespread at the beginning of the 1950s.[24] Much more concern existed amongst teachers in high status schools, as will be shown in later chapters, with the adequate preparation of a minority for the Oxbridge entrance and scholarship examinations.

Secondly, the eleven to sixteen curriculum in mathematics was differentiated within the selective schools by 'ability' (and, therefore, given the relations existing between IQ, streaming and social origin,[25] also by socio-economic status) and by sex. There is considerable evidence of this in the Inspectorate's publication, already referred to. In relation to 'ability', for example, it was reported that some schools felt the alternative (Jeffery) syllabus was suitable only for 'their abler groups', others that it was most suitable for their 'weaker groups'.[26] This document which, in the tradition of Spens and Norwood, was supportive of 'ability' grouping, also reported that different sets were, and should be, receiving different courses.[27] A less 'academic', more 'practical', course was recommended for the less 'able' in the grammar school.[28] Various remarks suggest that the reality in many schools tended to be a mainly arithmetic-based course for these pupils.[29]

The Crowther Report also noted that setting was 'almost universal' for mathematics.[30] This the Committee supported without reservation as it enabled pupils of different 'ability' to progress at different rates.[31]

Evidence on differentiation by sex is also provided by the examination statistics summarized by Crowther:

> Elementary mathematics at ordinary level is taken by more boys than any other subject except English language; by more than twice as many boys as take physics. It is safe to say that it is attempted by virtually every boy in a grammar school sixth form. The pass rate for boys in the three years 1956–8 averaged

59.5 per cent ... It is fairly safe to assume that the great majority of boys who subsequently enter the sixth form secure their passes in elementary mathematics. Additional mathematics in these years was taken by 14 per cent of the boys who secured passes in elementary mathematics ... Among girls on the other hand, it is not nearly so universal for mathematics to be taken at ordinary level. Using the entries for English language as a basis for comparison, the proportion of boys taking elementary mathematics was 87 per cent and of girls 53 per cent for the period 1956–8. Clearly mathematics is taken for examination only by the abler girls at this subject. The others do not give up the subject altogether, but in fact, a good many confine themselves to arithmetic.[32]

It can be tentatively concluded, therefore, that girls and the less 'able' were more likely to receive arithmetic only, while boys and the more 'able' were more likely to receive 'mathematics'.

I have now described, although from necessity only briefly, various aspects of the selective school mathematics curriculum of the 1950s. I have said nothing of the processes whereby the reformed independent model of the early 1900s came to be imitated throughout this sector by this decade, nor of how girls had come to study mathematics to the extent that they then did (compare Taunton's reference to 'sons'). Neither have I space to provide an account of how mathematics came to secure its position, and increase its status, after the 1860s. As I argued earlier, my concerns must force me to take much as given. I have, however, indicated the role of the Mathematical Association, a grouping representing mathematics teachers in the higher status selective schools and the university mathematics dons, in these processes. Having thus outlined the nature of one mathematical subculture based in the selective school/university relationship, I shall now proceed to provide a similar descriptive account of the other.

The Non-Selective School Mathematics Curriculum

If the selective mathematics curriculum of the 1950s might be seen loosely as deriving from Taunton's suggestions for the first grade of education, that is, as an amalgam of the 'academic' and the 'practical', with the former more heavily weighted, then that received by most pupils in the non-selective schools after 1944 might be seen as deriving from Taunton's third grade and the Revised Code, that is, as being concerned almost entirely with the 'practical'. This simple picture was, of course, becoming complicated by the increasing tendency during the 1950s for pupils in the secondary modern schools to be entered for GCE examinations.[33] This resulted in some pupils in these schools receiving a course of mathematics similar to that of grammar school pupils up to the age of sixteen.

I shall show that the sources of the post-war secondary modern mathematics curriculum are to be found in the practices of the senior departments of the inter-war elementary schools, and the associated official literature. Many of the general subjects teachers who taught mathematics in the secondary moderns had been recruited from these schools,[34] and many of these had been trained specifically to teach in them. Because of this important link, before turning to a contemporary survey of the work of the secondary moderns, I shall briefly describe the 'mathematical' work recommended for the senior departments of the elementary schools before the 1944 Act. The *Handbook of Suggestions for Teachers* (1937) states:

> The course will fix and extend the knowledge and the skill in arithmetical operations gained in the junior school, and teach the children to apply their new powers to the affairs of daily life and school; it will also have to prepare them to deal with situations requiring numerical knowledge that lie ahead of them. Their experience of accounts, gained in school affairs such as meals, concerts, savings banks and societies, school journeys, excursions, gardening or poultry-keeping, will introduce ideas that are current in the larger world of finance, and will be used to lead up to such questions as buying by instalments, investments, pensions and insurance. The use of graphical methods will provide them with a new means of representing and interpreting arithmetical data. Their work in practical subjects, mechanical drawing, surveying and design will provide material that will serve as a basis for the study of geometry.[35]

The practical, non-academic orientation is clear. The Handbook goes on to suggest the following specific topics: more complex multiplication and division, decimals, ratios, percentages, rates, proportions, averages, factors, square roots, some geometry 'through practical activities', simple graphical representation of statistics, various examples of applied arithmetic, basic logarithms and some very basic algebra.[36] The course was clearly intended to be arithmetic-based. As such, it will be seen to have had much in common with the secondary modern curriculum of the 1950s. Indeed, one early book on the secondary modern school,

Education in the Secondary Modern School, by Dempster, the Chief
Education Officer for Southampton, had no section on 'mathematics',
only one on 'arithmetic'.[37] Nor did 'mathematics' appear in this book's
list of contents or index.

In order to illustrate the continued importance of this arithmetic-
based tradition in the secondary modern schools, I shall now draw on
Chapman's (1959) survey of 1600 of them.[38] It is clear from his results
that, by this time, 'mathematics' comprised a substantial part of the
formal curriculum (see Table 2).[39]

Table 2:   Average time (in hours) spent on mathematics in 1600 secondary
modern schools in the late 1950s

	Year 1	Year 2	Year 3	Year 4
A-Stream	3½	3½	3⅓	3⅓
Others	4	4	3⅔	3⅔

Chapman summarized his data on the nature of the mathematics
taught thus:

> It would seem that a rough division acceptable to schools, is that
> half the time should be spent on arithmetic and the other half on
> geometry and algebra, with a greater proportion on geometry
> than on algebra.[40]

This summary, however, does not adequately convey the extent of
curricular differentiation existing within these schools. His case studies
make it quite clear that this summary refers to no real 'average' pupil:
the curriculum was clearly differentiated by 'ability' and sex. As a first
example, we can consider the boys' school he chose to illustrate the
scope of mathematical work in the modern schools:

> Here the content of mathematics appears under three headings:
> the mathematics *necessary* for everyday life, as, for example,
> money, simple length, time, etc; mathematics *useful* in everyday
> life, as, for example, in interest rates, proportions, averages and
> statistics; and mathematics as a *mode of thought*, as in problems
> in arithmetic, algebra and riders in geometry. This school
> provides all except the near-ineducable with the first of these
> mathematical aims, and as many boys as possible with the
> second. Only, however, with a few of the boys is it possible to
> attempt the third aim. The claim of any topic for inclusion in

this mathematical scheme of work depends not only on the categories to which it belongs but on whether it is within the powers of comprehension of a boy.[41]

Of another (mixed) school, where 'the "A" class children are expected to reach a standard of mathematics not much lower than that attained by the lower forms at a grammar school' and, by implication, follow a similar course, he reported, quoting from the reply to his questionnaire:

> On the other hand, in the 'D' stream, we shall be struggling with pupils to whom the manipulation of figures is almost a closed book. It is reasonable to assume that the demands of mathematical ability will be very small on these latter children. The ability to reckon up their wages and to obtain correct change for purchases made will be the limit of mathematical demands upon them. It is, therefore, of paramount importance that the teacher has in mind the subsequent demands that are likely to be made upon the child.[42]

Such differentiation of course and aims appears throughout his report. The 'A' stream often, but not always — it depended on the school's attitude to the GCE — received a mathematics course broadly of a grammar school type, while the lower streams received courses in the elementary arithmetic-based tradition. The description of one (mixed) school's scheme of work illustrates the latter approach:

> This minimum consists of the four rules, with numbers one to a hundred, the four rules with very simple fractions, the four rules with money, weights and measures, simple proportion, a knowledge of the meanings of decimal and percentage notation, simple square measure, simple protractor drill, and knowledge of simple angles and names of common figures, both plane and solid. To these essentials can be added interest, the planning of incomes, the use of time, a knowledge of local and national finance, simple accounts, both household and personal, and the relation of three fractional notations.[43]

It is in this area of applied arithmetic that clear evidence of sex-based differentiation appears. Under the very significant heading 'Adapting Mathematics for Girls', Chapman describes the following topics from a girls' school's scheme of work:

> household arithmetic of furnishing, the covering of areas of floors and walls, curtain calculations, heating and lighting, and calculations relating to apparatus and equipment for third year

children, and for the fourth year, household accounts and the planning of a household budget.[44]

Not all girls' schools, however, saw the futures of their pupils as limited to the home. In some cases reference was made outside of the immediate domestic setting. One school, for example, reported:

> Topics are grouped under three headings of the community, the house and the girl. Under the heading of community, the list of topics includes taxes of all kinds ..., and the Budget. Topics under the heading of the house include the renting and buying of a house, various forms of savings clubs, insurance of all kinds, plans of houses and rooms with decorations and furnishing, weekly household budgets, costs of fuel, ... the use of catalogues for buying by post and hire purchase. Under the heading of the girl, the school aims to show how to plan weekly spending, monthly salaries and the yearly budget, and items concerning holiday charges and expenses ...[45]

But, nevertheless, in the schemes for boys' schools, we can discern a different emphasis. Paid work figures more prominently. For example, in one school, staff aimed 'to encourage the boys to pass later on to an apprenticeship; mathematics helps to build a bridge between education and industry'.[46] Similarly, 'practical surveying' is often mentioned in schemes for boys but not in those for girls. And, in relation to 'domestic affairs', a different emphasis can be noted. For the first of the above boys' schools, for example:

> So far as domestic affairs are concerned, the scheme points out that there are always plenty of jobs in a house awaiting the householder who has had a school training in handicraft, requiring such skills as space measurements and planning to ensure an economical use of materials.[47]

References to the Budget appear, as they did for girls. References to domestic finances more often tend, however, to avoid everyday spending and to point beyond this to 'such investment schemes as national savings, building societies, assurance companies and the like' or 'investments, local and national finance, mathematics in business ...'.[48] The mixed schools' schemes are similar in the above respects to those for boys (although, of course, much differentiation may have occurred within these).[49]

This evidence suggests, then, that not only was 'mathematics' for many pupils in the non-selective schools a different subject from that in the selective schools, but also that it was highly differentiated within the non-selective sector, especially between schools, by sex, and within them, by 'ability'. If we now move on to consider pedagogical practice, where obviously Chapman's self-report data may be considerably less valid, we find that many schools reported a 'practical' approach. Some rural schools, for example, based their mathematics around farm and garden concerns.[50] Others reported attempts, as recommended in the Board of Education's *Senior School Mathematics* of 1934 and again in the section on 'ordinary pupils' in the Inspectorate's *Teaching Mathematics in Secondary Schools* of 1958, to link work in mathematics with work in other subjects (especially technical drawing, geography, craft and gardening).[51] It is clear that the 'A' streams, if taking the GCE, would have been exempt from these lower status activities. It is beyond much doubt, however, that in many schools the pedagogic emphasis was on rote-learning and routine solutions to arithmetical problems. The Inspectorate's publication notes that 'some' modern schools had emphasized 'a rigorous and exclusive insistence on the practice of mechanical skills, in long sequences of similar sums'.[52] Furthermore, one of my informants for this study, R. Morris, a member of the Inspectorate at the time, emphasized that, in his experience, only a minority of modern schools were seriously working within other approaches than this in mathematics lessons.

Further evidence on the differentiation of the mathematics curriculum in these schools, in the late 1950s, can be obtained from the 1961 survey carried out for the Newsom Report, in which data were collected for fourth year pupils.[53] Clear sex-based differences were found to exist in relation to the amount of 'mathematics' studied, both between single sex schools and within mixed schools:

> The simplest way of expressing the difference is to say that boys in boys' schools spend on the average the equivalent of half a morning a week more in the mathematics and science field than do the girls in girls' schools, who in turn spend a correspondingly greater amount of time on the practical subjects. In co-educational schools, the difference still exists, but is roughly halved.[54]

The amount of 'mathematics' received also varied by 'ability'.[55] The relation was not, however, a simple one. Some schools gave more 'mathematics' to the 'more able', while others reversed this. Agreement existed, though, that pupils of varying 'ability' required different 'treatment' in 'mathematics'.[56]

The Report also allows us to throw more light on the differential distribution of the 'mathematics' taught (see Table 3).[57] It appears, from this table, that, not only did girls do less 'mathematics' than boys on average, but also that they were much more likely, if in a single sex school, to be restricted to arithmetic. A relationship also existed here with 'ability':

> Naturally, it is for the most part the weaker pupils who only do arithmetic, but less than half of the forms (44 per cent) concerned are in fact the bottom forms in the fourth year of their schools, while in six schools no fourth year girl does any mathematics as opposed to arithmetic.[58]

We can conclude this section, therefore, by noting that, in the secondary moderns, the majority of pupils, especially of the girls, were receiving a 'mathematics' curriculum grounded in the elementary arithmetical tradition. The 'more able', especially boys, were, however, quite likely to have been initiated into the selective school version of mathematics as schools increasingly entered pupils for the GCE.

In the next part of this chapter, I shall discuss the 'perspectives', to use Esland's term, or, at least, the 'mainstream' perspectives, that served

Table 3:   Time given to 'mathematics' for fourth year pupils in single sex and co-educational secondary modern schools

Minutes per week	Boys (%)	Co-ed (%)	Girls (%)	All (%)
320–360	4	2	—	2
275–315	3	4	1	3
230–270	51	25	10	27
185–225	39	53	33	47
140–180	3	16	45	19
95–135	—	tr	11	2
50–90	—	—	—	—
Less than 45	—	—	—	—
	(n=119)	(n=345)	(n=116)	(n=580)
Average number of minutes per form	260	215	180	205
Percentage of forms doing only arithmetic	10	12	31	15
Average minutes per week in these forms	225	200	130	175

to legitimate some aspects of the differentiation of 'mathematics' so far described.

Mainstream Perspectives on Differentiation

I shall consider here the assumptions of 'mainstream' mathematical educators in relation to curriculum differentiation. By 'mainstream' I wish to indicate primarily those in official positions associated with the Ministry, such as members of the Inspectorate, and those actively involved with the Mathematical Association. The somewhat different perspectives of activists within the rival Association for Teaching Aids in Mathematics will be discussed in chapter 4. I shall consider first differentiation by 'ability' and then, more briefly, differentiation by sex. I shall be concentrating on the non-selective sector as it was pupils from these schools that were seen as problematic by those holding these perspectives.

Differentiation by 'Ability'

The pedagogical perspective displayed in writing for, and about, mathematics teaching in both the selective and non-selective sectors at this time employed a psychological model of the child which closely approximated to Esland's psychometric ideal-type:

> The psychometric model endows the child with an 'intelligence', a capacity of given power within which his thinking develops. He is a novitiate in a world of pre-existing, theoretical forms into which he is initiated and which he is expected to reconstitute. The teacher monitors his progress by means of 'objective' evaluation and he is differentiated from others by its objective criteria.[59]

Thus, these writers can be seen as working within an overall set of assumptions in keeping with those of the Spens and Norwood Reports.[60] According to the writers of the latter document, not only, intellectually speaking, did there exist three distinct types of child but, furthermore, each should receive appropriately different educational offerings. These ranged from an academic curriculum for the most 'able' to a concrete or practical one for the least 'able'.[61] In one important respect, however, the perspectives of the mathematical educators, especially of those associated with the Teaching Committee of the

Mathematical Association, differed from this. In line with the A-B-C schema, all pupils were seen, at least at Keddie's 'educationist' level,[62] as needing to move through an experimental or practical stage in their learning of any mathematical topic. Rote-learning was, to some extent, frowned upon. 'Understanding' was recommended. An underlying adherence to a psychometric view is demonstrated, however, in their assumption that many less 'able' pupils will progress no further than stages A and/or B.

I shall now illustrate these features by referring to various key mainstream documents. *Senior School Mathematics* had, in 1934, expressed very clear views on 'ability' in its discussion of the elementary school curriculum:

> The variation of pupils in natural capacity needs no elaboration ... The plan of dividing the senior school into two, three or even four streams ..., with appropriate differences in curriculum, timetable and methods of teaching, has become common practice, and mathematics is rightly considered as one of the chief subjects in which differences of treatment must be made ... The chief point that it is desired to emphasize is that wide differences in ability must be met by syllabuses which differ not only in content and difficulty, but also in outlook and treatment, and that each senior school must normally provide at least two alternative courses in mathematics.[63]

This official position was supported in mainstream books published up to the end of the 1950s. In *The Teaching of Modern School Mathematics*,[64] for example, by James, of Redlands Training College and Secretary of the Mathematical Association's Sub-committee on Secondary Modern School Mathematics, we find:

> Not many modern schools have a mathematics staff large enough to allow the pupils to be placed in sets for mathematics. A few schools divide their pupils into streams using mathematical ability only for carrying out the streaming. The advantage in mathematics is obvious ... It must be said in favour of 'mathematical' streaming that no other subject is so difficult to teach to a class with a wide range of ability.[65]

And, in his chapter on the 'modern school child', he wrote:

> For most modern school pupils the mathematics course must be based on practical situations with the mathematical ideas growing out of these. Indeed for many of our pupils we shall never

get away from this; the less able the pupil, the more tied to practical considerations the mathematics course must be.[66]

More specifically, he argued of geometry that:

... geometry should be taken with all streams. The difference will be in the treatment given and the range covered. Whereas some of the work of the 'A' stream can be deductive and can deal with generalisations, that of a 'C' stream will be entirely practical, measurement and observation taking the place of intellectual activity.[67]

Similar views were expressed by Olive Morgan, Deputy Head of a Middlesex comprehensive school, in her *The Teaching of Mathematics in the Secondary Modern School*, which she described as a 'practical guide for the non-mathematician'.[68] I shall quote at length to illustrate her (somewhat ambiguous) perspective:

The majority of people who teach in the secondary modern schools were taught in the grammar schools, and were, by definition, above the average in intelligence. The secondary modern school is the school for the average and below average child, the slow learner, the 'non-academic type', the child with handicaps of all kinds — essentially the child who needs all the skill a resourceful teacher has at his command.

For the so-called 'bright' child, ability to leap from concrete experiences to generalisations and abstract ideas is the hallmark of intelligence. It is an intellectual process which demands great mental effort, and the difference between the bright, nimble-minded, intelligent child and the 'dull', or 'slow' or 'non-academically minded' child is the difference in his ability to make this effort.

In the secondary modern school there will be some children who have the innate ability to think easily in abstract terms, but the majority will have to be trained to do so, and trained by very carefully graded steps. There will be some children who will never be able to perform any but the simplest exercises in abstract thought, because they are either unwilling or unable to make the necessary mental effort.[69]

She also favoured setting:

In large schools ... the best method of arranging the mathematics lessons is to have all the lessons for one age-range taking place at the same time, and to reshuffle the classes into 'sets' of approximately homogeneous ability. The work can be suited to the child by this method, and the able children can be made to work to their capacity, while the weaker ones can receive the attention they need.[70]

The Mathematical Association's (1959) report on the teaching of mathematics in the modern schools also shared this perspective:

> Pupils entering the modern school are generally quite unready for the kind of mathematical syllabus associated with grammar school courses. Some may attain readiness for an intellectual approach later in school life, but many will never do so.[71]

And, in line with the A-B-C schema:

> It is against a background of experience that mathematical ideas take shape and notations gain meaning. At advanced levels the experience itself may be mathematical but most of the work appropriate to the modern school pupil is closely related to his practical experience ... We feel strongly that all pupils need actual experience and experiment again and again ... Only the older abler pupils in modern schools are mature enough mathematically to pursue very far the study of mathematics as an abstract system and even these benefit from frequent recourse to experience.[72]

Renewed official backing, in the form of the Inspectorate's *Teaching Mathematics in Secondary Schools*,[73] was given to these ideas in 1958:

> The outstanding problem to be faced in the modern school is that of the wide range of the ability of the pupils ... Their [teachers'] task is simultaneously to do justice to the abilities of some who could well tackle courses in grammar schools or technical schools, to serve the needs of those who are really dull, and, while not neglecting either of these minorities, to provide the best education possible for the large, but by no means homogeneous, middle block of those, who may be slow at their work and not academic in their interests, but who respond remarkably to sympathetic and appropriate treatment.[74]

And, on setting, it was argued:

> In large [modern] schools classes are often formed by grouping together pupils of comparable general ability. Although there is evidence that some correlation exists between general ability and mathematical ability, it is sometimes found to be advantageous

> ... to group together pupils of similar mathematical ability into 'sets' or 'divisions' for their mathematical work. The teaching in these sets is usually more effective, and the arrangement allows the pupil to follow suitably differentiated syllabuses.[75]

This need for 'appropriate' syllabuses was also seen as being shared by 'weaker' pupils in the grammar schools. It was argued that those grammar school pupils 'whose mathematical ability seems really weak' will need a course 'which may differ substantially from that offered to the abler pupils in its content, its sequence and its method of presentation'.[76] The approach must 'appear practical', as must that for the modern school.[77]

It must be stressed of these documents that, while they were all 'reformist' in the sense of wanting non-selective pupils to receive something more than arithmetic in their 'mathematics' courses, they simultaneously provided a set of legitimatory principles explaining why such pupils would not actually be able to progress very far beyond arithmetic. Such comments as James' 'the solution of right-angled triangles using sine, cosine and tangent is as far as most modern school pupils will go in trigonometry' and Morgan's 'it will be only the minimum number of children who will be able to tackle algebra with understanding' abound.[78] In this respect they echoed official statements within the elementary tradition. *Senior School Mathematics*, for example, had stated:

> For most senior school pupils, any systematic geometry based on definitions, axioms and postulates, is unsuitable either as a means of disciplining their minds or of giving them a knowledge of space. In any case, they will gain far more, mentally and practically, from a study of the useful and interesting applications of geometry.[79]

The above discussion has demonstrated that influential figures within the Mathematical Association and the Inspectorate operated, in the late 1950s, broadly within the Norwood philosophy. I shall now, more briefly, discuss equivalent perspectives on the sexual differentiation of the mathematics curriculum.

Curriculum Differentiation by Sex

In respect of sex, more of a mismatch between mainstream perspectives and curricular reality seems to have existed in this period. I shall show that, while the pre-war publications of the Board of Education had made fairly explicit suggestions for curricular differentiation by sex within the senior school curriculum, the writers discussed above had, by the end of the 1950s, come to lay much more emphasis on the desirability of both sexes receiving broadly similar courses in mathematics.

The Board's *Senior School Mathematics*, while stressing that 'it is not lightly to be assumed that girls have less natural capacity for the subject than boys', and noting that girls had previously given less time to mathematics and had lacked the help provided by the study of woodwork and physical science, had argued in its section 'the course for girls':

> The occupations of girls and women, in and out of school, make, generally speaking, less specific demands on mathematics than do those of boys and men ... Any large expenditure of time on mathematics unassociated with applications and practical work is perhaps more greatly to be deprecated for girls than for boys. With a small time allowance it becomes all important to scrutinize carefully the content of the syllabus and to ask what mathematics is essential for girls, how this may best be treated and how far it is desirable or possible to go beyond the utilitarian minimum. There is very little in the foregoing pages which is essentially unsuitable for girls.[80]

In spite of the last sentence, however, curricular differentiation by sex was clearly officially acceptable. Indeed, the writers later added:

> All those applications of arithmetic ... which are in any way allied to Housecraft or to the usual occupations of women will naturally be selected in building up the girls' course.[81]

And:

> Illustrations of the use of branches of mathematics other than Arithmetic and Mensuration ... can be drawn from topics of special interest to girls.[82]

The carrying of these views into the early secondary moderns by teachers trained for, and experienced in, the elementary sector presumably goes some way towards explaining the differentiation by sex described by Chapman and Newsom. Attitudes were, however, at least in educational circles, clearly changing in the 1940s and 1950s. This can be illustrated by referring to the writers discussed earlier.

Morgan, notwithstanding her previous *Real Life Arithmetic for*

Girls, lists topics relating to the house and to work but claims their suitability for both sexes.[83] She does, however, add such comments as 'the boys will probably be more ready to work in groups and produce some original ideas', and 'hobbies, to boys, are an important part of their life, but girls of this age tend to be more interested in passive occupations'.[84] James specifically argues that girls should have greater access to areas of mathematics previously reserved for boys, such as practical drawing and surveying.[85] The appropriate report of the Mathematical Association, produced by a Committee comprising seven men and five women, similarly argued for boys to do some housecraft and girls some gardening in order to allow the possibility of a more common mathematics course.[86] In particular, they argued against the exclusion of girls from geometry.[87] The Inspectorate's publication of 1958 was more equivocal. While it argued that girls had previously been disadvantaged in mathematics, it did not simply suggest a common course. Rather, it argued that girls would benefit from a more appropriate selection of material. Their specific interests should be 'borne in mind'.[88]

This brief review suggests that more of a shift in perspectives had occurred in respect of gender than 'ability' over the years 1935 to 1960. While curricular differentiation by 'ability' was still, broadly speaking, supported by mainstream writers, differentiation by sex was often less clearly acceptable to them. To this extent, some aspects of existing practice, especially the grouping and differential curricular treatment of pupils in terms of 'ability', were still seen as legitimate, while others, especially sex-typed syllabuses and rote-learning, were less so.

I shall now consider the relationship between selective school and university mathematics, a central issue in the intra-subject debates of the late 1950s and early 1960s.

Selective School and University Mathematics

The discussion so far has been limited to what, for various categories of pupils, counted as school mathematics. This section will briefly discuss the differences between the mathematics of the selective secondary sector and that practised in the university mathematics departments at this time.

Most of the mathematics taught in the selective schools in the 1950s had been developed before 1800.[89] Many more branches and topics of 'pure mathematics' had, however, been created, and others further developed, since that time and were, by the 1950s, being taught, alongside the earlier material, in the universities.[90] Examples included nineteenth-century varieties of vector analysis, matrix algebra, the 'modern' algebras of sets, fields and groups, and non-Euclidean geometries. The schools were providing elementary introductions to much pre-1800 mathematics, such as the calculus, but not to more recent material.[91] Pupils whose study of mathematics ended at school would, in most cases, have remained unaware of these post-1800 developments.

It was not, however, only the content of university courses that had changed. A major change in the approach to the study and development of pure mathematics had also occurred in the late nineteenth and early twentieth centuries. Compared to pre-1800 emphases, mathematicians had come to stress abstraction, structure, rigour and the use of the axiomatic method. According to Bell:

> Mathematics after Gauss (1777–1855), and partly during his own lifetime, became more general and more abstract than he conceived it. Interest in special problems sharply declined if there was a general problem including the special instances to be attacked . . . Mathematics after Gauss turned to the construction of inclusive theories and general methods which, theoretically at least, implied the detailed solutions of infinities of special problems.[92]

One strand of this nineteenth-century development was the creation of algebras with operations, other than the arithmetical, on elements, other than the natural numbers, in which the 'normal' laws for the combination of elements might not hold. (In matrix multiplication, for example, it is not normally true that $AB = BA$ under 'multiplication'; that is, the commutative law does not apply.[93]) The resulting concepts, such as fields and groups, were well-known to research mathematicians by the late nineteenth century. They increasingly turned to the study of the 'structure' of these algebras. I shall quote from Bell to illustrate the meaning given to 'structure' in this mathematical context:

> A group G is a set S of elements a, b, c . . . x, y . . . and an operation O, which may be performed upon any two (identical or distinct) elements a, b of S, in this order, to produce a uniquely determined element aOb of S, such that the postulates (1)–(3) are satisfied.
>   (1)   aOb is in S for every a, b in S.
>   (2)   aO(bOc) = (aOb)Oc for every a, b, c in S.
>   (3)   For every a, b in S there exist x, y in S such that aOx = b, yOa = b. . . .

Consider two groups, with the respective elements a_1, b_1, c_1 ... and a_2, b_2, c_2 ... and the respective operations O_1, O_2. These groups are said to be simply isomorphic, or to have the same structure, if it is possible to set up a one-one correspondence between the elements such that, if $x_1O_1y_1 = z_1$, then $x_2O_2y_2 = z_2$, and conversely, where x_1, y_1, z_1 are the respective correspondents of x_2, y_2, z_2.

This definition is probably the simplest example of what is meant by the 'same structure'.[94]

Klein, in 1872, produced his unification of several diverse geometries using such an approach.[95] One way of summarizing this is to say that some mathematicians increasingly studied the relations between things, and theories, rather than those things themselves.[96]

Another aspect of this change of approach, part of a developing concern with the fundamentals of mathematics, related to the degree of rigour expected in theoretical work. Hilbert, in his work during the 1890s on the foundations of geometry, had argued for an axiomatic, or postulational, approach to proof.[97] Here the object is to state, in the most unambiguous way possible, the assumptions on which eventual conclusions are based. Specifically, the mathematician must define the laws which his undefined terms are to obey. The rest is then logical deduction.[98] Bell has described the consequences of Hilbert's crusade for a revived Euclidean method thus:

> With a minimum of symbolism, Hilbert convinced geometers, as neither Pasch nor Peano had succeeded in doing, of the abstract, purely formal character of geometry; and his great authority firmly established the postulational method, not only in the geometry of the twentieth century, but also in nearly all mathematics since 1900. Again we emphasize that intuition was not ousted from mathematics by the abstract attack. Nor were the applications of postulational analysis more than a small fraction of twentieth-century mathematics. But they were a potent catalyst for that mathematics, and they attracted hundreds of prolific workers.[99]

The introduction of these trends into English universities was well under way by the first world war. Hardy's well-known *Pure Mathematics* (1908) was used to teach the rigorous analysis of the mid-nineteenth century to undergraduates at Cambridge and elsewhere and, from then on, the other ideas of the nineteenth century were gradually introduced into degree courses.[100] The French group of mathematicians writing under the pseudonym of Bourbaki were one major pressure group advocating such changes from the 1940s onwards.[101] By the 1950s, the newer approach was seemingly secure in England. Howson and Griffiths write:

> Many of the younger university teachers now found analysis entirely natural, in a 'third generation' way: their PhD work had taught them modern algebra, the axiomatic method, and other great ideas of the nineteenth and twentieth centuries. At the very least, this made them want to teach even old-fashioned syllabuses (where these were still laid down) in a different, more rigorous way.[102]

The resultant widening paradigmatic discontinuity between the mathematics practised by some university mathematicians and that taught in the selective schools will be seen to have been one important factor in the sequence of events analyzed in this study.

Changes had also occurred in the practice of 'applied mathematics'.[103] I shall only discuss these briefly here as details will emerge in chapters 5 and 6. New branches such as game theory, linear programming, numerical analysis and some newer topics in statistics, many relying on the increasingly available computer technology, were being taught in some university and technical college departments by the mid to late 1950s.[104] They were also being used in commercial and industrial settings.[105] Much earlier applied mathematics, especially that based on the calculus developed from the late seventeenth century onwards, was simultaneously being taught to mathematicians, scientists and engineers.[106] Modern axiomatic approaches had not, however, affected the practice of applied mathematics, which tended to occur not only in academic settings, to the same degree as that of pure mathematics. In applied mathematics, the obtaining of a solution *per se* was often seen as much more important than an adherence to any particular method.[107] Furthermore, the computer had made possible the practice of approximate, numerical methods for the solving of equations.[108] One result was an increasing stress on 'mathematical modelling'.[109] The schools' applied mathematics course at 'A' level reflected few of these developments (excepting some in statistics if an alternative syllabus was chosen).[110]

I shall now consider some mainstream responses to this situation up to about 1957. In particular I shall examine the reports published by the Teaching Committee of the Mathematical Association, the Inspectorate and the Assistant Masters' Association. I am particularly interested, given later developments, in their attitude to the possible inclusion of the newer topics and approaches in the school curriculum. (The opinions of ATAM activists will be examined in chapter 4.) I will show that these mainstream mathematical educators, although concerned about the discontinuity between school and university, tended to argue that the newer branches of mathematics were not appropriate material for study in schools.

This can be illustrated by an examination of the Mathematical Association's reports of the 1950s. First, however, it should be recalled that the early campaigns of the Association had been explicitly aimed at the reform of the Euclidean, and hence axiomatic, approach to geometry that had then dominated the selective schools' mathematics curriculum. In their *A Second Report on the Teaching of Geometry* (1938) which, like the first in 1923, emphasized the importance of stage A and stage B work in school mathematics, the importance of the axiomatic approach in contemporary fields of advanced geometry was recognized but was held to be inappropriate for school study since one was 'faced with a different problem, viz. the first recognition of geometrical facts and the development of the powers of geometrical perception'.[111] This concern with an intuitive approach, coupled with an apparent belief that post-1800 content was also inappropriate, was maintained by the Teaching Committee, with its largely high status selective school membership, through to the mid-1950s. This is probably partly explicable in terms of the 'agreed' purpose of the reports. In that of 1953 on *The Teaching of Higher Geometry in Schools* earlier reports are described thus:

> With the exception of the 1923 report on the teaching of geometry, these have been concerned mainly with methods of presentation. They have been based on extensive experience gained in the classroom and on the interchange of ideas between teachers at meetings of the Association and its Branches. A report has in fact expressed the considered opinions of the general body of teachers and has put on record various details of classroom procedure which have proved to be effective in practice.[112]

This was not a procedure likely to lead to radical proposals. The 1953 report, subject to a considerable university influence in its writing, was, in this respect, somewhat deviant. It claimed:

> A large part of this report is addressed to those teachers who are unfamiliar with the ideas of abstract geometry and much material is included which is not intended for the pupil. Unless

this is realized, it will be thought that the later stages of the
report set a standard that can not possibly be achieved or even
approached, and the contents will be dismissed as visionary and
unrealistic. The object of the writers ... has been to suggest a
view of geometry for the consideration of the teacher, not to
prescribe a particular mode of approach by the pupil. They have
endeavoured to present ideas which will act as a stimulus to the
teacher and to provide material from which he can make
selections.[113]

Having described this as a change of policy, the report went on to
recommend 'abstract' geometry. This was seen, however, as 'suitable
only for mathematical specialists and those specialists in science or other
subjects who have marked mathematical ability'.[114] This approach was
seen as likely to 'render less abrupt the transition from geometry as
taught at school to that taught at the universities' since 'most of this
material is included in a first year's work' in the latter, and few schools
do it.[115] This reference to 'abstract' geometry was not, however, a
reference to the early nineteenth-century work of Gauss, Bolyai and
Lobachewsky nor to the later work of Klein and Hilbert.[116] Rather, it
was used to describe the Cartesian geometry of the 1600s, that is,
algebraic analytical geometry.[117] It was the study of this branch of
mathematics that would, according to the writers, provide 'some sort of
bridge across the dividing gulf'.[118]

A similar stress on pre-1800 work is demonstrated in the Association's *The Teaching of Algebra in Schools*.[119] This had originally been
published in 1934 and, after seven reprints, was again reprinted in 1957,
but with 'some revision'.[120] Algebra here means generalized arithmetic,
not structural approaches. In fact, the report argued:

The joys of pure mathematics, the study of algebraic form, the
appreciation of an 'elegant' method are for the pure mathematician and not for the average boy.[121]

And, more specifically:

Of the formal laws of algebra the only one which it may be
useful to mention in the classroom is the law $p(a*b) \equiv pa*pb$.[122]

As this implies, axiomatic approaches were not favoured for use in
schools by the mainly school-based Committee which produced this
Report. In their discussion of directed numbers, they argued:

Formal proofs of the laws of operations and the determination
of a minimum set of laws from which the others can be deduced

is wholly unsuitable work for schools; only the exceptional sixth form boy will be interested in it.[123]

Lastly, in this context, we can examine the Association's *The Teaching of Algebra in VIth Forms*,[124] prepared by a Committee including, as university representatives, Ledermann (the writer, while at Manchester in 1948, of *Introduction to the Theory of Finite Groups*[125] — a book for second and third year undergraduates at that time) and Newman (who in the late 1930s had suggested that some linear algebra might be taught in schools[126]). The position on the newer mathematics was clearly stated, but may have represented a compromise:

> As a general rule school teaching should not be in a hurry to adapt itself to new trends in the more advanced parts of mathematics, but the basing of algebra on independent axioms of its own has the advantage of leading to treatments of many topics that are simpler and more natural than those that make it a part of analysis ... It is thought that a brief account of the axiomatic foundations of algebra may be welcome to some readers, and this has been given in the Appendix. No more is done than to state the axioms and discuss their meaning very briefly. It need scarcely be said that it is not suggested that any of this material should find its way into the school course.[127]

And:

> Any attempt to state the postulates of algebra, and derive everything from them in the same clear and exact way as in geometry, would lead to notions lying outside the range of school teaching.[128]

Interestingly, given Newman's earlier arguments for linear algebra, matrices were considered as a possible school topic. They were, however, only introduced in the Report, it was claimed, for 'the interest of those who wish to introduce something on this topic into the last few months of school work'.[129] Furthermore, it was only the 'better pupils' who could 'usefully be introduced to the idea'.[130]

All of the above positions can be seen to be broadly in keeping with the Mathematical Association's established pedagogical perspective, as embodied in the A-B-C schema. The Report reiterates this:

> In university teaching of pure mathematics it is a basic principle that topics shall not be introduced until they can be handled rigorously. No such principle is valid in school mathematics ...[131]

This brief discussion of the Teaching Committee's publicly agreed position in the 1950s demonstrates that the Association remained 'officially' committed to a radical discontinuity of approach between school and university. This was legitimated by reference to the pedagogical perspective established in earlier reports. Furthermore, nowhere in these reports are such post-1800 concepts as sets and groups discussed as potential topics for school mathematics.

Individual university-based members were, however, beginning to suggest that some elements of modern approaches might not be inappropriate for study at school. Hodge, Professor of Geometry at Cambridge, had, for example, in his presidential address of 1955, argued that some introduction to axiomatic methods might occur at school, at a stage when pupils took easily to new ideas.[132] Many school-based members were not, however, ready to accept such suggestions for change. As an example, we might consider the subsequent presidential address of Parsons, an independent schoolmaster, in 1956.[133] He argued that there had been enough change. Consolidation was now needed. The move from Euclid had gone too far. More emphasis on accuracy in arithmetical calculation was needed. He felt this situation has arisen from Jeffery's extension of the syllabus to the calculus: 'the process of extension of the syllabus has dangers which need to be closely watched'.[134] He summed up his views thus:

> I sometimes wonder whether we have not gone so far towards removing the so-called drudgery that we haven't removed the accuracy as well.[135]

Snell, another schoolmaster, had made similar points, though more indirectly, in his presidential address of 1953.[136]

The Assistant Masters' Association's Report of 1957, *The Teaching of Mathematics*, written by a Committee on which the Mathematical Association was well-represented, was similarly conservative in relation to content.[137] As the introduction to the revised edition of 1973 made clear in its discussion of the original Report:

> With the exception of statistics there was no mention of the newer topics which have found their way into mathematical syllabuses, nor of some of the newer methods of teaching which are being used increasingly in schools.[138]

The Inspectorate's publication of 1958, written, according to one of my interviewees, by Rollett, a mathematician active within the Mathematical Association, took a similar stance.[139] The 'problem' was noted:

> A pupil leaving school at sixteen may not have heard of any branch of mathematics less than 250 years old. A future mathematician may enter the university ignorant of groups, matrices, tensors, symbolic logic or topology.[140]

Problems arising from the discontinuity of approach, the 'plunge' from the particularities of school to the generalities of the university, and the restricted nature of school applied mathematics were also referred to.[141] Reference was also made, during a discussion of the moves towards an increasingly analytical geometry at school level, to the readiness of examiners to 'move the content of syllabuses away from what is dying to what is alive and growing'.[142] No suggestion was made, however, that 'modern' topics should appear in the general school course. After referring to the work of nineteenth and twentieth century mathematicians as being stage C in nature, and arguing that the teacher should know something of it, the writer posed the question whether the teacher should pass it on to his pupils. The answer given was that only a very little should be dealt with:

> A lesson or two of Boolean algebra (or another modern algebra) with its novel operational rules might reveal more clearly, by contrast, what ordinary 'algebra' is and does, and also give a taste of symbolic logic to those whose appetites and digestions are suited to it.[143]

Clearly, these mainstream publications, representing what Hughes, in 1962, termed the 'weight of authoritative opinion', were not, at this time, in favour of any radical changes with the aim of bringing 'modern' content and approaches into the schools.[144] But, as Bucher and Strauss stress, such documents represent compromises between segments with different missions and, as I noted earlier, some individual university-based members of the Mathematical Association were beginning to publicly criticize this 'consensus'.[145] Furthermore, some school-based members of this Association would also have been members of the ATAM whose leadership was to champion 'modern mathematics' at the end of the 1950s.[146] Individual members of the Teaching Committee may also have favoured some change in this direction. Certainly one member, Quadling, of Marlborough College, was to help found SMP. Articles on post-1800 mathematics, but not on the teaching of it in schools, did appear in the *Mathematical Gazette*, the Mathematical Association's journal. Its Assistant Editor after 1956, Cundy, of Sherborne School, was particularly interested in recent European and American work on mathematics education involving modern algebras, and was also to help launch SMP.[147] But, overall, the Association's stress on a 'good practice' approach to producing its reports, and its having become the representative association for older and senior selective school teachers, whose careers had been successfully constructed within the context of existing practice, made it seem a 'conservative' force to many of those who began to advocate curriculum reform in the late 1950s and early 1960s.[148] Those interested in change were going, as we shall see in later chapters, to bypass the Association in achieving it.

Conclusion

This chapter, dealing with what will be taken largely as 'unexplained givens' in this study, has shown that, in the 1950s, secondary school mathematics was clearly differentiated by 'ability' and, to a lesser extent, by sex. The main boundary was between what I have termed selective and non-selective school mathematics but there was also differentiation within these, especially the latter. There was not, however, a one-to-one correspondence between these two subject subcultures and the selective and non-selective school sectors. As the 1950s passed, more and more pupils were being entered by the secondary modern schools for the GCE and, as a consequence, the most 'able' pupils within these schools were being brought into contact with the selective mathematics tradition. Broadly speaking then, at this time, two versions of mathematics were being taught to two different categories of pupil, largely in different types of school, by teachers who, again broadly speaking, had been educated in two different types of post-school institution: the university and the teacher training college. The latter teachers were more likely to be non-specialists.

On this basis, it can be suggested that the two mathematical educational subcultures existed both at the level of ideas and at the level of social relations. The first, the selective, was a part of Lawton's 'public school tradition'; the second, the non-selective, of his 'elementary tradition'. It was also shown that the pedagogical perspectives held by mainstream mathematical educators, broadly 'psychometric', were such as to legitimate the broad outlines of a curriculum differentiated by 'ability' (but not so clearly its differentiation by sex).

Lastly, it was shown that a discontinuity of both content and approach existed between selective school mathematics and some currents within university mathematics, especially pure mathematics. It was suggested that part of the explanation for this might lie in the

Mathematical Association's continuing commitment, at least at the level of their reports, to the pedagogical strategy embodied in the A-B-C schema, that is, to an initially intuitive approach in the classroom. The Association's commitment to the principle of publicizing good practice in its reports was also seen as important here.

Such commitments must, however, be regarded as compromises, always likely to be changed, between the perspectives and interests of different segments within an association. As Bucher and Strauss argue in relation to the 'codes of ethics' of professional associations, in a process-orientated conflict approach:

> these products of professional activity are not necessarily evidence of internal homogeneity and consensus but from this viewpoint, such things as codes of ethics ... become the historical deposits of certain powerful segments.[149]

They note that different emerging segments will compete for control of such definitions.

In the case of the Mathematical Association, many of the older school-based members will have constructed their careers in terms of existing definitions of school mathematics and, if the arguments of the sociologists of science are correct, will have had an interest, all other things being equal, in resisting changes which might be seen as leading to the relative devaluation of their 'knowledge'. Some university mathematicians, on the other hand, especially those pure mathematicians teaching the post-1800 algebras, were beginning to express some concern over the nature of school mathematics. One example, Hodge, Professor of Geometry at Cambridge, has already been noted, and the inclusion of a discussion of the axiomatic basis of algebra in the 1957 Report discussed earlier might also be seen as reflecting such a trend. In terms of the model outlined in the last chapter, this might be seen as an expression of concern by university mathematicians about the subject socialization of their potential students. For several reasons, it might also have been expected, and will be seen later to have been the case, that some of the younger teachers in the higher status selective schools might become allies of those in the universities beginning to press for change. This would be expected because, first, they would have been socialized into a version of mathematics nearer to that of the university 'modern' pure mathematicians than that of their elders and because, secondly, they would have had a potential interest in changes that could, within schools, challenge the seniority of their elder colleagues or, at least, they would have had less of a vested interest in current practice.

The Mathematical Association was not, however, the only Association existing for secondary school mathematics teachers at this time. Members of the Association for Teaching Aids in Mathematics, drawn from a wider range of locations than members of the Mathematical Association, were also vigorously involved in discussing the nature of secondary school mathematics, both selective and non-selective versions. In the next chapter I shall turn my attention to the perspectives and interests of members of this more recently-formed association.

Notes

1 ARCHER (1979), pp. 44–5.
2 See, for example, GRIFFITHS and HOWSON (1974), p. 158.
3 LAWTON (1973), p. 79.
4 MACLURE (1973), pp. 89–97.
5 *Ibid.*, pp. 92–3.
6 *Ibid.*, p. 93.
7 *Ibid.*, p. 94.
8 *Ibid.*, p. 94.
9 *Ibid.*, p. 95.
10 *Ibid.*, p. 80.
11 See MINISTRY OF EDUCATION (1958), p. 1.
12 I have drawn on three main sources in preparing this section. These are: MINISTRY OF EDUCATION(1958), ASSISTANT MASTERS' ASSOCIATION (1973) and GRIFFITHS and HOWSON (1974).
13 This table has been compiled from information given in the introductions to the various reports of the association. Fuller details of these are given in the bibliography.
14 See, for example, MATHEMATICAL ASSOCIATION (1938), pp. 1–12.
15 See, for example, MATHEMATICAL ASSOCIATION (1953), pp. 4–5.
16 See, for example, MINISTRY OF EDUCATION (1958), pp. 16–19.
17 *Ibid.*, pp. 19–20.
18 *Ibid.*, p. 20.
19 Quoted in MINISTRY OF EDUCATION (1958), p. 17.
20 *Ibid.*, for example p. 51 and pp. 58–9.
21 See BERNSTEIN (1967).
22 See, for example, HALL (1955) or PARR (1950).
23 MINISTRY OF EDUCATION (1951), p. 38.
24 See MACLURE (1973), pp. 330–1.
25 See, for example, although for a slightly later period, FORD (1969), p. 36.
26 MINISTRY OF EDUCATION (1958), p. 20.
27 *Ibid.*, p. 24.
28 *Ibid.*, p. 103.
29 *Ibid.*, for example p. 104.
30 See CENTRAL ADVISORY COUNCIL FOR EDUCATION (1959), p. 219.
31 *Ibid.*, p. 219.
32 *Ibid.*, p. 212.

33 *Ibid.*, p. 76.
34 Many of the secondary modern schools had their origins in pre-war senior elementary departments. See, for example, Rubinstein and Simon (1969). On secondary modern teachers generally, see Taylor (1963).
35 Board of Education (1937), pp. 144–5.
36 *Ibid.*, pp. 534–64.
37 See Dempster (1949).
38 Chapman (1959).
39 *Ibid.*, p. 111.
40 *Ibid.*, p. 120.
41 *Ibid.*, pp. 113–4.
42 *Ibid.*, p. 112.
43 *Ibid.*, p. 114.
44 *Ibid.*, p. 117.
45 *Ibid.*, p. 117.
46 *Ibid.*, p. 112.
47 *Ibid.*, p. 112.
48 *Ibid.*, p. 112.
49 *Ibid.*, for example p. 118.
50 *Ibid.*, p. 118.
51 Board of Education (1934), pp. 24–6, and Ministry of Education (1958), p. 104.
52 Ministry of Education (1958), p. 111.
53 Central Advisory Council for Education (1963), Part Three.
54 *Ibid.*, p. 234.
55 *Ibid.*, pp. 235–6.
56 *Ibid.*, pp. 235–6.
57 *Ibid.*, p. 240.
58 *Ibid.*, p. 240.
59 Esland (1971), p. 89.
60 Board of Education (1938) and Board of Education (1943).
61 See Maclure (1973), pp. 201–2.
62 Keddie (1971), p. 135.
63 Board of Education (1934), pp. 15–16.
64 James (1958).
65 *Ibid.*, p. 5.
66 *Ibid.*, p. 7.
67 *Ibid.*, p. 82.
68 Morgan (1959).
69 *Ibid.*, pp. 14–15.
70 *Ibid.*, pp. 21–2.
71 Mathematical Association (1959), p. 6.
72 *Ibid.*, p. 19.
73 Ministry of Education (1958).
74 *Ibid.*, p. 105.
75 *Ibid.*, p. 108.
76 *Ibid.*, p. 103.
77 *Ibid.*, p. 103.
78 James (1958), p. 105, and Morgan (1959), p. 20.

79 BOARD OF EDUCATION (1934), p. 47.
80 *Ibid.*, p. 58.
81 *Ibid.*, p. 59.
82 *Ibid.*, p. 60.
83 MORGAN (1959), p. 135.
84 *Ibid.*, p. 136.
85 JAMES (1958), p. 137 and p. 210.
86 MATHEMATICAL ASSOCIATION (1959), p. 31.
87 MATHEMATICAL ASSOCIATION (1959), p. 65.
88 MINISTRY OF EDUCATION (1958), p. 108.
89 See, for example, BELL (1945).
90 See GRIFFITHS and HOWSON (1974).
91 See ORGANIZATION FOR ECONOMIC COOPERATION AND DEVELOPMENT (1961a).
92 BELL (1945), p. 198.
93 See, for example, COHN (1958), p. 32.
94 BELL (1945), pp. 215–6.
95 *Ibid.*, p. 217.
96 *Ibid.*, p. 211 and p. 266.
97 See, for example, MESCHKOWSKI (1968), pp. 7–11.
98 See, for example, STEWART (1975), p. 113.
99 BELL (1945), pp. 334–5.
100 See, for example, GRIFFITHS and HOWSON (1974), pp. 109–10.
101 On Bourbaki, see HALMOS (1968).
102 GRIFFITHS and HOWSON (1974), p. 109.
103 See, for example, LIGHTHILL (Ed.) (1978).
104 See below, chapters 5 and 6.
105 See below, chapters 5 and 6.
106 See, for example, the mixture of the old and the 'new' in STEPHENSON (1961).
107 See below, chapters 5 and 6.
108 See, for example, WILKES (1966).
109 On 'models', see chapters 5 and 6 below, and HALL (1978).
110 See chapters 5 and 6 below.
111 MATHEMATICAL ASSOCIATION (1938), p. 5.
112 MATHEMATICAL ASSOCIATION (1953), p. ix.
113 *Ibid.*, p. ix.
114 *Ibid.*, pp. ix–x.
115 *Ibid.*, p. x.
116 See BELL (1945) on the development of geometry.
117 Descartes lived from 1596–1650.
118 MATHEMATICAL ASSOCIATION (1953), p. x.
119 MATHEMATICAL ASSOCIATION (1957a).
120 *Ibid.*, p. 2.
121 *Ibid.*, p. 8.
122 *Ibid.*, p. 10.
123 *Ibid.*, p. 100.
124 MATHEMATICAL ASSOCIATION(1957b).
125 LEDERMAN (1949).

126 NEWMAN (1937).
127 MATHEMATICAL ASSOCIATION (1957b), p. vi.
128 *Ibid.*, p. vi.
129 *Ibid.*, p. 34.
130 *Ibid.*, p. ix.
131 *Ibid.*, p. v.
132 See HODGE (1955).
133 See PARSONS (1957).
134 *Ibid.*, p. 5.
135 *Ibid.*, p. 6.
136 See SNELL (1953).
137 ASSISTANT MASTERS' ASSOCIATION (1957).
138 ASSISTANT MASTERS' ASSOCIATION (1973), p. 1.
139 MINISTRY OF EDUCATION (1958).
140 *Ibid.*, p. 135.
141 *Ibid.*, pp. 146–7.
142 *Ibid.*, p. 93.
143 *Ibid.*, p. 145.
144 HUGHES (1962), p. 26.
145 HODGE (1955).
146 See chapter 4 below.
147 See THWAITES (1972), p. ix.
148 See GRIFFITHS and HOWSON (1974), p. 130, and chapter 10 below.
149 BUCHER and STRAUSS (1961), pp. 331–2.

4   The Association For Teaching Aids In Mathematics

My purpose in this chapter is not to provide a detailed historical account of the development of the ATAM nor an explanatory account of its origins but rather to present, broadly in terms of the model outlined earlier, a brief analysis of the perspectives and activities of its activist members in the mid to late 1950s. This is necessary here in order to provide part of the background for the events of 1959 onwards which will be analyzed in later chapters. It will be seen, in chapter 10 in particular, that members of the ATAM played a significant role in the development of new textbooks and syllabuses, especially those of MME.

The period covered in this chapter included many other important events, such as the Oxford and Liverpool conferences — to be discussed in chapters 5 and 6. Hence this, and the subsequent two chapters, consider parallel periods of time. This non-chronological approach is a necessary device to achieve some clarity in presenting the context for events after 1959.

It will be seen that the Association, founded by a small group of members of the Mathematical Association who shared a mission they saw as unrealizable within that Association, experienced rapid growth into lower status sectors untapped by the Mathematical Association and then a consequential growth of dissension between differently located members. In Bucher and Strauss' terms, the ATAM became, like most established associations, a 'battleground' in which 'different emerging segments compete for control'.[1]

Drawing on secondary sources, I shall first very briefly discuss the founding and growth of the ATAM. I shall then discuss the perspectives of its activist members in some depth, drawing mainly on the journal of the Association and then, again briefly, the strategies for achieving their mission employed by the leadership, in this period. I shall then speculatively analyze the material presented in the chapter in terms of the model developed in chapter 2.

Foundation And Growth

According to the AMA's publication *The Teaching of Mathematics in Secondary Schools*,[2] produced by a Committee having Birtwistle of the ATAM as Chairman, the ATAM:

> was started by a small group of enthusiasts in 1953 under the influence of the International Commission for the Study and Improvement of the Teaching of Mathematics ... The initial emphasis on aids and materials constituted in part a reaction against the sterile and 'academic' treatment of mathematics in so many classrooms: partly again it arose from a desire to demontrate that children really can explore and represent mathematical situations for themselves in the concrete.[3]

Howson and Griffiths present a similar account, arguing that, because of the increasingly 'conservative' nature of the Mathematical Association, a 'number of educators', led by Gattegno, 'came together to form the Association for Teaching Aids in Mathematics'.[4]

Key personnel in the early years included Gattegno, who had sat on the Mathematical Association's Primary School Sub-committee in the early 1950s, J. Peskett, T.J. Fletcher, R.H. Collins and I. Harris. Their work led to a rapid growth in membership, which, by early 1959, had reached 1058.[5]

By the late 1950s, one sociologically significant difference from the Mathematical Association was the greater number of key members from relatively low status educational locations. The April 1958 election results (Table 4),[6] if compared with the Teaching Committee membership of the Mathematical Association (Table 1) (page 38), demonstrate this clearly. The range of locations is also striking.

Perspectives on Teaching, Learning and the Subject

In this section some elements of the perspectives of activist members of the ATAM will be described. My sources will be primarily articles and book reviews appearing in the journal of the Association, especially during the period 1957–59.

The mission of the founding members had been explicitly con-

Table 4:   ATAM Officials in April 1958

		Location
President	C. Gattegno	University
Chairman	R.H. Collins	Grammar school (1963)
Secretary	Mrs.R.M. Fyfe	Grammar school (1959)
Treasurer	Miss B.I. Briggs	Senior secondary school (1962)
Committee	C. Birtwistle	Technical school (1958)
	Miss J. Clarkson	Primary school (1963)
	R.H. Fielding	Comprehensive school (1958)
	T.J. Fletcher	Sir John Cass College
	Miss. Y.B. Guiseppi	Comprehensive school (1957)
	I. Harris	Grammar school (1957)
	C. Hope	Worcester Training College
	R.D. Knight (librarian)	Uncoded
	J.V. Trivett	Secondary modern school (1957)
Coopted	Miss I.L. Campbell	Uncoded
	D.T. Moore	Secondary modern school (1962)
	J.W. Peskett	Sandhurst
	L.A. Swinden	Retired

cerned with pedagogical reform, but it will be seen that, by the end of the 1950s, many in the leadership had become equally concerned to promote change in the school mathematics syllabuses. I shall concentrate the discussion on actors who were involved in the events of the early 1960s to be analyzed in later chapters.

The very name of the Association indicates precisely where the original members' concerns lay — in the 'improvement' of mathematics pedagogy through the increased use of such teaching aids as films and structural apparatus. Early members, such as Gattegno, Fletcher and Peskett, were already, or about to become, well-known for their work in this area. This concern with pedagogy remained a key element of activist members' perspectives during the 1950s. Hope, for example, a lecturer at Worcester Training College who was to jointly found MME in 1961, argued in the April 1958 issue of *Mathematics Teaching*, the journal of the Association:

> We are not concerned with mere instruction designed to convince the child sufficiently for him to accept the teacher's

dogmas, but with the child's creative activity by which he discovers and convinces himself and others of the truth and importance of his discoveries.[7]

In the same issue, in another contribution, he attacked contemporary textbooks and classroom practice.[8] Having noted the uniformity of available textbooks and the enormous demand for them, he continued:

> Mathematics teaching is thus assailed from two flanks: on the one hand the textbook, on the other the public examination, and both work together to defeat the teacher who would go forward. The examination provides the framework which justifies the uniformity of the text.[9]

He argued that mathematics teachers did not have to follow this preordained strategy of bookwork plus drill plus bookwork. Rather, topics could be partly determined by children's interests and stage of development. 'Some' sequencing might be necessary but he would prefer an approach through 'problem-solving'. If, because of the shortage of teachers, a textbook was necessary for the use of weaker teachers, then:

> It is necessary that the bookwork should at least force the reader to recognize that a problem interesting enough to solve at that stage exists and to provide opportunity for attempting a solution before a ready-made effort tailored to the needs of certain examination topics is supplied. One would like to see more reference to things to make, experiments to carry out, fields of mathematics to investigate. One would like problems included which would provide an opportunity for reference to and natural explanation of more advanced mathematics or of modern topics of mathematical investigation, for example, algebra as a theory of structure, new number fields, geometries without measures, etc, general methods of solution, etc.[10]

He ended by calling for pressure to be applied to publishers' representatives for such texts to be produced, for more comment on the need for them in the educational press and, lastly, for reviewers to attack 'poor' texts more systematically.

Similar views on pedagogy were voiced by many other activist members. Fyfe, in 1958, argued for a 'working together' of teacher and pupil in the classroom 'in order to arrive at a cogent discovery, or towards the gaining of mastery'.[11] She was reported, in the same issue, by Wheeler, as favouring a 'learner-centred' approach. In particular:

She suggested that because there were so many failures in mathematics at 'O' level, even among the top 10–20 per cent of the school population, the conventional methods of drilling in techniques had been proved inefficient. She had decided she would never teach a technique unless the mathematics involved were first understood by the pupils: a serious obstacle was the excessive impregnation of all branches of mathematics with complex arithmetical calculations.[12]

Various members who shared these basic pedagogical assumptions seem to have also shared Hope's views on how to use review columns. Briggs, for example, discussing J.D. Hodson's *Introductory Comprehensive Mathematics* of 1956, wrote in 1957:

The text, in general, leads the pupil to work according to certain rules, without real understanding of the mathematical situation; and in the geometrical field to a passive acceptance of relationships rather than a real awareness. This is a criticism of mathematical textbooks in general ...[13]

Having, by implication, argued for a new approach, she continued:

All single triangles and parallelograms drawn in the book have one side parallel to the bottom of the page and all separate right-angled triangles are drawn with the sides containing the right angles parallel and perpendicular to the bottom of the page. It is not surprising that some children think of the hypotenuse as the sloping side ...[14]

And, in the same issue, Meetham, reviewing Keith and Martindale's *Know Your Mathematics*, wrote:

A careful examination of Book 3 leaves no doubt that the authors' aim is to lull the enquiring mind of the child into permanent apathy, and to substitute for mathematics a respect for the mechanicalness of the manipulation of arithmetic.[15]

These writers were, in Esland's terms, providing a 'degree of public legitimacy' for those mathematics teachers interested in an alternative 'definition of subject and its methodology'.[16] They were clearly, in relation to contemporary classroom practice, presenting a deviant perspective on learning and the pupil's role in the process. Pupils here are not seen, as in Esland's psychometric ideal-type, as passive, as vessels to be filled with knowledge. A didactic pedagogy is, in fact, explicitly rejected. Rather, Esland's 'epistemological paradigm' captures many elements of their position. This paradigm:

is explicitly concerned with how the child actively constructs and arranges his knowledge of the world in his developing interpretational schema.[17]

In this paradigm, a concern with 'intelligence' is replaced by a concern with 'curiosity and motivation'. 'Discovery' becomes a central issue. 'Interests' are relevant to the selection of content. Esland's paradigms were, of course, intended as ideal-types and, in this particular case, do not, in fact, capture in a fully adequate manner the activists' perspectives. In spite of their adherence to some key elements of his epistemological paradigm, they also shared elements of his psychometric idealtype.

For example, while there were many attacks in *Mathematics Teaching* on the practice of testing, such as in Hope's review of K. Anderson's *Arithmetic Tests for Fourth Year Juniors* in November 1958:

> it is not Mr. Anderson's fault, but his book will perform a valuable service if, in its most comprehensive and admirably constructed tests, tests which fulfil their purpose one might say 'almost to perfection', it shows up the futility and the triviality of the mathematical aims of so many of our primary schools,[18]

it is nevertheless the case that, almost without exception, writers in the journal adhered to a capacity model of intelligence. Hope, for example, was reported as having informed a group meeting that differences between children should be emphasized, and that groups of 'like standard' must be taught together. But, in the same talk, he argued that experiences in learning must be more often arranged by the learner, hence reflecting elements of both Esland's paradigms.[19] Elsewhere in the journal, contributors use the terms 'backward boys', 'slower streams' and the like quite unselfconsciously. Key elements of the perspective of the Norwood Report remained unchallenged by these members' positions. One of the few exceptions was Gattegno himself who outlined his ideas to a meeting at the London Institute in 1957, reported by Fyfe in the journal.[20]

He wanted both teacher and learner involved in the learning process. He did not believe in 'grading children according to ability'. Children are all thinkers, but with different modes of thought.

A study of the journal, however, reveals him to have been in a very small minority on this issue. Most key members in schools and training colleges seem to have accepted some of his views but not those totally at variance with the assumptions regarding 'ability' of the mainstream perspective described in chapter 3. Given that Hope, and others, were working in training colleges where, at this time, Piaget's ideas were receiving much support,[21] it may not be implausible to suggest that the detailed nature of the perspectives of the activist members can only be accounted for in terms of the variety of elements combined in them — including the Mathematical Association's stress on the importance of stage A work, Piaget's psychology, and the Norwood-type thinking of many mathematics teachers — and in terms of the variety of audiences addressed within the Association.

Evidence for the suggested influence of Piagetian ideas can be found in discussions of educational research in the journal. There were several articles in *Mathematics Teaching* which either took Piagetian ideas as given or specifically aimed to disseminate them to teachers. Terms such as 'mental structures' and 'stage of development' are used freely. Illustrations can be taken from the issue for November 1957. An article by Dodwell discusses Piaget's work in relation to the evolution of number concepts in the child.[22] And, in a letter from Brookes, later to be an important member of the Association, we find, in a discussion of 'reversibility' and school algebra, a very Piagetian vocabulary:

> At every turn the relation which exists between a mathematical structure and the mental structure created in the mind of the child is the ultimate arbiter of our teaching method.[23]

But, as I have already noted, such Piagetian perspectives on the proper approach to the study of intelligence were not held by all members and, furthermore, even those making some use of the Piagetian paradigm often worked simultaneously with psychometric 'capacity' models.

Having now discussed activist members' pedagogical and, more specifically, psychological perspectives, I want to turn to the 'subject' *per se*. What views of school mathematics and its purposes were adhered to? Esland's 'subject perspective' agenda raises the important questions here.[24] I shall concentrate on certain of these. I shall also concentrate on the views of the leadership and other active members.

The existing paradigms within university mathematics at this time were briefly discussed in chapter 3. For those seeking reference points, choices were available between the 'elegant' axiomatic modern algebras and the increasingly computer-orientated applied mathematics, with its problem-solving focus. 'Modern' content existed within both sub-disciplines. As I have already remarked, during this period, some of the ATAM leadership, possibly as a strategy for increasing the legitimacy of their mission (which changed in the process) and increasing their resources through alliance with high status university mathematicians, moved towards supporting the introduction of some of this content into school mathematics. Between 1956 and 1959 a dozen articles in *Mathematics Teaching* appeared which probably served to introduce 'modern mathematics' to many teachers in the schools.[25] Many of the topics discussed in these articles, later to appear in such texts as those of SMP and MME, were explicitly presented with the school classroom in mind. Others were presented as new mathematics for members to study. (As was seen in chapter 3, no parallel support for those wishing to bring such material into schools was forthcoming from the publications of the Mathematical Association at this time.) The legitimation of these new topics drew on various sources. The editorial of April 1958, which discussed the Mathematical Association's *The Teaching of Algebra in VIth Forms*, well illustrates this variety:

> The present shift in algebra is away from emphasis on complicated manipulation towards a more general study of operations and structure ... Is it too much to hope that we may adopt this attitude in school? The attempt is being made in France, and it is being made in the USA. There is little evidence for the view that the latest parts of mathematics to develop historically are the most difficult for the pupil to grasp. Indeed much modern research in pure mathematics has been directed towards putting the foundations of the subject on a simpler logical basis, and much of the psychological work of Piaget suggests that many of the essential notions of modern algebra (which are regarded as a university study) have to form in the pupil's mind before he is even ready to undertake the study of number ... Such topics as the algebra of sets or relations might be taught with profit not merely in the sixth form but lower down the school as well. In other countries they are learning how to do this, and unless we learn too we shall be left behind.
>
> Of course, such ideas have to be presented in a suitable way. The formal axiomatic way in which groups, rings and fields are presented to pure mathematicians at university would never do in school. The idea must be presented in terms of concrete applications with a similar structure.[26]

Illustrations of applications must be given — 'up to date uses' — for these topics. The editorial ends by referring to the 'needs' of future scientists, a crucial issue within educational and political arenas at the time[27]:

> The traditional, abstract and formal methods of teaching algebra have not had much success with them in the past, so can we hope

that they will succeed any better in the future? But we need these boys and girls increasingly, and we have to teach them to think systematically about real-life situations, to appreciate the formal structure of problems, to devise mathematical techniques to describe them, and to interpret the final solutions in everyday terms. The teaching of algebra in sixth forms will not be on a sound basis until it is doing all of this ... [28]

This editorial, from an Editorial Committee consisting of Fletcher, Hope, Gattegno, Guiseppi and Fyfe, is, at first sight, confusing. It simultaneously advocates abstract modern algebra and attacks abstract and formal methods. It stresses mathematics for its own sake and applications. In fact, it brought together many of the issues then under discussion by mathematicians and others concerned with mathematics.[29] The emphasis on abstract algebra, for example, reflected the involvement of members of the ATAM in the Europe-wide meetings of the International Commission for the Study and Improvement of the Teaching of Mathematics (ICSITM). At these meetings, university-based modern algebraists had much influence and hence, although one focus was on pedagogy and teaching aids, the possibility of bringing 'modern' topics into all levels of school work was also being discussed.[30] The emphasis on modelling and applications reflects the discussions of the important conference held at Oxford in 1957 between actors from universities, schools and industry to which both Harris and Hope refer in *Mathematics Teaching* in support of their arguments for change.[31] But, alongside both of these elements, there remains the stress on the founding mission of pedagogical reform. In spite of this being a primary commitment, however, the impression gained by an examination of the journal at this time is that Harris was reflecting a broadly-based consensus — amongst the leading activists — when he wrote, in November 1957, that 'important new trends in mathematics' should be 'reflected in the teaching of mathematics in schools'.[32] In the same issue Hope also recommended several newer branches of mathematics for the new three year course in the training colleges.[33]

Lastly, before turning once again to the issue of the differentiation of the curriculum by 'ability', the centrality of 'applicability' for many members must be noted. This was a major concern for many of the leadership. Collins, for example, later to be involved with Hope in MME, stressed, in a series of articles on the place of mathematics in the curriculum, the role that the subject played in scientific and technical thought.[34] He wrote, in 1958:

When I finally come to consider this particular theme (that is, mathematics is the basis of the scientific mode of thought) I find myself of the opinion, that properly understood, it will provide the most satisfactory aim for the teaching of the subject to all children and in every type of school.[35]

Harris had experimented with numerical methods and calculating machines at Dartford Grammar School.[36] Other members, for example, Brookes, Collins, Fyfe and Tammadge, attended the Liverpool conference of 1959, at which applicability was a central issue.[37] This concern with the uses of mathematics was to be reflected in the development of MME.[38]

Perspectives on the Differentiation of Content and Pedagogy

I shall now turn to those elements of ATAM activists' perspectives relating to the differentiation of the curriculum by 'ability'. Relative to the Mathematical Association, the ATAM exhibited a greater concern with the teaching of mathematics at all levels of age and 'ability'. As can be seen from Table 4 (page 71), key members were drawn not, as in the case of the Mathematical Association, largely from the universities and prestigious independent schools and grammar schools, but from a wider range of locations, some of which were, sociologically speaking, of considerably lower status. To a much greater extent than in the case of the Mathematical Association, key figures might be associated with the non-selective mathematical subculture. Furthermore, it will be seen later that the interests of such members were well-represented in debates within the Association as a whole. Although the pages of *Mathematics Teaching* also contain many articles, and report many meetings, concerned with the primary sector (and primary teachers may well have influenced debates within the Association on pedagogy), I shall, since this is my main concern, concentrate here on material relating to the secondary sector.

A number of emphases can be discerned. The overall impression is of a commitment amongst members to a mathematics-for-all, as opposed to a mathematics-for-some and arithmetic-for-others, approach, but with the meaning of 'mathematics' varying, and the degree of commitment wavering, according to members' particular locations, current occupational problems and reference groups. I shall illustrate this by, first, considering the positions held within the Association on the 'mathematics' appropriate for secondary modern pupils and the place of the subject in these schools and then, secondly, on the relevance of teaching aids to pupils of various 'abilities'. It will be seen that, especially in relation to the second issue, the leadership and the general membership were, by the late 1950s, beginning to hold different positions. These possibly reflected their somewhat different locations and occupational problems.

In relation to the first question, that of the nature of secondary modern mathematics, there is considerable evidence that what most occupied secondary modern-based activists in this period was not the issue of 'modern' content but of 'mathematics' — as opposed to arithmetic — *per se*. This was associated with a desire to establish mathematics departments and the taking of the GCE in their schools. Such concerns were clearly expressed at the annual conference of the Association at Blackpool in 1958.[39] In fact, Collins, not himself working in a modern school, was, according to one report, 'shocked by the demand of the secondary modern schools that they should take the GCE: their attitude seemed to be one of wishing to tie themselves to a syllabus'.[40] It is clear that a number of secondary modern members publicly disagreed with him on this. Their disagreement was expressed in terms of the incentives offered to teachers and pupils by examinations. It is clear, however, from the work of both Taylor and, more recently, Goodson, that often associated with or underlying these claims was a tendency for teachers in these schools to use an examination-orientated strategy as part of an attempt to increase their status and access to resources, that is, as part of a strategy for individual and collective mobility.[41] In fact, in the two discussion groups at this conference addressing 'difficulties in the secondary modern schools', a concern to increase the status of mathematics teaching through an increased degree of subject specialization and an examination orientation was clearly displayed. The first group was mainly concerned about large class sizes, poor timetable allocation, the apathy of parents and indiscipline. They felt, according to the report, that under the 'new Burnham arrangements':

> a head of the mathematics department should be appointed, even in the smallest school, to take charge of all mathematics throughout the school. He should be responsible for the schemes of work within the subject, coordinating the work at every stage, and holding regular meetings of the mathematics staff to discuss syllabus content and method. Whether the GCE should be taken in the modern schools and the syllabus designed to this end was not resolved, but it was generally felt that the children should have an incentive.[42]

In the second group examinations were also discussed, along with staff turnover. The existence of non-specialist staff 'having ... to teach the subject when they had no interest in it' was regarded as a special problem.[43] Given these expressed concerns and the situation in these schools at the time, it is not implausible to suggest that many general subject teachers and mathematics specialists will have been involving themselves and their schools in activities aimed at establishing their careers and/or their school's status in the new subject-specialist and GCE-orientated climate.

Not all those in the secondary moderns, however, gave up the claim to be providing a distinctive but equal education. Elements of this position can be discerned in an article by Moore on the organization of the mathematics course in the modern school.[44] He shared some ground with those whose views were described above. Having argued that the two most important factors are the selection of mathematics suitable 'for the 75 per cent ... not destined for an examination' and the 'shortage ... of specialist mathematics teachers', he went on to argue for the establishment of heads of department. He wanted specialist rooms stocked with equipment for practical work, homework to 'ensure' parental interest, and a pedagogy emphasizing the 'understanding of concepts and techniques' through experience. But he wanted a syllabus designed in relation to special local interests, such as rural studies, and for the 'average or middle groups in the school'. This should be modified for the 'less able', but the syllabus should not be designed for the 'best children' and then be 'cut ... down to suit slower or less able pupils'. He concluded:

> Despite the dozen or so years that have passed since the secondary modern schools were created, mathematics is still in the experimental stage in these schools, and we must see that it becomes a study in its own right and not a watered-down version of grammar school or technical school mathematics.[45]

His article makes no reference to the 'modern' topics being discussed in the journal at that time. In fact, he recommends James' book[46] and the relevant report of the Mathematical Association.[47] Here, then, the move to imitate the grammar schools in order to raise the status of the secondary moderns through increased GCE entries and passes is not given priority. But such voices from within the modern sector were increasingly in a minority as the decade passed and it was instead non-secondary modern-based activists, whose status was more secure, who provided arguments against the move towards the GCE and subject specialization in these schools.

Birtwistle, for example, Deputy Head of a technical grammar school, wrote, in an editorial of July 1959, of the advantages of an increased division of labour in society but claimed to be worried about the associated tendency for over-specialization to increase: 'it is we who are the humanizers of society' he argued, but we are becoming 'victims of this move to specialisation ourselves'.[48] His subsequent comments demonstrate that the relationship between specialization, status and resources was well understood:

> No longer do we regard ourselves as teachers; instead we are 'mathematicians', 'chemists', 'mathematics specialists', ... heads of department and so on through a whole list of pretentious titles. We do really believe that we are the people described by these titles. Any secondary school headteacher knows that an advert for a teacher of general subjects would produce little or no response. We are all anxious to teach 'our subject', we are 'mathematicians', so we must teach that subject.[49]

He concluded by arguing that a danger existed of putting 'subject' not education first, and of not adequately considering the relations between subjects.

Again, it was other non-secondary modern-based activists who argued, at this period, for some 'new' mathematics to come into these schools. For example, in *Mathematics Teaching* for April 1958, Walker, in an article on statistics aimed 'mainly at the grammar school', stressed that what he had said would 'apply equally well to technical and modern schools, and so far as the latter are concerned even more so since they are not usually geared to and impeded by university syllabuses'.[50] Harris, of Dartford Grammar School, was reported in the same issue as having spoken on the advantages of a 'dynamic' approach to geometry for the modern schools.[51] This outsider's approach is perhaps best illustrated, however, by Hope's piece in 1959 on the Mathematical Association's Report on the modern school mathematics course.[52] He first noted that 'A' stream work for the GCE had served to move the mathematics curriculum of these schools away from mere arithmetic plus, as the 'high-water', a little graphical work:

> Many children received an unrestricted, if somewhat repetitive diet of commercial arithmetic, a repertoire of tricks, methods and catches, rote-learnt to no purpose, and in many cases just a repetition of primary experience.[53]

He continued:

It is not surprising that advisory literature has not yet caught up with the schools, for there have been only two previous books about the secondary modern mathematics course: one which has not caught up with 1945 ... and one by Mr. James of Redland which copes with the 'B' streams of three years ago.[54]

Hence:

We looked forward to this report with some expectation of learning about recent developments. In some directions expectations have been fulfilled, whilst in others there is a feeling of disappointment. The report has almost nothing to say about the 'A' children.[55]

He went on to the details of his review. He largely approved of Part One on 'purpose, approach and organization', but added:

There is nothing new in the proposals and one is struck by the need for more thought about the way to select topics and to relate them to mathematics and the other subjects of the school curriculum. One feels that a syllabus formed by projecting mappings of mathematics on different planes, on other planes, might serve better the muse of integrated mathematics than a sequence of topics which are on account of their sequence studied seriatim in time.[56]

His main criticisms were, however, reserved for Part Two:

The second part of the book is one of the best treatments of Stage A geometry and algebra which has been published. There are brief sections on mechanics and statistics but their brevity makes them mere mentions. Surveying, navigation are given a full treatment. Having said that, one has to admit that this section is sadly lacking in mathematics and vision. The report might have given treatments of the ideas of calculus and coordinate geometry analogous to the infant treatment of number, and mathematics which one could introduce and which would help the children to understand something of the underlying rationale of the various industries which would employ them. There is a lack of Stage B collection of results into a pattern which has some reasonable basis however slight. There is no dovetailing of topics. One has the feeling that the report is concerned to reinforce existing textbooks rather than to break new ground. It is, in fact, rather behind what the schools themselves are developing. But, having said all this, it remains a landmark in the teaching of secondary modern mathematics. It will find an honoured place on staff library shelves and will be well-used by the teachers. It will serve as a valuable source for much of the B and C stream mathematics. Nevertheless, many teachers will bemoan its lack of forward vision, which reaches out to a new concept of secondary mathematics stressing mathematical ideas and principles in a form which enables modern developments to be glimpsed if not appreciated, and at the very least will ask why the Jeffery Report has had little influence on it. To quote the Spens Report of 1938 we must 'treat mathematics as a science in which the topics are chosen so as to develop a grasp of mathematical ideas, and . . . these topics should be suggested and introduced by the examination of practical questions which in their day have been of urgent interest and utility to man in his affairs'. It is perhaps in realizing this suggested development that our own Association might supplement the efforts of the Mathematical Association.[57]

Within this attack, which also provides a rationale for the separate existence of the ATAM, and especially in his comments on the 'A' stream, can be discerned a belief on Hope's part that 'modern mathematics' of some sort should be brought into the secondary modern curriculum.

It is clear, then, that at least a difference of emphasis, if not of opinion, existed between activists from different locations at this time. Those in the secondary moderns were primarily interested, for a mixture of 'educational' and material reasons, in the establishment of a mathematics curriculum leading to the GCE, consisting of much more than arithmetic, and to be taught by specialist teachers. It was to be a few years yet before they became greatly concerned with the introduction of 'modern' content. On the other hand, some members in selective schools and training colleges, as part of their development of the founding mission, were already beginning to argue for the inclusion of such material in these schools' schemes of work. Others, usually based in the selective schools, were arguing against the move within the modern schools towards the GCE.

Having now discussed the general issue of appropriate content for non-selective pupils, I shall turn to the second question: that of pedagogy and 'ability'. I shall show that, while the activist members tended to argue for the relevance of their favoured pedagogic approach to all pupils, the general membership, once the Association had grown to about a thousand, often did not accept this. For example, a discussion at the 1958 conference was reported thus:

> It was the unanimous opinion of the group that practical work was invaluable with children who found difficulty with the subject. Opinion was divided as to whether it would assist the brighter child.[58]

Similar 'shop-floor' disagreement, but in respect of all children, can be inferred from the report of a one-day conference at the Dick Shephard School in 1958. Fyfe, amongst others, had given a demonstration lesson, with nine year-olds using geoboards:

> The ... lesson aroused a good deal of discussion. Considerable conflict of opinion about the depth of understanding achieved by the pupils was evident. Some deplored the absence of a formal definition of the figures involved; others countered with the view that understanding having been achieved, verbalisation was not essential until the pupil desired it. To some, the lesson was valuable time wasted, and to others, an exposure of a lack of understanding in the child frequently unnoticed by the teacher. The discussion showed clearly that those who thought the lesson largely wasted would have had different aims in the same situation, and failed to judge accurately the end-product because they were not in sympathy with Mrs. Fyfe's aims.[59]

It can be hypothesized here that, as the Association grew, many would have joined and attended meetings, not because of a commitment to the original mission, but rather because it would have been expected of promotion-minded teachers, or to receive helpful journal articles, and so on. If so, this would account for the critical response to Fyfe and others which developed within the Association at this period. To some extent, the more radical members now found themselves having to defend their positions. In *Mathematics Teaching* for April 1959, for example, we find Fyfe writing, in a piece on using aids in the grammar school:

> A critic tells me that aids are 'for playing about' and that there is not time for this in the grammar school, and then adds that, anyway, they ought not to be necessary.[60]

She argued, in reply, that schools, after 600 hours, currently failed many of their pupils, those who fail to understand mathematics. She was not, however, concerned to use aids 'solely to help those who would otherwise fail'. Enough was not taught to the rest, nor to an adequate depth of understanding. She concluded that, 'wisely-used', aids saved time and made 'the children inclined to work much harder than they did when I relied exclusively on the blackboard and the written work they did in their exercise books'.[61]

Here she appealed to criteria of success which were presumably widely-held amongst mathematics teachers. A similar position had been taken by Swinden in the November 1958 issue. He had been asked by the Editor to contribute an article 'explaining my aims in making models and the use I have made of them in teaching'. He wrote:

> I have spent most of my career with the slower streams and my aims in using models have been to lighten the burden for these children and help them reach a creditable standard.[62]

He added that 'enjoyment' was also a consideration and that models are a 'tremendous help to the slower child' and 'do no harm to the quicker ones'.[63]

There is some evidence, then, that as the ATAM grew in size (and 'respectability'), there was increasing conflict within it over pedagogy. As with the Mathematical Association, an early radicalism was to be, to some extent, diluted by an influx of teachers ready, for a variety of reasons, to resist major changes in approach. In particular, it appears that, by the late 1950s, a range of opinions existed amongst the membership on the question of the differentiation of pedagogical strategies by 'ability', especially in relation to the use of teaching aids.

Strategy

To some extent, the activities of the ATAM activists have been described above. I shall, therefore, only briefly discuss the major strategies employed by these members in the 1950s. These were: publishing a journal, expanding membership, holding meetings and conferences, and aiming to be represented in various settings.

The journal was started in 1955, having been preceded by a few duplicated bulletins. It contained articles aimed at both primary and secondary teachers. These presented accounts of the use of teaching aids, of newer mathematics, of psychological and educational research, and translations of European material of the same sort. The review columns were employed to attack 'traditional' textbooks and to provide welcoming reviews of books concerned with newer content and/or broadly 'epistemological' pedagogies. To this extent, the journal provided elements of a 'plausibility structure' for teachers in schools who favoured reform, as well as being simultaneously an attempt to 'convert' others. Various pamphlets were also published.[64]

Meetings and conferences were the other main activity. They usually took the form of either lectures on the use of aids, followed by discussion, or demonstration lessons. Harris, Trivett, Fyfe, Guiseppi, Hope, Collins, Clarkson and Birtwistle seem to have been the main contributors. Fletcher specialized in the use of film. Local branch meetings often took a similar form, with invited speakers. The setting-up of these branches was a major aim of the leadership. From 1957 onwards, the Association also ran annual conferences at Easter. For these, speakers were often invited from abroad, through the ICSITM. This range of activities quickly ensured the existence of a well-informed network of supporters of reform. The more 'conservative' consequences of this rapid growth in membership seem to have quickly followed.

Partly as a result of this growth in membership (in a context where the Mathematical Association was seen by many teachers as primarily concerned with sixth form and university mathematics), the ATAM had begun, by the end of the 1950s, to be taken seriously by mathematical educators. The achievement of this 'respectability' is perhaps best demonstrated by Hope's having been one of the four United Kingdom participants at the influential Royaumont Seminar of 1959.[65] Further-more, he was also to be one of the 'group of experts', sponsored by the OEEC, that produced the influential *Synopses for Modern Secondary School Mathematics* during 1960.[66] That members of the Association also contributed to the events of the early 1960s which led to the development of 'reformed' textbooks will be shown later.

Conclusion

I shall now, somewhat speculatively, interpret the material presented in this chapter in terms of the model developed in chapter 2.

The ATAM had originally been founded by a small group with a particular mission — to 'improve' the teaching of mathematics through pedagogical reform. The founders were located in a range of educational organizations, were mostly members of the Mathematical Association, with which some were dissatisfied as a vehicle for 'improving' mathematics teaching, and derived some support and encouragement from their links, through Gattegno, with the International Commission for the Study and Improvement of the Teaching of Mathematics. Their chosen strategy for achieving their mission, the building of an Association in which the emphasis would be on classroom practice at all levels, quickly led, in the context of the partially strategic moves by teachers within secondary modern schools towards specialist examination-orientated teaching and the Mathematical Association's perceived concern with elite selective schools, to a rapid growth in membership. After 1955, this growing membership was reached through a regularly produced journal, in which leading members mounted attacks on current practice. The ideational and social bases of a 'plausibility structure' supporting change were therefore beginning to be constructed.

Not all of the increasing membership, however, shared the founders' original mission in full. Those in the secondary modern schools in particular were frequently more immediately concerned with the establishment of mathematics departments, with the associated resource-generating consequences, in their schools. This led to a certain amount of conflict at the annual conferences, began in 1957, and at other meetings. Many grammar school-based members argued, for a mixture of ideological and material reasons I am unable, for a lack of relevant evidence, to disentangle here, against such moves.

At the same time that the nature of the membership, and hence the segments in conflict, was changing, some of the leadership began to combine an interest in 'modern' pure mathematics with the original mission of radical pedagogic reform. The most likely source of this change was the involvement of members with the ICSITM. The 1957 meeting in Spain, which Fletcher and Harris attended, included amongst its speakers, for example, Professor Choquet of the Sorbonne, an advocate of the teaching of modern algebra in schools, and Servais, who in 1956 had published work on physical models for teaching Boolean algebra.[67] Furthermore, in the Report of this meeting, Harris explicitly noted that the display of models from Britain, unlike those from other European countries, had not been concerned with 'modern trends in mathematics'.[68]

Now, generally, in educational interaction, lower status actors tend to imitate the practices of those of higher status. As Davies, for example, has noted in respect of paradigms, 'no weak society can afford to ignore dominant ones if it wishes to stay in the premier league of research'.[69] And, for example, in relation to the curriculum, Bell has argued that:

> Because of its high prestige, an elite's curriculum can very often ... influence teachers outside that elite's own institution.[70]

Such tendencies are probably best understood partly in terms of processes of deference to 'legitimate' reality definers within subject communities, but also partly in terms of the resources, including those of status by association, controlled by those imitated. In this particular case, it can be hypothesized that some of the leadership of the ATAM, as well as deferring to the status of 'better mathematicians' such as Choquet, might also have seen in the advocacy of 'modern mathematics' a strategy which would serve to further legitimate their critique of current school mathematics. First, the latter could now be attacked as 'out of date' in relation to university mathematics. Secondly, it was possible, as will be seen again in chapter 7, to forge links between the advocacy of modern algebra and the favoured Piagetian psychology, thus strengthening the mission. Thirdly, some may have seen a potential for alliance with high status groups in the universities who were beginning to attack school mathematics. It will, however, be seen in chapter 8 that some members were to resist this redefining of the mission.

By the end of the 1950s, then, the ATAM, in so far as it had moved towards including within its membership a range of institutionally-based interests, rather than being a disparately located group agreed on a mission, was beginning to meet Bucher and Strauss' description of associations as 'battlegrounds', and to experience considerable internal conflict over aims.

It was noted earlier that, just as the advocacy of 'modern mathematics' was utilized to help de-legitimate current practice, Hope and others began, after the Oxford conference of 1957, to use the results of the debates between university mathematicians and employers of their graduates that occurred between 1957 and 1959 to further legitimate their demands for change.[71] In the next two chapters, I shall consider the two major meetings at which this potential resource was generated.

Notes

1 BUCHER and STRAUSS (1961), p. 331.
2 ASSISTANT MASTERS' ASSOCIATION (1973).
3 *Ibid.*, p. 17.
4 GRIFFITHS and HOWSON (1974), p. 130.
5 See *Mathematics Teaching* (July 1959), p. 22.
6 See *Mathematics Teaching* (April 1958), facing p. 1.
7 HOPE (1958a), p. 11.
8 HOPE (1958b).
9 *Ibid.*, p. 21.
10 *Ibid.*, pp. 21–2.
11 FYFE (1958), p. 25.
12 WHEELER (1958), p. 33.
13 BRIGGS (1957), p. 48.
14 *Ibid.*, p. 49.

15 MEETHAM (1957), p. 47.
16 ESLAND (1971), p. 86.
17 *Ibid.*, pp. 88–9.
18 HOPE (1958c), p. 31.
19 See ESLAND (1971), pp. 87–98.
20 FYFE (1957a), p. 39.
21 See, for example, CENTRAL ADVISORY COUNCIL FOR EDUCATION (1967), pp. 192–3 and p. 235.
22 DODWELL (1957).
23 BROOKES (1957), pp. 25–6.
24 ESLAND (1971), p. 86.
25 See, for example, HARRIS (1956), WALKER (1957), FYFE (1957b), SILLITTO (1957), BROOKES (1958), and FLETCHER (1959).
26 Editorial, *Mathematics Teaching* (April 1958), p. 3.
27 See, for example, VIG (1968).
28 Editorial, *Mathematics Teaching* (April 1958), p. 3.
29 See chapters 5 to 9 below.
30 See, for example, the report of the eleventh meeting of the Commission in *Mathematics Teaching* (November 1957), and chapters 7 and 8 below.
31 See Hope's editorial contribution in *Mathematics Teaching* (November 1957), p. 3, and HARRIS (1957), p. 29.
32 HARRIS (1957), pp. 28–9.
33 HOPE (1957), p. 2.
34 See COLLINS (1956) and subsequent articles in the journal.
35 COLLINS (1958), p. 24.
36 HARRIS (1957).
37 On the Liverpool Conference see chapter 6 below. The individuals mentioned appear in the Conference Register. See *Mathematics, Education and Industry* (1960).
38 See chapter 10 below.
39 See the report in *Mathematics Teaching* (July 1958).
40 *Ibid.*, p. 31.
41 See TAYLOR (1963) and GOODSON (1983).
42 Report of the Blackpool Conference, *Mathematics Teaching* (July 1958), pp. 38–9.
43 *Ibid.*, p. 39.
44 MOORE (1959).
45 *Ibid.*, p. 20.
46 JAMES (1958).
47 MATHEMATICAL ASSOCIATION (1959).
48 BIRTWISTLE (1959), p. 2.
49 *Ibid.*, p. 2.
50 WALKER (1958), p. 10.
51 See the report of the Richmond Weekend Conference, *Mathematics Teaching* (April 1958), p. 32.
52 HOPE (1959).
53 *Ibid.*, p. 37.
54 *Ibid.*, p. 37.
55 *Ibid.*, p. 37.

56 *Ibid.*, pp. 37–8.
57 *Ibid.*, p. 38.
58 Report of the Blackpool Conference, *Mathematics Teaching* (July 1958), p. 33.
59 See the report of the one-day conference at the Dick Sheppard School, *Mathematics Teaching* (July 1958), p. 42.
60 FYFE (1959), p. 17.
61 *Ibid.*, p. 18.
62 SWINDEN (1958), p. 15.
63 *Ibid.*, p. 15.
64 For a list of the first eight of these, see *Mathematics Teaching* (July 1961), p. 59.
65 On Royaumont, see chapter 7 below, and OECD (1961a).
66 OECD (1961b).
67 SERVAIS (1956).
68 Report of the eleventh meeting of the ICSITM, *Mathematics Teaching* (November 1957), p. 37.
69 DAVIES (1973), p. 324.
70 BELL (1971), p. 23.
71 See footnote 31.

5   Movements For Change: The Oxford Conference

The last chapter was concerned with processes and events within the boundaries of mathematics education. The actors involved were located entirely in educational organizations. In this and the next chapter, I shall consider relations across the boundary of this arena during the 1950s, specifically the relationships between selective school and university mathematicians and some sections of commerce and industry. Primarily, I shall be describing, in some detail, two major conferences of school and university mathematicians and personnel from industry held at Oxford (1957) and Liverpool (1959). Retrospectively, these meetings have been seen by some of those involved in the reform movement of the early 1960s as something of a watershed in the development of secondary school mathematics. Thwaites, for example, wrote in 1972:

> To my way of thinking, the source of SMP can be traced back to 1957 when a conference was convened on the personal initiative of Dr. John M. Hammersley, a fellow of Trinity College, for the purpose of bringing together, virtually for the first time, those who taught mathematics in schools and those who used mathematics in real life.[1]

I also, however, have more theoretical reasons for examining these conferences in detail. The issue raised in chapter 2 of the role of 'industry' in subject definition can, I would argue, only be fruitfully examined if attention is paid to the detail of the demands put forward by the employers of labour in their interaction with educational personnel. In the absence of attention to such empirical detail, sociologists are likely to continue to operate in the field of largely unsubstantiated and vague generalizations. The availability of detailed, often verbatim, minutes of the Oxford and Liverpool conference makes such an analysis possible here. In chapters 5 and 6, I shall therefore be able to examine the relationships between participants' occupational locations and their preferred definitions of the mathematics curriculum as well as the manner in which potential redefinitions are negotiated in such arenas of interaction. First, however, I shall briefly describe those changes in the use of manpower and the climate of opinion that led to 'industry' being seen by some mathematicians, usually from the 'applied' segment of the subject, as a potential source of allies and resources in their attempt to advance their version of the subject.

The government and the opposition were, at this time, increasingly concerned with the adequacy of arrangements for teaching and research in scientific and technological areas and, in particular, with potential shortages of manpower in these fields.[2] This official concern was demonstrated in a series of post-war reports.[3] Some indication of the accentuation of this concern in the late 1950s is given by Vig's analysis of questions in the House Of Commons (see Table 5).[4] Increasingly, Vig shows, many politicians and commentators assumed that Britain's economic success would depend centrally on the application of scientific research to industrial processes.

Table 5: Questions in the House of Commons on industrial, agricultural and medical research

Parliamentary sessions	Number of questions			Average per session		
	Con	Lab	Total	Con	Lab	Total
1945/46 – 1949/50	24	29	53	5	6	11
1950/51 – 1954/55	19	58	77	4	12	16
1955/56 – 1958/59	168	277	445	42	69	111

In this context, a concern was increasingly expressed by many in educational organizations, with a variety of interests in the expansion of post-school mathematics education, about possible and perceived shortages of specialist teachers of the subject and about the adequacy of the mathematical education of non-specialists. *The Supply of Mathematics and Science Teachers* (1956), produced by a Subcommittee of the ATCDE, was one key document of this type.[5] The changes which were used to legitimate these claims can be fairly briefly described. In previous decades most mathematics graduates had found work in educational, rather than commercial or industrial, settings but, after the war, as result partly of the increasing employment of mathematicians in connection with computing, a variety of other careers became possible. The figures quoted in the government's manpower planning paper of 1959 illustrate this trend clearly (see Table 6).[6] It can be seen that, over three years, while those employed in education had risen by about seven per cent, those employed in industry had risen by approximately forty-eight per cent. This shift in employment patterns was the likely structural basis of the increased interest in mathematics education expressed by industrial employers in the late 1950s. The result would be the introduction of new actors, with major resources at their control, into the social processes of subject redefinition.

Another important change, occurring alongside these, was an increase in the number of pupils in the sixth forms and, in particular, possibly in response to the new opportunities for mathematicians and scientists, of the number taking external examinations in mathematics (see Table 7).[7] These figures could also be used to legitimate the demands of various groups that the training of mathematicians, especially for teaching, be expanded.

These trends and possible educational responses, discussed in the context of a media-supported concern with a threat, both economic and military, from the USSR and other industrial societies, will be seen to have featured centrally in the conference debates to be analyzed here. It is, however, important to emphasize that the interest of several industrial concerns in mathematics — demonstrated by their support of these

Table 6: Graduate level mathematicians employed in Great Britain

	Industry	Central Government	Local Authorities	Education
1956	1387	840	32	9302
1959	2049	957	24	9955

Table 7(A) Pupils aged seventeen in schools in England and Wales (thousands)

	Boys	Girls	Total
1947	18.0	14.0	32.0
1955	24.9	19.9	45.0
1956	26.8	22.1	49.0
1957	28.8	22.5	51.3
1958	30.2	23.0	53.2

Table 7(B):   Numbers taking examinations in mathematics

GCE 'O' level					
1951	1953	1955	1957	1959	1961
84,798	119,099	125,410	135,241	177,596	203,281

GCE 'A' level					
1951	1953	1955	1957	1959	1961
12,329	17,659	21,467	29,441	34,388	44,395

conferences — was, to some extent, part of their wider interest in the recruitment of suitably prepared scientific and technical staff. In this more general respect, Waring has noted that it was 'the changed climate of the 1950s that turned the attention of industry to school science and mathematics', their interest previously having been expressed in the support of initiatives in further and higher education.[8] In particular, she describes the work of ICI, in the early 1950s, with the Science Masters Association and the setting-up, in the mid-1950s, of the Industrial Fund for the Advancement of Scientific Education in Schools by, amongst others, Shell, Vickers and Courtaulds.[9] This fund, which was later to help SMP, originally concerned itself with the establishment of new science laboratories in independent and direct grant schools. As a result of these activities, many mathematicians, both in these schools and in the universities receiving their ex-pupils, must have become much more aware, seeing the success of their science colleagues, of the resource-generating possibilities of relations with these major companies.

Another major set of issues under debate in the educational locations from which the majority of the conference participants came, i.e. the universities and the higher status selective schools, related to university entrance requirements and procedures, and their effects on schools. Montgomery has described how various organizations and committees, representing school-based interests, expressed concern about the complexity, variety and standards of entrance requirements throughout the 1950s and early 1960s.[10] Many candidates had not only to satisfy entrance requirements in the form of 'A' levels but also, to receive grant support, to take further competitive scholarship examinations. Some universities had started, in the case of mathematics, to demand adequate performance in the latter as an entry requirement.[11] Problems for many schools less well-endowed with the resources necessary to compete successfully for the scarce resource of university places were further exacerbated by Oxbridge's reliance on internally set examinations for the selection of various categories of entrants. (Some university-based educationists, for example, Peterson, critical of 'specialisation', were beginning to use this climate of opinion to further their own missions.[12]) The conference debates will be seen to have also reflected these concerns and interests. The potential that existed for relating them to the 'manpower' issue can be seen by considering figures produced by Montgomery, drawing on the Crowther report:

> There were no less than 2,500 unfilled places in the British universities in 1955, partly because of inefficient entry methods. At the same time, similar numbers of applicants were formally qualified but not selected.[13]

Many mathematics teachers and headmasters, who can be seen to have had a variety of interests in gaining more university places for their pupils, were in fact, over the next few years, to take their criticism further than the issue of 'inefficiency' and to accuse the universities of demanding too much of entrants. They were often to legitimate these attacks by referring to the 'resulting' shortages of manpower, including that of mathematics teachers.[14]

Having briefly discussed the climate of opinion and some of the occupational and demographic changes in various arenas which, taken together with the changes in university mathematics described earlier, constituted the context in which the debates of the 1950s must be understood, I shall now turn to the conferences. These will be examined, since the nature of the data makes this worthwhile, in some detail. This approach will inevitably produce an uneven balance between the reporting of these events and others, especially those which occurred outside of English settings. Since, however, I wish to follow Young and Esland's suggestion that such conferences, where possible, be hypothetically treated as key arenas in which what counts as curriculum knowledge is negotiated, the detailed reporting becomes a necessary device for capturing the perspectives of particular actors and segments.[15] I also want to be able to make detailed comparisons with the curricular proposals of SMP and MME in chapter 10. For similar theoretical reasons, it is necessary to provide detailed analyses of participants' occupational locations. Furthermore, as I have already noted, the particular conferences have been chosen because, with the benefit of hindsight, they can be seen to have been especially important events in the process of redefining school mathematics. Apart from the activity of the ATAM, the major organized source of de-legitimation of current definitions was to be, until late 1959, these conferences.

The Oxford Conference Of April 1957[16]

This Conference was conceived and organized by Hammersley, an Oxford statistician who also worked as a Principal Scientific Officer at Harwell. Like Thwaites, who organized the important Southampton Conference of 1961 to be discussed in chapter 8 and, during the 1950s, worked both at Winchester College and in the universities, Hammersley's occupational activities straddled what were normally well-defined boundaries. Because of this, he would have been particularly aware of any conflict of opinion about the nature of mathematics education between university mathematicians and those using mathematics in research and development applications outside of the universities. His own mission will be discussed in detail below, but I shall first describe the participation at this meeting.

Participation and Support

It can be seen from Table 8 that the participants were drawn largely from the higher status locations of the educational system.[17] The debates were therefore to be concerned almost entirely with the mathematics of the selective schools and the universities. From Table 9, it can be seen that Hammersley and his fellow organizers saw school teachers primarily as an audience. Reality was to be defined for them. (Further support for this conclusion is available from the analysis below of Hammersley's opening address.)

Before leaving this section, it might be noted that a number of future SMP writers were present.[18] Thwaites gave an address; Quadling, then on the Teaching Committee of the Mathematical Association[19] opened a long discussion; Jones summed up for the teachers. Durran also attended.

The organizations supporting the conference were mainly private companies from the electrical, engineering and chemical sectors of the economy (see Table 10). Presumably, Hammersley's academic and occupational credentials, coupled with his commitment to focus on applications of mathematics, enabled him to successfully tap this available resource.

The Conference Debates

I shall start with a detailed account of Hammersley's opening address in which he successfully linked his concern with applied mathematics to

Table 8:   Institutional affiliations of all participants at the Oxford Conference

University:	Mathematicians	7	
	Educationists	2	
	Others	4	
University examination boards		3	(including 2 university mathematicians)
Colleges of technology		4	
Private industry		16	
Government scientists/nationalised industry		8	
HMI		2	
Schools:	Independent boys	28	
	Independent girls	2	
	Direct grant boys	5	
	Direct grant girls	2	
	Mixed grammar	6	
	Boys' grammar	10	
	Girls' grammar	4	
	Total	103	

Table 9:   Institutional affiliation of programmed speakers at the Oxford Conference

University:	Mathematicians	7
	Educationists	1
Colleges of technology		4
Private industry		13
Government research		6
Nationalised industry		2
Schools:	Independent boys	2
	Girls' grammar	1
	Total	36

Table 10:   Organisations supporting the Oxford Conference

Major private companies	12
Nationalised industries	2
Government research establishments	3
Ministry (of Supply)	1

the contemporary climate of opinion. Amongst his several themes, he basically argued from national decline to a national interest in producing scientists to the schools' current failures to the need for reform to the holding of the conference. He began with the 'crisis' affecting Britain:

> Most people are aware of this country's perilous position. Our material resources are inadequate for the size of our population; our foreign assets are depleted; our political influence is waning. To eat and to escape anarchy, we must pay for our imports with our only substantial indigenous commodity, the skill of our hands and of our heads. So we can not afford to fall far behind the United States and Russia in industrialisation and technology, and we must maintain an adequate technological lead over the less developed countries, such as India and China, who have lower densities of population, lower wage scales, greater material resources, and little compassion for us.[20]

He expressed certainty about the centrality of mathematics education in this competition:

> Our national prosperity will waste away if our supply of technologists does not flourish. In our technological supply line, the schools are an irreplaceable link. Again, in a scientific education, there is much besides mathematics; but, at the school level, mathematics is the main single essential ingredient. That is why the mathematics school teachers are so important. If they fail, the schools fail. If the schools fail, the country fails.[21]

These remarks reflected both the climate of opinion already described and his concern with the subject socialization of potential students.

He emphasized, in several places, the changes that had, in his opinion, occurred in 'real life' to which the schools had not yet adjusted. In particular he stressed the growing use of the computer in industry. It was because of such changes that action was necessary: 'we must take practical action in the schools now to provide the trained technologists needed for the 1980s'.[22] He went on to outline the current inadequacies of school mathematics as he saw them. First, he saw many of the topics then covered in the selective school as redundant. Referring to the 'mere twenty years available for teaching ... the unbounded bulk of useful and interesting knowledge', he added, in an attack on pure mathematics:

> Therefore, although we may casually have time for learning specialist trivia such as the nine-point circle, we can not afford time for teaching them.[23]

Perhaps more important, however, was the inadequacy of the existing pedagogical approach. He blamed this on the requirements of examinations coupled with the fact that few school teachers had ever used mathematics in 'practice'. Specifically:

> Mathematical examination problems are usually considered unfair if insoluble or improperly described; whereas the mathematical problems of real life are almost invariably insoluble and badly stated, at least in the first instance. In real life, the mathematician's main task is to formulate problems by building an abstract mathematical model consisting of equations, which shall be simple enough to solve without being so crude that they fail to mirror reality ...[24]

He added that computers broadened enormously the fields in which such modelling was possible but that knowledge of computers and statistics had not yet 'penetrated to schools'. He reserved his strongest criticisms for the applied mathematics curriculum:

> At school, statics and dynamics is frequently the only example of applied mathematics; and even then is generally emasculated by the removal of the model-building side, for the pupil is rarely left to make his own assumptions on the weightlessness of rods and the smoothness of planes, say. Further, at school and university, there is too much preoccupation with the detailed techniques of mathematics and far too little thinking about mathematics, about its uses, about its values, and about its meaning.[25]

In spite of this reference to university curricula, it was primarily school mathematics he wanted to see changed:

> This conference is intended to help broaden school mathematics. It is not a refresher course. Changes in school syllabuses and examinations are best brought about from within the teaching profession; and good changes can only be expected if school teachers are acquainted with real-life mathematics.[26]

In his remarks, then, Hammersley can be seen to have drawn on the twin resources of the contemporary climate of opinion and his alliance with those employing mathematicians outside of the universities to argue for the version of mathematics he represented, that is, problem-orientated applied mathematics.

The Perspectives of 'Real-Life' Users of Mathematics

I shall deal with the contributions of these speakers by theme. The patterns of their addresses were similar: most first described some of the uses to which mathematics was put in their occupational location and then discussed the implications, as they saw them, for the school curriculum. Most of the discussion was concerned with the use of mathematics by those in higher professional and administrative positions, and hence with those pupils likely to move from selective school to university. I shall deal first with comments on content, then with those on pedagogy.

Content[27]

Several points must be stressed. Many speakers pointed out that they employed primarily scientists, engineers and technologists rather than mathematicians *per se*. Their interest in mathematics education therefore related to the preparation of the former and the preparation of mathematicians to work with them in the formulation of problems and their solution. Others, however, did express a desire to employ more mathematicians, especially statisticians. The branches of mathematics that were repeatedly mentioned as being increasingly used were computing and numerical analysis, statistics and probability theory, linear programming and matrix algebra, calculus (especially differential equations) and, much less frequently, modern algebra such as group theory.

Several speakers argued that more of these branches should now appear in school and university syllabuses. For example, Felton, of Ferranti, having argued the need for both graduate mathematicians and, increasingly, for 'non-graduates with a mathematical bent' to work with computers, went on to argue:

> There is a case for the wider teaching of good numerical processes and systematic arrangement of calculations, and for critical reappraisal of conventional school arithmetic.[28]

Owen, of the British Iron and Steel Federation, also wanted changes at school level. Because of increasing demand, he wanted the principles of computing introduced, but he was mainly worried by the 'grave lack of statistical knowledge' amongst science graduates:

> I therefore plead for a greater emphasis on the notions of probability throughout the training of all scientists: we need people with statistical sense, and I believe that much more could be done in the schools and later to introduce probabilistic concepts.[29]

Griffiths, of Rolls Royce, talking mainly of university mathematics, wanted to see more stress on numerical methods of solution, errors and matrix applications. The latter could, in his opinion, be introduced through the study of matrices in the sixth form.[30] Herne, of the National Coal Board, argued similarly:

> ... the teaching in sixth forms, or even earlier, should include the elements of statistical ideas ..., the school should [also] emphasize that arithmetic and numerical methods are always with us and not something given up in the lower forms.[31]

However, although a majority of these speakers wanted new topics introduced into the school curriculum, not all did so. Kerruish, of British Thomson-Houston, an electrical company, argued that the use of mathematics by engineers and physicists greatly exceeded that by mathematicians in industry and, that for the former, classical 'orthodox' mathematics was necessary.[32] He argued that the Conference, whose purpose was to 'increase the number of scientists, engineers and mathematicians produced by the schools', might have an unintended opposite effect because:

> by exposing a wide gap between the mathematics used in practice and the orthodox mathematics used in schools it might discourage the schoolmaster by making him feel that what he taught was never going to be used afterwards. To counter-balance this feeling, if it exists, it is important to point out that in the electrical industry, the vast majority of engineers and physicists do need and use the orthodox mathematics they learn at school and university.[33]

He mentioned draughtsmen and higher level engineers as examples, concluding:

> During the past week several speakers have indicated that a drastic revision of mathematical syllabuses in schools should be made. We in the electrical industry take the opposite view that

most of the school mathematics is necessary in later work, and
the only modifications we would advocate at the school level are
relatively minor ones. For example, it would be a great improvement if some numerical analysis were introduced in the school
syllabus, but not at the expense of some of the more classical
methods ...[34]

Others from the electrical industry had, however, described uses of
'modern' mathematics. Taylor, of Metropolitan-Vickers, for example,
had described the uses of topology and matrix algebra, as well as the
classical calculus, in electrical circuit theory.[35] Clearly, therefore,
amongst the speakers at this meeting (who may not, of course, have
been representative of 'industry') different perspectives on mathematics
education existed, at least in respect of appropriate content. Nevertheless, the dominant view here was that some changes were needed if their
requirements were to be satisfied.

Another, more general issue, which will serve to move this
discussion towards more pedagogical issues, was raised by Lewis, of
ICI, amongst others. He was against premature specialization. Talking
of university curricula, he argued:

Certainly we do not want to encourage universities to push
more and more specialised mathematical training into their
ordinary degree courses, which are over-crowded already. *A
fortiori* we should hate to see school education becoming more
specialised than it is now. We should rather like it to become less
specialised.[36]

With few exceptions, this concern for a good 'general' background in
mathematics for their scientists was shared by the speakers.

In spite of a strong concern with content, however, it was perhaps
in relation to pedagogy that the most radical suggestions for change
were made.

Pedagogical Issues

The main issue here was introduced in Hammersley's address. These
speakers were concerned primarily with the application of mathematics
to 'real' problems. They clearly felt that current school practices were a
hindrance to this. In particular, they were worried about 'attitudes' and
pedagogical practices, including examining methods. On 'attitudes', for
example, Scott, of English Electric, had this to say:

The important requirement is to create the right attitude of mind
in the pupil in respect of the value and purpose of his mathema-

tics ... The mathematical specialist must be taught to think in terms of physical problems. He should be stimulated to take an interest in some of the applications of mathematical techniques, so that he wants to work with scientists and understands their point of view.[37]

He went on to illustrate how schools, in his opinion, might achieve this by a problem-solving approach to the teaching of mathematics.

The assumed for-its-own-sake attitude of pure mathematicians was to receive many more implicit, and sometimes, explicit critiques. These generally came during discussions of 'modelling'. Most of the suggested new topics for the curriculum, such as numerical analysis, matrix algebra and statistics, owed their increasing importance to the growing use of 'modelling' of real life situations (made feasible by the computer). The views of several speakers are well-represented by the remarks of Griffiths of Rolls Royce. First, he argued that graduate engineers and direct intakes from 'schools and technical colleges should have a good mathematical background', and then, secondly, that the 'powers of discrimination' needed to make models should be fostered by teachers at all levels:

> All too often the student is presented with problems in, say, statics and dynamics where the discrimination is already done. It should be possible to present problems with more factors than are needed for the solution, leaving the student to select those he considers most significant. At present the student entering the aero-engine industry has to orientate his outlook from the convenient world of exact solution, presented to him during his education, to an inexact environment where the commonest problems are not amenable to classical methods of approach nor allow for exact solutions. Moreover he must use numerical techniques to get solutions.[38]

Hopkins, of the Armaments Research and Development Establishment, echoed these views.[39] Many of those expressing such opinions also stressed the 'need' for flexibility and adaptability in their mathematical employees. The causes of the perceived inadequacies in this respect were viewed as rooted in the lack of concern of mathematical educators with those who were likely to want to use mathematics in other fields. Lewis, of ICI, for example, argued, in what might be considered an attack on the control of the socialization of mathematicians by university pure and applied mathematicians:

Teaching is geared too much to the future professional mathematician. I suggest that much might be done to draw out mathematical ability in people without a real flair for the subject if a more practical approach were taken to teaching it.[40]

In particular, he wanted to see a less abstract approach:

People who are not going to be professional mathematicians ... would ... profit greatly from the presentation of mathematical ideas as a means of manipulating essentially realistic practical problems.[41]

More obviously related to the stress on 'modelling', and on inexact, numerical solutions, he also wanted less stress to be laid on formal proofs:

In fact, if only teachers concentrated more on showing the highly pragmatic and inductive methods by which mathematicians actually arrived at their theorems before they set about working out a formal proof the whole subject would be much more lively and interesting to the pupil ...[42]

Generally then, it can be seen that the speakers from industry, often from research and development departments, and those from government research establishments were in broad agreement, with notable exceptions, that the school and, possibly, the university mathematics curricula were in need of reform. Furthermore, the reforms they sought can be seen to have reflected the uses of mathematics within their industries. In Young's terms,[43] existing 'academic' criteria for the status of knowledge were under attack here.

Before leaving these speakers I shall briefly describe their apparent assumptions in relation to gender. Although they normally talked of males when specifying sex, they also made some remarks on the role of female mathematicians within industry. Many of them seem to have taken it for granted that different positions in the division of labour were appropriate for men and women. I shall merely illustrate these features of their perspectives here.

Taylor, of Metropolitan-Vickers, for example, remarked that the Conference was concerned with:

The teaching of mathematics to boys who wish to become scientists and engineers, that is, boys whose main interest is not in mathematics as such but who will need to use it as a tool.[44]

However, it was in relation to computing that the most explicit comments on sex roles were made. Kerruish had spoken of the increasing use of 'lady mathematicians'. The jobs they were doing involved using 'desk-calculating machines' and, with the future in mind, computer programming.[45] Both of these were fairly routine. Herne, of the National Coal Board, after listing the advanced mathematics used by researchers in the mining industry without reference to sex, continued:

> There may be a third and still smaller need for computers [human, that is], chiefly girls from school with an 'A' level in mathematical subjects.[46]

Again, routine work is specified for women. Most of the male speakers appeared to assume that men constituted the pool for advanced mathematicians. A paper from a Mrs. Hoare, of Armstrong-Vickers, 'communicated' to the Conference, however, argued that a shortage of women mathematicians existed within industry.[47]

Educators' Perspectives

Under this heading I shall consider the perspectives of the following three groups: university mathematicians; university educationists; and school teachers.

First, it must be noted that the prior arrangements for discussions and lectures indicated a certain range of concerns on the part of the organizers. The university mathematicians each delivered a series of lectures, for example, in which the topics covered were (i) the mathematical study of random phenomena; (ii) types of fluid flow; (iii) linear programming; (iv) Monte Carlo methods; (v) the theory of games; and (vi) non-linear oscillations.[48] All the topics were, therefore, 'applicable' mathematics, essentially matrix algebra and probability theory plus some applications as well as some other applied mathematics. For the teachers, these lectures must have further legitimated the industrial speakers' demands for more of these topics plus 'modelling' to appear in curricula.

The discussion sessions concerned with school mathematics reflected, in their emphases, the concerns of the members of the Advisory Committee and the participants in general with those pupils likely to study at university. This Committee consisted of Hammersley and the lecturers referred to above (all, bar one, Oxford mathematicians and including the President of the Mathematical Association), a senior mathematics master from an Oxford boys' grammar school, an Oxford Professor of Mathematics, Hirst (an Oxford educationist), two more

Oxford men and Rollett, an HMI. The main sessions were concerned with the following:[49]

(i)   The purpose of learning mathematics (unfortunately scarcely reported in the minutes).

(ii)   School and scholarship examinations (several sessions).

(iii)   The mathematical education of scientists (led by the President of the Royal Society).

(iv)   Teacher shortage.

(v)   The mathematical education of girls (led by the secretary of the Mathematical Association).

There were also smaller discussion groups set up to report back to the final session on:[50]

(i)   Mathematical topics studied outside of the school syllabus.

(ii)   Choice of specialist subjects at 'A' and 'S' levels.

(iii)   Closer relations between schools, university and industry.

(iv)   Allotment of periods for mathematical specialists.

(v)   The streamlining of mathematics and physics courses.

It can be seen that the main concern was with those pupils who would (i) study 'A' level mathematics; and (ii) go on to university to study mathematics or science. In looking in more detail at the views expressed, it will become clear that entrance to Oxbridge was a central concern of the teachers as well as of the organizers.

There were also sessions on technical colleges and technological education but (i) few participants were directly concerned with these; and (ii) they received only a few pages in the published report of the meeting.[51] Furthermore, the four speakers from this sector were given one 'symposium' session to deal with four separate topics. All of this suggests that the over-riding concern was with pupils from high status institutions. I shall now discuss, by theme, the views expressed in these sessions.

Examinations and the Curriculum

This formed a major area of discussion, reflecting the occupational interests of both school and university teachers in the content and form of examinations. The discussion is looked at here in some detail in order to demonstrate the ways in which university influence on school practice was variously encouraged, accepted or resisted by differently located school teachers; and also to show that the representatives of the examination boards who spoke were certainly not against change in general.

In his talk, Thwaites, of Winchester College, who was later to organize SMP, summed up his reaction to the first two days of the Conference. He argued that examinations dominated a school's curriculum and that, unless they changed in parallel, any reform of school mathematics teaching would achieve little:

> If, for example, the 'A' and 'S' level mathematics papers were rearranged to give greater prominence to, say, numerical methods and realistic physical affairs, and to subordinate certain traditional studies such as pure geometry, the schools would rapidly fall into line.[52]

It will be seen that other speakers from the schools tended to support his position, sometimes explicitly, and sometimes implicitly, in that what they said indicated a strong concern with teaching for examination success and Oxbridge entry.

The session on school examinations started with a long discussion of the fairness of JMB's alternative 'A' level papers. Then Cobb, of Malvern College, moved to more general issues:

> Any major change that we make in teaching apart from differences in attitude must be preceded by changes in the examinations because in the nature of things we teach for examinations and it is not possible to envisage getting away from that at present.[53]

Dr. Powell, a Cambridge mathematician and a member of the Cambridge Board, suggested, however, that examinations were not the major cause of the lack of change in school mathematics. Explaining that the Board had a Mathematics Committee to discuss and settle syllabus issues which consisted of two-thirds school teachers and one-third university representatives, he argued:

> While not naturally conservative, they had to go rather slowly, because one must not move faster than schools can follow. But for schools who want to go faster, several routes were possible. One was an alternative syllabus. They were only too glad to put it in if the schools wanted it . . . If we are satisfied with it, we set papers. This is the way for the really adventurous school to do something quite different. It often happens in science, but not in mathematics.[54]

These remarks, with the benefit of hindsight, might well be seen as an invitation to potential reformers in the higher status schools. Then, after considerable discussion of specific contents and whether they should be included or excluded at 'A' level, Dr. Lightfoot, an applied mathematician who was then Principal of Chelsea College of Science and Technology, as well as being associated with the JMB, noted that there was apparently no consensus on the issues under discussion:

> It seems to me that to get any result from a conference such as this, it is necessary for the teachers' organizations to reach a conclusion as to what they would like and put their ideas up to the board, when they certainly will be considered.[55]

Similar assumptions to those of Thwaites, on the part of teachers, were apparent during the discussion of the Oxbridge scholarship examinations. Quadling, of Marlborough College, later to help found SMP, argued, for example:

> We do rely on the scholarship examinations to give us ... guidance ... We look to the universities in this respect to indicate to us what are the trends in the university. For example, is projective geometry coming in or ... going out.[56]

Blakey, of Bolton School, also agreed that these examinations affected school practice:

> The open scholarship did have very considerable prestige, and was bound to influence teaching in schools.[57]

Unwin, of Clifton College, agreed they 'were guided very largely by the university scholarship exams'.[58] He argued that, in the national interest, changes in mathematics and science curricula should be carefully controlled. We should not leave:

> science and mathematics to chance in this peculiar sort of way. I feel very strongly there should be some closer liaison between universities and schools. It should not be left to this haphazard business.[59]

It was not just a question of cramming, he continued, but of streamlining a system of education through the schools into the universities. Herbert, of Eton, agreed and added:

> If we establish a closer contact between the examiner and the school much less time will be wasted in the study of subject matter no longer considered important by the examiners. I am in favour of schoolmasters and candidates being able to obtain

copies of recent scholarship papers. I am in favour of our knowing as much as possible concerning the nature of these examinations ... It must be borne in mind that it is through these scholarship papers that the universities can let the schools know what they require of them.[60]

The above speakers clearly looked to the universities for authoritative statements on what now counted as mathematics. In doing so, presumably partly because of the status to be gained by schools in successfully competing for Oxbridge places, they were also clearly deferring to university mathematicians, and thus accepting a hierarchy of rights in subject definition.

One school-based dissenter from this (elite) consensus was reported. Waddams, a grammar school headmaster — from a lower status location than most of the above speakers, said of Quadling's remarks:

If he is speaking on behalf of us, then I think we should all be ashamed. If the universities are to be left with the idea that we run about at their behest, I am sure it is quite wrong. In the vast majority of schools, it is just not true. It may be for those schools which are fortunate enough to keep mathematicians separate for three or four years and guide them on the straight and narrow path, but not in the majority of schools ... I am very much in favour of the universities experimenting. I am against issuing a syllabus.[61]

There were other dissenters. The Report notes briefly that several (unidentified) schoolmasters argued that the prestige attached to the number of open awards gained by the independent schools was the main cause of the problems in mathematical education.[62] Hammersley, however, supported Unwin's position, continuing:

Schools might not know of the changes taking place at the universities. For instance, in Part 1 of the Mathematics Tripos it was now possible to take numerical analysis as an alternative to projective geometry. Numerical analysis had proved much the more popular option, and might soon be permeating into sixth form work from the Cambridge end.[63]

The university scholarship examiners made several contributions. Powell, for example, felt that the schools appeared not to fully understand the situation. While the examinations set by the boards were discussed by interested groups, such as teachers, on syllabus committees, the situation with scholarship examinations was quite different:

In practice a body of examiners, a small group of men, are brought together for the purpose of setting papers in one examination. When that is over, the body is dissolved. There is therefore, no consistently continuing policy: the thing just happens. I think it is quite wrong to suppose we are examiners considering what the university desires. We are just doing a job of work. Many of the scholarship examiners have no other contact at all with the schools. They don't feel any responsibility and often have no knowledge or appreciation of the side effects their exams have on schools. It is a fact, I am afraid.[64]

He went on to claim that, given their concern for 'picking out the best men', they had to set questions which would be understood by the majority:

Therefore we never venture into new fields. We must stick to what we believe is safe. If you see something that is new, it is a mistake. We thought you did it, and you don't.[65]

Maxwell, a Cambridge mathematician and also a scholarship examiner, prominent within the Mathematical Association, thought this to be too black a picture. Those examiners who had more contact with the schools did influence, or at least attempt to, the others.[66] Busbridge, for the Oxford women's colleges, argued that they tried to allow for the differences between the schools in terms of teacher quality and syllabus covered.[67]

The impression gained is one of some confusion, probably a reflection of the separate setting of papers by different groups of colleges. Powell, of Caius, for example, was 'horrified' to hear that Mauldon, of Corpus Christi, used scholarship examinations to select 'commoners'.[68] It can be seen, however, that, in spite of Maxwell's claims and Powell's later comments to the effect that if schools did make protests they were 'remarkably effective', the content of scholarship papers was likely to tend to respond over time to the changing interests of university mathematicians, leaving the schools to follow as best as they could. That only some schools had access to the resources, including recently socialized and highly qualified graduates, that would have made this relatively easy possibly accounts for much of the difference in opinion between Quadling and Waddams.

Further evidence for the influence of these examinations on the school curriculum can be seen in the attention paid in the discussion to the issue of the General Paper.[69] Again the university comment was mixed. Mauldon 'did not pay a great deal of attention to the General

Paper, except in selecting commoners'.[70] Powell said that 'in his group nobody who fails in the General Paper can have a scholarship'.[71] Again, the groups of colleges differed. This must have tended to increase the teachers' anxieties, even given the practice of relating to a given group of colleges over time. Similarly, concern was exhibited by the teachers in relation to the physics paper taken by mathematics pupils.[72]

Unwin, Maxwell and Quadling concluded the discussion. Unwin, perhaps on the defensive after Waddam's remarks, argued:

> I just feel that there is not sufficient contact. We should like more guidance in the kind of thing we ought to teach and the kind of way to teach it, so that a boy or girl going up to university can get the most out of the university course. It is not a question of prestige. That does not come into it at all. There have been enormous changes and there has always been this time lag before we get on to those changes.[73]

It is clear that this speaker not only accepted the universities' right to define 'mathematics' in the selective schools but also felt that they could do this more effectively than at present. Maxwell then claimed that the universities were busy creating new material; there was not much time for increased contacts. These already existed, however, through the Mathematical Association in whose Teaching Committee 'universities and schools get together and issue reports as to what they consider proper material for teaching in schools'. He favoured this 'informal and friendly way' of tackling the problem.[74] Quadling, however, a member of this Committee, added that:

> The Mathematical Association in its reports, always tries to avoid saying what should be taught and specifying syllabuses.[75]

But, he went on, when teachers in schools saw certain topics appearing in university scholarship papers, they tended to see this as something important and therefore as something to teach to their pupils.

In conclusion, the representatives of the public schools clearly regarded university influence on school syllabuses as legitimate, and thus provided a possible channel for university influence on selective school mathematics at this time. This probably reflected their advantageous position in the competition for university awards, but also their being 'good mathematicians' in terms of their own degrees. (There were apparently five double firsts at Winchester at this time, for example.[76]) As a result, they would both have been less threatened by possible change and have been more likely to have taken university mathematicians as a reference group. It was also seen above that various examinations were seen by all the teachers to strongly influence the school curriculum, and that it was a speaker from the lower status and less well-resourced schools, who might be seen as disadvantaged in the competition for university places, who seems to have been ready to publicly criticize this situation. In relation to later events, it is also important to emphasize that several university-based representatives of the examination boards seemed very ready to support some syllabus reform.

Having now discussed the issue of university influence on schools' work in a general way, I shall now move on to consider more detailed opinions expressed on the inclusion of particular mathematical topics in syllabuses and, to a lesser extent, on more pedagogical issues. As I argued earlier, such attention to empirical detail is necessary if sociologists are to be able to move beyond vague generalizations on the process of subject redefinition. It is in such debates as those at Oxford that actors come to understand the demands of significant others.

Before I begin this analysis, however, it is important for the reader to note that Hammersley, as organizer, structured much of this detailed discussion in his summing-up of the preliminary debate by proposing a set of suggestions for curriculum reform as a 'tentative basis for discussion'. His own mathematical interests as an applied mathematician, as well as some 'modern' pure mathematics, were well-represented in these suggestions. Basically, he proposed less arithmetic, less manipulation of formulae in statics and dynamics, less Euclidean geometry and coordinate geometry, and more numerical analysis, formulation of problems, statistics and probability, abstract algebra (matrices, groups), vector analysis and descriptive topology. Many of the later comments must be seen as references to these suggestions. I shall begin with the references made to statistics and probability theory.

Statistics and Probability Theory

Interesting points emerged here. In the discussion of the JMB's alternative papers it was pointed out that of 3,000 who usually took the examination, just two dozen took statistics, even though the syllabus had existed for several years.[77] Lightfoot, for the Board, seems to have been hinting that the GCE boards could not be held solely responsible for any lack of change in school mathematics: he had previously stressed the degree of teacher representation and claimed that schools were listened to during the drawing-up of syllabuses. Cobb, of Malvern College, responding, thought the situation might now change, indicating that the Conference might be having its intended effect on teachers:

It may be that a new situation has been created by our own meeting. It has been emphasized by very many speakers that statistics is a subject that is wanted and that may very well be something that we shall investigate ... We can not of course teach half the boys mechanics and half statistics at the same time very easily. I think we should be allowed a considerable amount of freedom until the thing has settled down.[78]

Powell, for the Cambridge Board, came in to argue that they had, for some years, offered statistics and probability as an alternative to certain parts of the mechanics syllabus but only a couple of schools had taken it up. They had also put it in their advanced and scholarship level papers but support had been very discouraging. Nevertheless, they had committed themselves to it.[79] Hammersley, himself a statistician, spoke last on this. According to the minutes:

He hoped special syllabuses such as statistics would not be allowed to die for lack of support in the early years. It naturally took some time for school teachers to orient themselves to new topics.[80]

It appears then, that, as far as statistics and probability were concerned, the university mathematicians on the committees of the boards were promoting change. The schools, however, were in general continuing with their traditional applied mathematics: statics and dynamics. Given the normal combination of mathematics with physics at 'A' level, and teachers' personal investment in current applied mathematics, this was perhaps to be expected. Apparently then, there was only a minority actively supporting statistics within the schools at this time.

Abstract Algebra

Maxwell, of the Oxford and Cambridge Board, thought there were 'possibilities' for the school curriculum in matrices and elementary vector theory.[81] Powell, of the Cambridge Board, thought, however, that matrices did not belong to the school syllabus, but that vector analysis might be done.[82] Geary, of Northampton Polytechnic, thought vector analysis 'highly desirable for sixth form work, but not for examinations'.[83] Little else was reported in this area except that Macro, in reporting back to the final session on the mathematics studied outside of the syllabus in the participants' schools, included matrices, group theory, two and three element algebras, and finite geometries. In his discussion group, the consensus had been that elementary vector analysis could give a false picture of the subject.[84]

Clearly, therefore, some of the university mathematics community, in line with the conclusions drawn from the discussion of Kuhn's ideas in chapter 2, favoured the introduction of some 'modern' linear algebra. Furthermore, some corresponding growth points existed in the schools.

Geometry

Maxwell thought 'we should not be too anxious to scrap geometry. Some idea of space was as important as some idea of number'.[85] Powell was more specific in his suggestions:

> I would like to be rid of much that appears in current syllabuses. I know that we live in a world of geometry, but let us teach it as mathematical physics. The nine-point circle, and all that old-fashioned account of triangles is quite out of place these days.[86]

Given his high status as a senior university mathematician, this choice of words must have given those teachers who looked to the universities for 'guidance' considerable cause for thought. Hammersley's earlier reference to 'specialist trivia', taken together with these remarks, must have tended to devalue or de-legitimate traditional school geometry in the minds of the teachers present.

Geary, however, thought they should be a 'little careful' about 'throwing out geometry'. One needed to think in three dimensions.[87] Again then, a lack of consensus existed. Teachers favouring traditional geometry could still find support amongst some mathematicians outside of the schools.

Numerical Analysis

Here too there were different opinions. Thwaites, in his talk, argued:

> The ideas of approximation, iteration, and so on are so difficult and subtle, and one can not readily see how they could be emphasized more than they already are in the school curriculum.[88]

Cobb, however, thought that 'there might be something in numerical analysis' for the school curriculum.[89] Geary, from outside of the schools, was more positive:

> Numerical analysis was a reasonable subject to take at advanced level, if schools could provide an examiner and one desk calculator for each candidate.[90]

Computing

Wooldridge, during the technical college symposium, described an experiment, funded by some of the industrial supporters of the conference, which had made computer facilities available to some schools. He was intending to run courses for sixth formers from the Wolverhampton and Staffordshire College of Technology.[91]

In later discussion, Cobb argued that computers were too expensive to easily allow computing to enter the school syllabus.[92] Maxwell thought the subject unsuitable for school examinations anyway.[93] Little else was reported on this area.

Pedagogical Issues and Modelling

I shall now discuss issues relating more to pedagogy than to content. Cobb stated that he had gained the impression from the various industrial and governmental speakers that 'the chief requirement they hope for is ability and willingness to learn, an attitude of applying mathematics to problems and an appreciation of the practical world.'[94] He thought the new 'mathematical tricks', since they were being used, must be better than the old. Powell agreed:

> Statics and dynamics as taught in schools had become mummified ... I should like to see a very drastic reduction in the statics and dynamics ... I don't think solution of problems is in the least important. I think formulation of problems and expression of problems in mathematical form are.[95]

The other main educational contribution in this area was from Hinshelwood, President of the Royal Society, in his address on the mathematical education of scientists. He echoed Powell's point of view, but he also wanted scientists to have this ability.[96]

There was little obvious support from the schools, apart from Cobb's comments, for such radical changes in pedagogical practice. According to Thwaites, then teaching at Winchester College, but also lecturing at Imperial College:

> Physical understanding is at least as difficult to teach and to acquire as mathematical technique. The assumption that mathematics is easier to understand if its physical relevance is explained is, as far as school teaching is concerned, quite false in my own opinion. Only when the student has acquired greater knowledge, maturity and experience at the undergraduate and postgraduate stage, can he begin to take a unified view of science and mathematics.[97]

Summary: The Educators' Views on Specific Topics

Some support for the introduction of new topics into the selective school curriculum, and for the removal of others from it, clearly existed amongst speakers from the schools and, more especially — as might be expected following Kuhn's analysis, amongst speakers from the university mathematics community. As would also be expected, however, from the discussion of the subject in chapter 2, there was no consensus on many of the issues discussed. There was disagreement amongst university mathematicians on the value of many topics in relation to school curricula and, while some growth points for change clearly existed in the schools, some teachers were more ready (and able) to introduce changes than others. In relation to one of the major demands for change emanating from industry, that more attention be paid to 'realistic' problems and 'modelling' in applied mathematics teaching, there was no obvious support forthcoming from the schools. Such a change would, of course, have represented a major threat to the occupational interests and practices of many teachers successful within current routines. Some support for such a change was, however, noticeable amongst university mathematicians, especially Hammersley. A continuing alliance of university applied mathematicians and actors from industry and commerce would, indeed, be forged around this issue. I shall now turn to two other issues discussed at Oxford, before describing the concluding session of the Conference.

Girls and Mathematics

Miss Cooke, SMM of a Slough grammar school, and Secretary to the Mathematical Association, gave a talk entitled 'Mathematical Prospects for Girls'. She referred to the tradition that girls did not like and could not do mathematics, claiming that it still existed. In fact, she said, girls did less mathematics in schools, and low expectations often produced failure. She wanted primary school teachers, mostly women, to receive a much better mathematical training in the colleges. 'Industry', in spite of crying out for mathematicians, was prejudiced against employing women to ease the problem.[98]

Speakers from industry argued in response that women did not apply in any numbers. Owen, from the steel industry, added that women were neater, more patient and more precise than men.[99]

Land, of the University of Liverpool, in the examinations discussion, wondered whether alternative papers, 'not necessarily easier', might encourage more girls to take 'A' level mathematics.[100] Blakey wanted to see more discussion of girls in relation to Oxbridge scholarship examinations.[101]

This, along with what was described earlier, is about all that was reported on this issue. It does not seem therefore to have been a central concern at this stage. Only about a dozen of the 103 participants, however, were from institutions educating girls, and the lack of attention the latters' mathematical education received may have reflected this as much as the participants' values.

Teacher Shortage

Land gave a talk based on his survey of the qualifications of students entering teaching in 1956, which had previously been published as part of the ATCDE's *The Supply of Science and Mathematics Teachers*.[102] He compared teachers of mathematics and arts subjects in grammar schools, pointing out that three-quarters of the latter had 'good honours' degrees compared with only one-quarter in mathematics and one-fifth in physics. Furthermore, he stressed, only 44 per cent of women in training colleges had 'O' level mathematics. Generally, he argued, a serious problem existed although, more optimistically, he added:

> 240 entrants to training colleges had 'A' level mathematics, and more should be done to encourage this better stratum to continue in mathematics.[103]

He wanted a mathematical diploma of General BSc standard to be instituted as an 'interim measure for the duration of the shortage only.'[104]

Miss Cooke asked whether the Mathematical Association should explore this possibility. Those members present favoured this with a show of hands.[105]

Speakers from industry responded favourably to suggestions that they should increase those facilities leading to teacher contact with industry.[106]

The issue of teacher shortage was not discussed outside of this session. For these schools, at this time, it appears not to have been a major problem.

Oxford: the Concluding Session

There were three main speakers at this session: Taylor, of Metropolitan-Vickers; Hammersley, the Conference organizer; and Jones, SMM at Winchester College. I shall report the main points made by them and by others in the subsequent discussion, perhaps the nearest this meeting came to producing agreed proposals.

After remarking that he thought many teachers had been surprised to learn of the types of advanced mathematics used in industrial research, and stressing the need for collaboration between the engineer and mathematician, Taylor emphasized that there was a need in industry for 'all grades of mathematical ability'.[107] In fact, he had in mind the range from 'engineer' to 'pure mathematician'. If the speakers were correct, he added, the latter would be increasingly needed, but the 'middle grade' and those whose abilities were not quite 'top class' would also be needed more and more in connection with the computer, which had made previously insoluble industrial problems mathematically soluble.[108] He then discussed at length the qualities industry wanted in its recruits. The large companies were not seeking vocational education. They would provide this in their own graduate apprenticeship schemes:

> In general, the details of school curricula are not of particular interest to industry. What industry does require, in view of the rapid changes in the applications of mathematics from decade to decade, is recruits who are capable of continuing to learn throughout their working lives. It is this training which is the most important function of schools.[109]

Smaller companies had different needs, which he believed were and would continue to be met by liaison between university engineering departments and companies, and between technical colleges and schools. There was a need for closer contact between schools and industry. He concluded by arguing that the 'national interest' demanded that more mathematicians, scientists and engineers be trained.

Hammersley, in his contribution, noted that the Conference had been an experiment.[110] He would welcome suggestions for a successor. In this respect, he raised a number of issues. Should the next conference be for mathematics and science masters? It was also important to consider the 'whole scale of teaching mathematics': should primary schools be involved? Should international delegates attend? And, 'should there be less of the educational cream and more of the milk'? Should there be more junior masters, with the future in mind?

Jones, later to help found SMP, commenced by referring to the lack of consensus amongst the school teachers on many issues.[111] He, and others, recognized the need from industry for more mathematicians but did not see how it was going to be met. The suggestion for a qualification, intermediate between 'A' level and an honours degree, was an important one. Perhaps, he hoped, a 'responsible body' would create such a diploma. An Institute of Mathematics might emerge for this purpose. He wanted industry to use mathematical talent more economically. They must welcome women. He reported that teachers hoped for other conferences of this kind 'bringing together industry and the schools with the universities as a link between the two':[112]

> No boy who leans towards a life in industry should be lost because he is unaware of the important part mathematics plays there ... Colleges of technology could be used for a wider range of boy.[113]

Teachers were encouraged by industry's wanting 'men with broad education', with minds 'capable of understanding the wholeness of a problem'. He noted that:

> Industry did not want schools to alter syllabuses drastically, but they did want schools to be aware of modern mathematical methods and wherever possible to visualize mathematics in a sort of physical setting.[114]

Closer contacts, he claimed, must be encouraged between schools and industry: visits and short courses for pupils and vacation experience for teachers should be encouraged. The Mathematical Association might provide space in the *Gazette* for articles discussing the industrial uses of mathematics. Many felt, he continued, that the school treatment of mechanics gave an unrealistic picture of the physical world. The industrial speakers wanted teachers to 'bring out that real problems are very rarely of an exact or formal nature'.[115]

There had been, he remarked, a failure to agree on whether some numerical analysis or statistics should displace some geometry, or whether mathematics teaching should emphasize the rigorous or the intuitive approach, and on the relation of mathematics to science teaching where problem formulation was concerned.

He said that 'there was no wide support for any significant changes in the GCE syllabuses'.[116] In relation to the Oxbridge scholarships, many would like to see more liaison, and it was certainly agreed that these examinations did 'strongly influence' sixth form work.

During the ensuing discussion, Unwin supported Hammersley's proposal to invite science masters next time. He felt secondary moderns should be considered before primary schools (the formers' only reported mention).[117] Davison, of Rotherham Grammar School, suggested that another Conference be held in the north of England. After (unreported) discussion, this was approved, and the following Organizing Committee nominated:[118]

Land (Convenor)	Department of Education, University of Liverpool.
Barwell	Staveley Grammar School.
Holman	Manchester High School For Girls, also a member of the Teaching Committee of the Mathematical Association.
Reuter	Department of Mathematics, University of Manchester.
Scott	English Electric.
Taylor	Metropolitan-Vickers.

Comments on the Oxford Conference

This meeting was primarily used by an alliance of university applied mathematicians, one segment of university mathematics, and representatives of employers of graduate labour to begin what was to become a sustained attack on secondary school mathematics, especially the teaching of applied mathematics at 'A' level. Some of the industrial speakers, generally from the research departments of major manufacturing companies, also criticized the 'abstraction' of university mathematics.

The discussion of examinations, in which teachers from the independent sector made it clear that they regarded university definition of mathematics as legitimate, suggests that Hammersley and his allies would have caused teachers to begin questioning their curricular assumptions and practices. Furthermore, a letter to Hammersley, thanking him for invitations to the meeting, from Jones, Quadling and five others, in which they stated that 'this conference has been of great value in re-shaping our outlook on the teaching of mathematics to those who will later use it in the industrial world' supports this suggestion.[119]

The discussion of scholarship examinations suggests that mathematics teachers in the relatively well-resourced independent schools, often well-qualified Oxbridge graduates themselves, would have welcomed increased university influence on their teaching syllabuses. This willingness to forego control, in the 'interests' of their pupils going on to study at university, might be accounted for, in terms of the model outlined in chapter 2, partly by their acceptance, within a hierarchical subject community, of the right of university mathematicians to define the subject, but also partly in terms of their being well-placed to succeed in the competition for scarce university places (a success on which the academic status of their schools depended). Waddams, from a less well-resourced sector, both in terms of mathematics teachers and contacts with Oxbridge, was less ready to accept university control of syllabuses as legitimate. He explicitly linked this with a reference to the less 'fortunate' condition of the 'vast majority of schools'. The minutes had summarized the ensuing discussion thus:

> Several school masters pointed out that prestige was the root of the trouble; and that as long as prestige was associated with the number of open awards gained by the independent schools, so long would the schools continue to struggle for these awards. A statement that 'a good school is one that gets good scholarships' was roundly condemned.[120]

In spite of this condemnation, perhaps best seen as at least partly rhetorical, one possible mechanism of university influence over the schools' syllabuses, rooted in their control over the scarce resource of entry, can be discerned here, especially if it is accepted that lower status selective schools, notwithstanding Waddam's remarks, tended, in practice, to attempt to imitate the more prestigious independent schools.

The two direct outcomes of this meeting were the proposal for another Conference and for a diploma to be run, at sub-graduate level, by the Mathematical Association, which had been well-represented at Oxford. Indirect outcomes, judging by the letter to Hammersley, must have included an increase in discussion within the independent and other higher status selective schools and the branch meetings of the Mathematical Association of the very nature of school mathematics.

I have already noted, in chapter 4, that members of the ATAM referred to the meeting, whose minutes were published, when arguing for reform. Any such effects of the proceedings on the climate of opinion in educational and political circles must have been considerably enhanced by the fact of *The Times* having run a leader (23 July 1957) on the issues when the official record was published.[121] As Hall *et al* argue, in their *Policing the Crisis*:

> Conversation in *The Times* or *Daily Telegraph* is conducted 'between equals'. The paper of this type can 'take for granted a known set of subjects and interests, based for the most part on a roughly common level of education'; they can 'assume a kind of community — in this society, inevitably either a social class or an educational group'. The position of *The Times* depends on its

power to influence the elite from within; its readership, though small, is select, powerful, knowledgeable and influential. It and its correspondents speak within the same conversational universe. In the letters it prints, therefore, it is making public one current of opinion within the decision-making class to another section of the same class.[122]

The leader, of which the same might be claimed, described how the mathematician was increasingly in demand within industry because of the requirements of the increasingly theoretical activities of research, design and development, especially now the computer had rendered his techniques applicable and useful. It described the conference in outline thus: 'Industry's needs were set before school masters and dons for the first time'. It then claimed that 'mathematical language has invaded the boardroom and future managers must learn it'. It bemoaned the lack of adequate teachers in the primary schools. This created problems in the grammar schools. 'Better teaching' was the first need.[123]

Interestingly, at this stage of the development of public concern about mathematics education, no correspondence ensued. Furthermore, unlike in later discussions in *The Times*, no explicit reference is made here to curriculum content, to what 'counts' as mathematics. Hammersley's success as a 'curriculum entrepreneur', to modify Becker's useful 'moral entrepreneur',[124] had, so far, been limited. Furthermore, in so far as he had succeeded in raising questions in the minds of influential teachers about the adequacy of selective school mathematics, these related mainly to applied mathematics and 'modelling'. This focus reflected the control of the conference's agenda of issues by the industrial participants and the applied mathematicians from the universities. Compared with the Southampton Conference, to be discussed in chapter 8, very little concern was evident in the reported discussions about the place of 'modern' algebras, with the exception of matrix algebra, in the school curriculum.

Notes

1 THWAITES (1972), p. viii.
2 See, for example, VIG (1968), chapters one and two.
3 See, for example, the extracts from the Percy (1945), Barlow (1946) and Crowther (1959) reports in MACLURE (1973).
4 See VIG (1968), p. 28.
5 ASSOCIATION OF TEACHERS IN COLLEGES AND DEPARTMENTS OF EDUCATION (1956).

6 The table is from ADVISORY COUNCIL ON SCIENTIFIC MANPOWER: COM-MITTEE ON SCIENTIFIC MANPOWER (1959), p. 31.
7 See, for (A), CENTRAL ADVISORY COUNCIL FOR EDUCATION (1959), p. 226, and, for (B), DES (1973), p. 5.
8 WARING (1975), pp. 158–9.
9 *Ibid.*, 160–2.
10 MONTGOMERY (1965), chapter 6.
11 *Ibid.*, p. 145.
12 A.D.C. Peterson ran a series of conferences, promoting a 'broader' sixth form curriculum, from the late 1950s. See, for example, *The Times* 10 April 1961 for a report of the third in the series, and MONTGOMERY (1965), pp. 161–4.
13 MONTGOMERY (1965), p. 148.
14 See chapter 6 onwards below.
15 See YOUNG (1972) and ESLAND (1971).
16 See the *Abbreviated Proceedings of the Oxford Mathematical Conference for Schoolteachers and Industrialists* (1957).
17 Tables Eight to Ten are derived from *Ibid.*, Appendix Two, the Conference Register.
18 *Ibid.*, Appendix Two.
19 MATHEMATICAL ASSOCIATION (1957b), p. ii.
20 *Abbreviated Proceedings* (1957), p. 8.
21 *Ibid.*, p. 8.
22 *Ibid.*, p. 9.
23 *Ibid.*, p. 9.
24 *Ibid.*, p. 10.
25 *Ibid.*, p. 11.
26 *Ibid.*, p. 11.
27 'Content' here is broadly Bernstein's 'curriculum', or 'valid knowledge'. See BERNSTEIN (1971), p. 47.
28 *Abbreviated Proceedings* (1957), p. 13.
29 *Ibid.*, pp. 59–60.
30 *Ibid.*, 64–5.
31 *Ibid.*, p. 77.
32 *Ibid.*, pp. 70–1.
33 *Ibid.*, p. 71.
34 *Ibid.*, p. 73.
35 *Ibid.*, pp. 40–4.
36 *Ibid.*, p. 80.
37 *Ibid.*, p. 21.
38 *Ibid.*, p. 64.
39 *Ibid.*, pp. 22–6.
40 *Ibid.*, p. 78.
41 *Ibid.*, p. 79.
42 *Ibid.*, p. 79.
43 See YOUNG (1971), p. 38.
44 *Abbreviated Proceedings* (1957), p. 100.
45 *Ibid.*, pp. 72–3.
46 *Ibid.*, p. 77.

47 *Ibid.*, pp. 34–5.
48 *Ibid.*, passim.
49 *Ibid.*, pp. 3–4.
50 *Ibid.*, p. 4 and pp. 97–9.
51 *Ibid.*, pp. 26–30.
52 *Ibid.*, pp. 30–1.
53 *Ibid.*, p. 82.
54 *Ibid.*, pp. 82–3.
55 *Ibid.*, p. 84.
56 *Ibid.*, p. 88.
57 *Ibid.*, p. 89.
58 *Ibid.*, p. 90.
59 *Ibid.*, p. 90.
60 *Ibid.*, pp. 93–4.
61 *Ibid.*, p. 92.
62 *Ibid.*, p. 92.
63 *Ibid.*, p. 93.
64 *Ibid.*, pp. 89–90.
65 *Ibid.*, p. 90.
66 *Ibid.*, p. 91.
67 *Ibid.*, pp. 91–2.
68 *Ibid.*, p. 93.
69 *Ibid.*, pp. 89–92.
70 *Ibid.*, p. 92.
71 *Ibid.*, p. 92.
72 *Ibid.*, p. 89.
73 *Ibid.*, p. 94.
74 *Ibid.*, p. 94.
75 *Ibid.*, p. 94.
76 See MINISTRY OF EDUCATION (1963), p. 9.
77 *Abbreviated Proceedings* (1957), p. 82.
78 *Ibid.*, p. 82.
79 *Ibid.*, p. 83.
80 *Ibid.*, p. 83.
81 *Ibid.*, p. 82.
82 *Ibid.*, p. 83.
83 *Ibid.*, p. 83.
84 *Ibid.*, p. 97.
85 *Ibid.*, p. 82.
86 *Ibid.*, p. 83.
87 *Ibid.*, p. 83.
88 *Ibid.*, p. 31.
89 *Ibid.*, p. 82.
90 *Ibid.*, p. 83.
91 *Ibid.*, p. 27.
92 *Ibid.*, p. 82.
93 *Ibid.*, p. 82.
94 *Ibid.*, p. 82.
95 *Ibid.*, p. 83.

96 *Ibid.*, p. 96.
97 *Ibid.*, p. 31.
98 *Ibid.*, p. 33.
99 *Ibid.*, p. 33.
100 *Ibid.*, p. 84.
101 *Ibid.*, p. 89.
102 ATCDE (1956).
103 *Abbreviated Proceedings* (1957), p. 58.
104 *Ibid.*, p. 58.
105 *Ibid.*, p. 58.
106 *Ibid.*, p. 58.
107 *Ibid.*, pp. 101–2.
108 *Ibid.*, p. 102.
109 *Ibid.*, p. 102.
110 *Ibid.*, p. 103.
111 *Ibid.*, p. 103.
112 *Ibid.*, p. 104.
113 *Ibid.*, p. 104.
114 *Ibid.*, p. 104.
115 *Ibid.*, p. 105.
116 *Ibid.*, p. 105.
117 *Ibid.*, p. 105.
118 *Ibid.*, pp. 105–6.
119 *Ibid.*, p. 107.
120 *Ibid.*, p. 92.
121 *The Times (23 July 1957).*
122 HALL et al (1978), p. 120.
123 *The Times* (23 July 1957).
124 BECKER (1963).

6   Movements For Change: The Liverpool Conference

Although the main purpose of chapters 5 and 6 is to provide detailed accounts of the two conferences at which the alliance of applied mathematicians and representatives of the employers of graduate labour initially attempted, in an organized way, to move selective school mathematics in a more utilitarian direction, it is necessary, before describing the second of these, held at Liverpool in 1959, to provide a brief account of other developments during the period 1957–1959, aside from those involving the ATAM, which were to prove important in the redefining of school mathematics.

Some of these occurred outside of specifically English arenas, and especially in the USA, but, given the international features of subject communities described by Davies,[1] were eventually to have substantial effects on English curricula in the period after the Liverpool Conference. Other developments, such as the increasing public visibility of the 'problem' of the supply of mathematics teachers, were nearer home. One of these, already discussed in chapter 3, was the publication of a series of documents from 1957–1959, representing the compromises achieved within the Mathematical Association between university mathematicians and selective school teachers before the occurrence of the debates described later in this study. Although, as was noted earlier, these documents advocated little of post-1800 mathematics for schools, one probable effect of the Oxford Conference can be seen in the HMI's *Teaching Mathematics in Secondary Schools* of 1958, written, according to one of my interviewees, by Rollett, who had helped organize the Oxford meeting. It refers to the new industrial applications of mathematics, adding 'sooner or later, the applied mathematics taught in schools and universities will have to reflect these changes'.[2] Reference was also made to the 'inadequacy' of the education of mathematics teachers at all levels as a 'vicious circle'.[3]

Before considering some of the results of the development of a social movement advocating 'modern mathematics' in the USA, it is important to note one other potential source of support on which various segments of the mathematics profession, insofar as they were able to influence its reports, were to be able to draw in subsequent years. Concern in the west over potential manpower shortages had intensified after the successful launch in late 1957 of the Sputnik satellite by the USSR. In this climate, the OEEC, formed shortly after the war, set up, in 1958, an Office for Scientific and Technical Personnel. It will be seen in chapters 7 and 8 that the perspectives dominant in the debates and reports sponsored by this body were to play an important role in the processes of redefinition of the early 1960s.

In the USA a number of important debates within the mathematics community had occurred in the 1950s.[4] These largely reflected the increasing influence within American university mathematics of the modern algebraists, and the issue of applications was not to be dominant.[5] There is no space here to attempt a detailed analysis of the origins and strategies of the movement amongst American university mathematicians aiming to reform school mathematics, although Kuhn's work on the socialization of 'successors' probably holds the key.[6] It is necessary, however, that I describe some of the recommendations of the various conferences and reports that resulted from their activities as they were to provide resources for protagonists in English debates.

The report of the Commission on Mathematics (1959), appointed by the College Entrance Examination Board in 1955, and having eight university mathematicians amongst its fourteen members, argued for less stress to be placed on manipulation in school algebra, and more on 'structure'.[7] It also wished to see the introduction of vectors into high school geometry. As such, it can be seen to have represented the perspective of mathematics of the modern algebraists. This view of what should happen to school mathematics was also supported by the School Mathematics Study Group (SMSG), a body of university mathematicians and school teachers, modelled on the Physical Science Study Committee, and set up as a result of two conferences attended by university mathematicians and held in February 1958.[8] The second had been called expressly to consider the adequacy of school mathematics. The SMSG's stress on. the importance of algebraic structure in mathematics teaching, as well as the views of the Bourbaki mathematicians, were to be well-represented in the seminars and reports of the OEEC from 1959–1961 (see chapter 7). Through the involvement of Hope in these seminars, and more generally through publication, these perspectives of the pure mathematicians were to receive considerable publicity in England after late 1959. Specifically, they were to provide an important resource for those arguing for the introduction of 'modern mathematics' into English schools, as well as persuading others to join them. American perspectives also received some publicity in England when, in 1959, the Mathematics Panel of the University of Birmingham's Gulbenkian Enquiry into 'A' level syllabuses, chaired by Professor Daniels, a statistician, published its recommendation that 'the algebra of sets' be introduced into 'A' level mathematics courses. The reports of the Commission on Mathematics were used to support this.[9]

Other American developments which were to become known in England were also well underway. Since 1952, Beberman had been running an experiment concerned with discovery learning in school mathematics at the University of Illinois.[10] (This was to be criticized by Newman in his presidential address to the Mathematical Association in 1959.) And, since 1953, a Committee, sponsored by the Mathematical Association of America, had been working to encourage colleges to introduce more 'modern' mathematics into undergraduate courses. As a result, textbooks were produced, as well as several articles in the *American Mathematical Monthly*.[11]

In England, after 1957, the issues of 'teacher shortage' in mathematics had received more publicity, largely because of the activities of Langford, Head of Battersea Grammar School and, in 1958, President of the Mathematical Association. He had devoted part of his presidential address to the 'problem'. *The Times* reported it thus (11 April 1958):

> He predicted that unless means could be found to assure in the next few years a sufficient number of capable teachers there would be a decline in the general standards of such teaching, a failure of government plans for technical education and a worsening situation in the schools.... Last year he asked for particulars of staffing and the scope of mathematical teaching in public and grammar schools of England and Wales. A summary of the replies from well over half made interesting and alarming reading. They showed that proportions of from thirteen to thirty per cent of the men teaching mathematics in the boys' schools had insufficient qualifications ... The girls' schools from which replies were received were in an even worse plight, and the information showed that far less teaching at advanced levels was available in such places. There was a prevalent belief that girls were in some mysterious way unable to learn mathematics, but he believed that given adequate teaching they were not unsuited to the subject.[12]

Langford had followed this up by speaking to the British Association meeting in September. According to the report in *Nature*, he argued:

> As the universities strive to carry their final year students right to the frontiers of knowledge in this rapidly developing field, the schools are expected to keep pace with what must inevitably be a rising standard of entry . . ., and this is occurring at a time when apparently less than one third of those engaged in the teaching of mathematics at school have specific qualifications in the subject. Mr. Langford indicated the possibility that in the near future there may be established an Institute of Mathematics comparable to the engineering institutes, which might offer a qualification capable of being acquired by teachers of mathematics who have not reached graduate standard, but are willing to improve their knowledge of the subject presumably while still engaged in teaching.[13]

To some extent then, the Liverpool Conference took place in a somewhat changed climate of opinion: one in which influential figures, possibly partly for strategic reasons (i.e., to gain further resources from government and industry), were beginning to articulate the view that a crisis was developing within mathematics education with enormous potential implications for the nation as a whole. Furthermore, as the news of the American developments filtered through, news of the possibility of new careers, in curriculum development, will have come with it.

The Liverpool Conference of April 1959[14]

In line with my treatment of the Oxford Conference, I shall begin by describing the locations of the participants and then, in the light of this information, analyze the debates. While the speakers from industry will be seen to have argued for similar changes as at Oxford, it will be seen that the school-based participants, from lower status locations than their Oxford counterparts, expressed somewhat different concerns.

Participation

This Conference, as was noted earlier, was the result of a suggestion made at the final session at Oxford. The eventual Organizing Committee differed considerably, however, from that nominated there (see

Table 11).[15] It can be seen to have comprised pure and applied university mathematicians, actors from industry, members of HMI, school teachers and a training college lecturer. It was chaired by an applied mathematician, Professor Rosenhead.

The distribution of participants was different from that at Oxford, reflecting the northern, non-Oxbridge, location of the meeting (see Table 12). Here the direct grant and maintained grammar schools, rather than the independent schools, predominated. The absence of secondary moderns was, however, still almost total. Again, there were relatively few girls' schools. Technical colleges were better represented. Taken

Table 11: Liverpool Conference Committee

Professor L. Rosenhead (Chairman)	Professor of Applied Mathematics (Liverpool)
Dr. F.W. Land (Vice-Chairman)	Senior Lecturer in Education (Liverpool)
E.D. Camier	Birkenhead School
L.V. Cocks	Unilever
Dr. P.C. Davey	HMI
Miss S. Harvey	Holly Lodge School (Liverpool)
Miss E.M. Holman	Manchester High School for Girls
R.C. Lyness	HMI
R.L. Plackett	Senior Lecturer in Mathematical Statistics (Liverpool)
W.E. Scott	English Electric Company
P.L. Taylor	Metropolitan Vickers Electrical Co.
Professor A.G. Walker	Professor of Pure Mathematics (Liverpool)
Miss D.B. Walker	St. Katherine's Training College (Liverpool)
Dr. T.J. Wilmore	Senior Lecturer in Pure Mathematics (Liverpool)
A. Young	Senior Lecturer in Applied Mathematics (Liverpool)
Dr T Kelly (Secretary)	Director of Extra-Mural Studies (Liverpool)

Table 12: Institutional affiliation of participants at Liverpool

University (mainly Liverpool)	18
Colleges of technology and further education	35
Colleges of education	5
Private industry	35
Government science/research	12
Nationalised industry	2
HMI	3
Schools: Independent boys	9
Independent girls	2
Direct grant mixed	1
Direct grant boys	20
Direct grant girls	7
Mixed grammar	15
Boys' grammar	26
Girls' grammar	17
Mixed technical grammar	2
Boys' technical grammar	2
Girls' technical grammar	—
Secondary modern (technical)	2
Secondary modern	1
Educational administration	1
Ministry of education	1
Unclassified	2
Total	218

overall, the occupational locations of the participants tended to be lower in the academic hierarchy.

The distribution of programmed speakers was very similar to that at Oxford (see Table 13). School-based participants and also, this time, those from the technical college sector were again an intended audience for messages from the universities and industry.

Of future SMP writers, Tammadge (associated with the ATAM) and Durran (present at Oxford) were present. Collins, of the ATAM, future joint instigator of MME, was also present.

Table 13: *Institutional affiliations of programmed speakers at Liverpool*

University:	Mathematics	4
	Education	1
Technical college		3
Private industry		12
Nationalised industry		1
Government science/research		5
HMI		1
Ministry of Education		1
Schools:	Boys' grammar	2
	Direct grant boys	1
	Total	31

Table 14: *Overlapping individual participation at Oxford and Liverpool: locations*

Private industry		4
Government science/research		1
University:	Mathematics	1
	Education	1
HMI		2
Schools:	Independent boys	1
	Direct grant boys	1
	Direct grant girls	1
	Boys' grammar	2
	Total	14

A number of those who had been present at Oxford (fourteen of 103) also attended the Liverpool meeting (see table 14). The effective degree of overlap can, however, be seen to have been much greater if organizations, rather than individuals, are considered (see Table 15). In

Table 15:   Overlapping organizational participation at Oxford and Liverpool

Private industry		10
Nationalised industries		2
Government science/research		3
University		1
HMI		1
Schools:	Independent boys	4
	Direct grant boys	2
	Direct grant girls	1
	Boys' grammar	1
	Total	25

fact, twenty-five organizations, some of which sent more than one representative, were represented at both meetings. Clearly, a group of large companies was maintaining an interest in mathematics education. Their willingness to fund these meetings supports this conclusion. Twenty-three organizations, of whom fourteen had also supported the Oxford event, supported the Liverpool meeting (see Table 16).[16] Both meetings were therefore basically supported by a core group of nine major private companies (being the British Iron and Steel Federation, British Thomson-Houston Co. Ltd., Bristol Aeroplane Co. Ltd., Courtaulds Ltd., English Electric Co. Ltd., Ferranti Ltd., ICI, Metropolitan-Vickers Electrical Co. Ltd., and Shell Petroleum Ltd.) together with state bodies of various types. A number of these companies had previously been involved in the support of school science through their membership of the Industrial Fund.[17]

The four independent schools represented at both meetings, all boys' schools, included Marlborough College, whose teachers were to help found SMP less than three years later.

Issues

Again, the agenda was set by a university applied mathematician. Rosenhead, in his Chairman's address, made it clear that, in his opinion, syllabuses were up for discussion, and that 'modelling' was crucially important:

Table 16: *Organisations supporting the Liverpool Conference*

Private companies	16
Nationalised industries	2
Government research/science	3
Government ministries	1
Liverpool Council of Education	1
Total	23

The words 'mathematics in action' embody the central idea of this conference. The more teachers know of the ways in which mathematics is used the more clearly will they be able to assess the value of current syllabuses of mathematics, and current methods of mathematical instruction, in relation to the needs of our rapidly changing society. The present day demands of industry, commerce, science and technology should not dictate the full content of school and university teaching, but those who help to mould the minds and characters of our young people should make themselves fully aware of the realistic industrial and intellectual requirements of our time...[18]

He seems therefore to have presented school mathematics as a servicing subject, continuing:

The most significant contribution which the mathematician makes to society is in the creation of 'mathematical problems' out of the 'real problems' of the world. This is called the 'making of mathematical models'. In order to make models of real value a mathematician has to become expert in the art of stripping complex physical and engineering situations of their irrelevances, and revealing the problems in their simplest possible form.[19]

It will be seen that, as in 1957, this was to be a central issue at the Conference. I shall now consider the contributions to the debates of the 'real world' speakers.

Issues: 'Real World' Users of Mathematics

Given the overlapping nature of the speakers, it is not surprising to find that similar themes emerged in 1957 and 1959. Because of this, I shall not go into such detail here as I did for Oxford. The speakers again discussed the various uses to which mathematics was put, again mainly by graduate employees, and the consequences of these, as they saw them, for mathematical education. The uses focused on involved 'modelling', linear programming, computing, numerical analysis and methods, statistics and probability, and matrix algebra. The speakers differed on the question of whether school syllabuses were in need of reform in respect of content, but most wanted to see changes in pedagogy and approach. A few particular points, some not aired at Oxford, will be stressed.

First, the focus was again very much on the use of mathematics by high level employees, mainly graduate scientists and engineers. However, at this Conference, one speaker, Langdale of ICI, devoted his talk to craft apprentices and their 'needs' in his company.[20] He noted that they came fifty per cent from modern schools, forty per cent from technical schools and ten per cent from grammar schools, adding that he was therefore really talking to the wrong audience. He divided them into four groups of trades with respect to their 'needs' for mathematics. The first group, mechanical fitters, turners and machinists, needed to be prepared 'to deal with problems in which the use of decimals and logarithms, simple algebra and trigonometry' were involved. The second, electrical fitters and instrument artificers, needed to be able to use simple equations and formulae. The third, platers and sheet metal workers, needed some fairly specialized geometry. The last, painters and bricklayers, basically needed arithmetic of area and volume. (This was all traditional content of school syllabuses in the selective tradition, though not necessarily taught in the modern schools.) His dissatisfaction related to the fact that these basics were 'nominally covered' but that extra instruction had to be given to recruits.

Secondly, as at Oxford, even within the discussion of graduate employees, some speakers emphasized that classical, and often elementary, mathematics was much used in industry by scientists and engineers. Beeching, of ICI, made this a key theme of his address.[21] He went on, however, to argue that the syllabus was not particularly critical, but that the approach to problems in the teaching of it was. Problem formulation, not just solution, should be covered. Bosanquet, also of ICI, made the same point, as, amongst others, did Scott of English Electric and Hastie of the Post Office.[22] Generally, there was a consensus on the need for the teaching of mathematics at all levels to emphasize problem formulation, the principles of modelling, and the relationship of mathematics to 'real life'. Bosanquet also argued that methods of thought, rather than techniques, should be stressed.[23] Alongside this group, expressing fairly neutral opinions on content, there was also a strong body of opinion demanding some changes in the syllabus. A number thought that statistics should be taught from the school upwards.[24] A smaller number wanted examples of numerical methods introduced at various levels from 'O' level upwards.[25] Others saw the principles of computer programming as a suitable topic for school syllabuses.[26]

As at Oxford, the ambiguity in the notion of the reform of school mathematics (content and/or pedagogy?) is clear here. A range of missions could be legitimated by reference to some industrial speakers' concerns, including a curricular conservatism.

Issues: Educators' Contributions

University Mathematicians

Apart from Rosenhead, three university mathematicians addressed the Conference. Young, a senior lecturer in applied mathematics, argued the case for more numerical analysis to be included in university curricula. His talk illustrates how a relatively low status content, which numerical analysis then was within the universities, can be legitimated by reference to the 'needs' of user groups:

> The case for training mathematicians in this branch of mathematics is easily justified on the grounds of national need. Despite this, numerical analysis is as yet a compulsory part of the undergraduate syllabus in only a few universities. Amongst many mathematicians, the belief is held that numerical methods are just techniques for doing unavoidable arithmetic, and can be picked up by the graduate if and when the need arises. I do not believe this belief is tenable by anyone who has a real knowledge of what modern numerical analysis is.[27]

He went on to list other, more intrinsic, justifications. It made reference to many other branches of mathematics. It involved considerable mathematical judgment. It had generated a multitude of research problems:

> Numerical analysis can thus be not only a unifying but also a stimulating influence in the university study of mathematics.[28]

In discussion, he suggested that some aspects of the subject could be introduced into schools. Wilmore, a university pure mathematician, disagreed. The relevant 'maturity of judgement' would not be available.[29]

In his own address, Wilmore argued for a change in pedagogic emphases in schools so that more 'intuitive' and 'inductive' reasoning could occur in classrooms. Deductive proof should come after this stage of conjecture.[30]

The last to speak was Jackson, who seems to have had some sixth form teaching experience, on 'the relation between the requirements of industry and the teaching of mathematics in grammar schools'. He began:

> The idea behind this conference is that perhaps greater weight should be given to industry than has been given hitherto. Mostly we shall be thinking of sixth form work, though not exclusively.[31]

He distinguished between the questions of 'what should be taught?' and 'how should it be taught?'. Under 'what', he listed suggestions that had come from representatives of industry: less Euclidean and coordinate geometry of a complicated kind, but more probability and statistics, three dimensional geometry, elementary vector algebra, numerical analysis and ('even') computer programming. He favoured some of these, not others. Under 'how', he argued for 'modelling', problem formulation, applications and links with physics as things to be stressed more in schools. He suggested the setting of under- and over-determined examination questions. Time could come from the streamlining of applied mathematics and physics courses. Not that problem solution should be neglected: it was as important as being able to set up the problem.[32]

Considering these three speakers together, we can note a general case being made for change, especially pedagogic change, in school mathematics. (Jackson's suggestion for reformed types of examination questions moved the debate into Bernstein's category of 'evaluation'.[33]) In terms of the theoretical framework employed here, the suggestion by Young, an applied mathematician, that numerical analysis, a quickly growing branch of mathematical research, be included in undergraduate courses to a greater extent might be interpreted as an attempt to use the resources inherent in the alliance with representatives of industry to advance the interests of some applied mathematicians.

University Educationists

Land, on the other hand, a senior lecturer in mathematics education and Vice-Chairman of the Conference, in choosing to focus on problems of staffing in his talk on 'the teaching of pure and applied mathematics in the schools of Great Britain' might be seen, in the climate of opinion partially created by the ATCDE, Langford and others, as seeking resources for either the subject in general or training departments in particular. He saw the issue of teacher supply, on which he had spoken at Oxford, as 'one of the most difficult and intransigent problems in education at the present time'.[34] He claimed that there was a 'critical shortage of mathematical specialists in the grammar schools', adding that 'virtually all' teacher training students, 'whether in training colleges, or universities, came from grammar schools, so that theirs is the key part in the supply of teachers'. He argued that a vicious circle existed. Teachers, mainly women, in the junior schools and those in the lower forms of the grammar schools were both poorly qualified and relatively uninterested in mathematics. This produced bored pupils who were less likely to continue their studies past 'O' level. The resulting low numbers of mathematics graduates, especially good honours graduates, perpetuated the problem of finding adequate grammar school staff. He claimed:

> A glance at the UGC report shows that mathematics is tenth on the list of subjects for which honours degrees are being granted in universities, pride of place being taken by history with 1017, and one wonders whether it is in the nation's best interests that the effort devoted, at the highest level, to delving into the past should be two and a half times that devoted to learning mathematics, which is largely the language needed to describe the present.[35]

Here the references to the national interest merge with attacks on other subjects. The high wastage rates within university mathematics, a problem internal to the subject, are not referred to.[36] He continued:

> Very necessary improvements in the teaching of mathematics from the infants' schools to the universities depend on finding more and better mathematics staff for grammar schools, and this is probably the greatest challenge to educational planners that exists today. The implications are becoming better appreciated, but the development of our whole national prosperity may well depend, ultimately, upon the boldness of the steps which those in authority are prepared to take to meet this challenge.[37]

He referred to two 'palliatives': the Ministry of Education's one-year supplementary courses and the diploma, mooted at Oxford, which the Mathematical Association was arranging to provide.

He also noted that the secondary modern schools were increasingly sending pupils into further education and therefore 'the quality of secondary modern mathematics teaching is of very great importance to the national manpower situation'. There was, however, a 'serious shortage' of specialist teachers in these schools. Furthermore, all types of girls' schools, which provided most junior teachers, found it difficult to obtain mathematics staff.

Clearly, in presenting such accounts of shortage and associated claims for extra resources for the subject, actors such as Land had to select legitimate criteria to support their arguments. Land emphasized the amount of mathematics taught in schools, and the importance of 'good honours' graduates in the middle and upper grammar school:

> Mathematics occupies about fifteen per cent of the grammar school timetable, and very large numbers are involved in both 'O' and 'A' level examinations. Since the war something of the order of 4.5 per cent of men and 3.8 per cent of women graduates in training who have first or second class honours degrees have been mathematicians.[38]

He then compared mathematics with other subjects on his 'good honours' criterion, giving the following figures for the entry of such graduates into teaching in 1957:

History	231
English	259
Modern Languages	289
Geography	211
Mathematics	57

In his terms, therefore, a strong case existed for special attention to be paid to mathematics.

He concentrated the rest of his talk on the specific needs of the more 'able' children of eleven to thirteen years of age. Here, the absence of suitable teachers was, in his opinion, threatening the production of nationally needed scientists.

Speakers from the Technical Colleges

The first speaker here, Varlow, a lecturer at Birmingham College of Technology, spoke on numerical analysis and methods.[39] He felt that, because of the increasing use of computers in industry, sixth formers should be taught 'some numerical methods'. Yet, he complained, only the AEB syllabuses currently included any papers on computations. Schools would need to be adequately equipped with desk machines 'as is the case in America, where even ten year-olds are taught to use a small hand operated calculator'. (Here he illustrates the use of supposed American practice as legitimation.)

The second speaker, Kerr, Head of the Mathematics Department at Salford's Royal Technical College, concentrated on 'mathematical contacts' between education and industry.[40] After bemoaning the fact, in his view, that, until recently, mathematics departments had been seen as merely servicing other subjects in the technical colleges, and that industry had therefore not bothered to develop any contact with them, he went on to outline how this situation might be changed. His proposals, which he claimed were already being implemented in some cases, included courses from HNC to postgraduate level in such areas as linear programming and its industrial applications, numerical analysis and statistics. Some should have a sandwich element. Lecturers should be placed for periods in industry, and industry should supply 'associate lecturers' for one or two days a week, as well as sponsoring research.

The third speaker, Loveday, a lecturer at Kingston-Upon-Thames Technical College, had previously worked in schools.[41] He used his talk to advocate statistics as an ultimately separate school subject. He began by presenting examination entry figures for the Northern Universities and London boards. Together, something over 800 candidates were entered in 1958 for alternative syllabuses containing statistics at 'O' and 'A' level. He contrasted this with the 300 entered in 1954, pointing out that statistics was increasingly being studied. He then referred at length to the first edition of the IAAM's *The Teaching of Mathematics* which, in 1957, had argued that statistics — as applied arithmetic — could well find a place in the school curriculum. It was more likely than formal geometry to interest the child, and it was equally 'logical'. In a final attempt to legitimate the subject, he noted that it also provided much practice in arithmetic. Given all this, he argued, teachers would need a good textbook because 'to the man who is feeling his way in an unfamiliar subject the right textbook is an anchor'.

Finally, after presenting some accounts from his own experience of how statistics had 'revived' pupils' interest in mathematics, he went on to argue against the IAAM's recommendation that the subject should be introduced gradually. He preferred 'the plunge', in order to avoid 'tedious and boring variations of the same question' in examinations, as already occurred in other branches of mathematics. There should be a new, separate subject.

His talk is interesting in indicating the extent to which statistics, notwithstanding the comments of speakers at Oxford in 1957, was gradually becoming accepted as a part of the mathematics curriculum in selective schools. This may have had much to do with the ease with which some aspects of the subject allowed teachers to generate routine numerical exercises.

Speakers from the Schools

There were four official speakers from the schools, but others offered opinions during discussion.

The first, Hodge, SMM at Manchester Grammar School, concentrated on the views of various philosophers on the nature of mathematics, and the relation of these to curricular issues.[42] He saw geometry and algebra as providing 'logical training'. He argued that most boys needed to have their mathematics related to something they can 'see or touch'. He agreed that more work in schools should be concerned with the setting up of equations as against routine solution. He would also favour less emphasis on rigorous proof, and more on intuitive reasoning.

In discussion of this, Camier, of Birkenhead School, defended Euclidean geometry, bemoaning that 'many boys did not appear to have the idea of a proper sequence of theorems'.[43]

The second speaker, Tomkys, SMM of a Bradford boys' grammar school, discussed 'present arrangements for the teaching of mathematics in schools'. He concentrated on 'ability' grouping and the transition of 'able' pupils to university.[44] He attacked what he saw as the inadequate use of setting in junior schools: the 'intelligent children' were being held back. He wanted more secondary moderns to follow the example of 'some of these schools' and provide more than arithmetic and geometrical drawing in 'mathematics'. In the grammar schools, setting could perhaps be further employed to 'enable the most able pupils to make the progress ... warranted by their ability'. He wondered whether the cooperation that existed between schools and examination boards might not 'bring, with its advantages, opportunities to resist change and so impede desirable progress'. He then raised the issue of the transition from school to university:

> In the sixth form the success achieved through the arrangements for teaching mathematics might, in the first instance, be measured by the extent to which the end-products satisfy the requirements of the university departments. Honours schools of mathematics in some instances suggest that our pupils find the

transition from school mathematics to university mathematics increasingly difficult to make successfully. The pupils find themselves without experience in modes of abstract thought and logic which must soon become a commonplace. Ought the schools to include in the sixth form such topics as:- ranges and pencils and the properties of the quadrilateral/quadrangle configuration; a more extended knowledge of plane curves, asymptotes; singular points, multiple points, etc; convergence; vectors and vector methods? Could they go further and, independently of examinations, introduce to the pupil such subjects as mathematical logic, set theory, and group theory?[45]

If the answer was yes, he saw a separate sixth form set as being necessary for potential honours students. And, if the course was to remain the same length, some topics would have to go: which ones 'should be made clear to the schools'. Ideally, those studying mathematics would have to be separated from those studying mathematics-with-science. He concluded by referring these issues to that of staffing:

> It might well be said that the dynamism of school mathematics teaching is threatened by the lack of teachers with training in modern mathematical requirements.[46]

Tomkys can be seen, as a result of his concern with the potential university success of his 'best' pupils, to have been ready to consider the introduction of new content into the sixth form. His reified usage, 'modern mathematical requirements' — actually certain segments' requirements, clearly indicates a tendency to equate 'mathematics' with university mathematics.

He was followed by Egner, Head of a South Shields technical grammar school, speaking on the same title, whose remarks can be seen to have possibly reflected his lower status, less well-resourced location.[47] Discussing timetabling, he noted that 'special provision for tuition for scholarship papers is rare'. Schools were lacking well-equipped mathematics teachers, this situation leading to unsatisfactory arrangements in the sixth form. He proposed a number of changes, several of which clearly reflected his location:

> (i) increase the supply of mathematics teachers and improve the sixth form staffing ratio; (ii) abolish scholarship papers in order to give all sixth formers a fairer deal; (iii) purge mathematical syllabuses at all levels, building them around mathematical methods; schools should be invited to submit special syllabuses in mathematics; (iv) reform textbooks, retaining collections of

examples, and including demonstration of essential mathematical method; (v) make university mathematics courses more attractive, and emphasize the attractions, not the difficulties of the subject; (vi) strengthen the liaison between the mathematics masters and mistresses and the staff of universities.[48]

The discussion focused on the staffing question. Part-time evening courses were discussed as one possibly helpful move.[49]

These three speakers were clearly ready to contemplate change, if differing as to its nature. The fourth, Brierly, from a Liverpool grammar school, was more cautious.[50] That change in content would, however, represent less of a threat to established practice, and hence the occupational interests of many teachers, than change in pedagogy is suggested by the following passage in the report of the proceedings. Scott, of English Electric, had just spoken on 'modelling' and its implications for school mathematics:

Later speakers said it seemed that a major difficulty in the mathematical formulation of practical problems was the disentangling of the irrelevant factors in the physical situation; whereas at school and university a student was always presented with problems which were clear-cut and without irrelevance. Could a case be made for the deliberate introduction of irrelevances in such problems? Mr. Scott thought to a certain extent that it could but was vigorously opposed by some teachers who said that it was difficult enough to teach some pupils and students even without the introduction of irrelevance.[51]

Also worthy of note is the apparently greater concern amongst these teachers, as against those at Oxford, with the 'shortage' of mathematics teachers. While there is evidence to suggest that the difficulty of appointing 'adequate' teachers may have been increasing during these years,[52] the importance of this in accounting for this concern, as opposed to changes in the climate of opinion brought about strategically or the lower status locations of these teachers, can not be accurately assessed here. Clearly, however, these factors would have worked in the same causal direction, especially as many actors, for example Egner, who in 1961 was to chair an IAHM working party on the 'shortage', would presumably have seen in the situation the possibility of successfully claiming extra resources for schools and the subject from the state.

Other Contributors to the Debate

Three other major contributions were made to the meeting: those of Flemming, a civil servant in the Ministry of Education, of Rollett, a senior HMI, and of Manders, a scientific civil servant. I shall not discuss the latter's talk although his topic, mathematics education in the USSR, and his stress on the rate of technological advance in that society, are interesting indices of contemporary official concerns.[53]

Flemming and Rollett both spoke on 'Measures needed to provide the mathematical specialists likely to be required in the next ten years', and are of interest here in that they can be seen as supplying the participants in the conference with an 'official' view, one that, because of the resources controlled by the Ministry, might have to be taken into account in any political moves that might be made.

Flemming, having carefully deferred to the notion of teacher autonomy by stating that it was not the sole function of the schools and universities 'to see that individuals enter particular callings', and that 'the tendency to regard them as factories for turning out qualified specialists or to speak of individuals as if they were simply units of scientific manpower is to be deplored', went on to discuss manpower statistics.[54] He focused on the increasing number of seventeen year-olds remaining at school, the increasing numbers taking 'A' levels, especially in mathematics, and the output of the universities in mathematics, science and technology. The output of mathematics graduates had not, he noted, kept pace with the increases in science and technology generally, remaining at a 'little over 400' from 1954 to 1957. He presented various projections, concluding that the school mathematics staffing situation was not likely to improve for several years. It was important to improve the supply of 'good non-graduate teachers' for the primary schools and some of 'the elementary work in the secondary schools'. As far as graduate teachers were concerned, there were some factors, such as the ending of National Service (graduates entering teaching had obtained 'indefinite deferment') and the approach of the 'bulge' to the sixth forms, that might worsen the situation. He concluded with a reference to the Kelsall Report of 1955 which had shown that the percentage of unfilled vacancies was much higher in university mathematics faculties 'than for all faculties taken together or for science faculties taken separately':

> If we are to get an increase in the numbers of graduates in mathematics, the schools and potential employers must see that sixth formers know about the careers to which a degree in

mathematics can lead, and the universities must see that their courses are as sound and attractive as they can be made from the wider educational point of view, and must ensure that no keen candidate is lost because he can not get admission to the first university of his choice.[55]

In this 'official' account of what was beginning to be labelled a crisis in mathematics education, the start of an attack on certain university practices can be discerned. This was to be followed up in Rollett's contribution. His talk also demonstrates that market factors were beginning to exert some pressures on the then partially sex-typed curriculum.[56]

He began by noting that, whereas Flemming had spoken from an administrative point of view, his task was 'to consider the same problem from inside the classroom'. He quickly restated and praised the 'tradition' of teacher autonomy in England, partly as an answer to 'criticism in some quarters' of his *Teaching Mathematics in Secondary Schools*[57] that it did not give adequate 'positive guidance to the man in the classroom'. It was intended to 'influence and stimulate, not direct'. He also praised the Mathematical Association, of which he was an influential member, whose 'reports and other publications [had] exercised a bigger and better influence on teaching than any official edicts could have done'. Arguing that 'curriculum reform' was a continuing process, he regretted that many teachers were not members of the Association (their 'professional responsibility') and also that, unlike America, the universities (and particularly the London Mathematical Society and the Royal Society) were not doing more to help the schools.

Having claimed that more mathematicians of 'all kinds' were needed, he specified three types: from single honours graduates down through mathematics as an ancillary subject in a degree to the proposed diploma students, and linked this point to a critical discussion of the transition from school to university:

I was recently in a provincial university which accepts sixty would-be mathematicians in a year but allows only fifteen to stay the full honours course, and I know that this state of affairs is a deterrent to the schools. One side at least knows too little of what is done on the other.[58]

And, later in his talk, he claimed:

The third discontinuity, which can be disastrous, may occur at the university, when freshmen with very mixed backgrounds (whatever the regulations for admission) are exposed at once to a battery of lectures without any survey of sixth form work from the university's higher standpoint, a survey which I personally believe to be vitally necessary.[59]

Then, after comparing school mathematics favourably with other subjects, he moved on to discuss pedagogy. He wanted to see more reference to 'experience' and 'practical applications' within 'boys' experience'. Pacing in relation to 'ability' was also crucial:

> The food offered for digestion must be suited to the recipient — milk for babes, meat for men ... Hurry is disastrous to the less able pupil; stagnation can be disastrous not only to the able pupil but to the nation.[60]

He also thought that more emphasis on discovery and creativity in lessons might be desirable.

He then discussed the teacher 'shortage', which he saw as prior to all other issues, including any curriculum reform:

> In order to produce more mathematicians we need more enlightened teaching all along the line from infant school to training college and university. Reform of curricula and examinations will follow automatically, but is not of prime importance. The better our teaching the greater will be the number of those coming forward to read mathematics, and the greater the number of those who will feel inspired to become teachers of mathematics.[61]

He considered a number of factors in, and possible solutions to, the 'shortage'. He regretted the 'nearly twenty women's training colleges without a mathematician on their staff', and that in the university departments of education only 'one in three at present has a mathematician as tutor'. He saw girls as a potential source of more mathematicians. He hoped that industry would not 'under-employ' the mathematics of those they engaged. He believed that short and supplementary courses were needed, and these had been started by the Ministry at various training colleges. He referred to the USA (whose 'need is greater than ours'), in particular to university-based vacation courses for teachers funded by the National Science Foundation. He thought that similar refresher courses 'may be necessary' for our grammar school teachers.

Comments on Liverpool

In many respects the debates here shared much with those at Oxford. The speakers from industry again argued for some reform of school and university mathematics in a utilitarian direction. Their emphasis was on pedagogy and the particular issue of 'modelling' but a number of specific contents were also favoured: statistics, numerical analysis and methods, computing, vectors and matrix algebra. Again, a number of speakers, including Beeching of ICI, mindful of the mathematics used by many 'non-mathematicians' in industry, reminded the meeting that classical mathematical techniques were also 'required'. Langdale, also of ICI, discussing the needs of lower level employees — ignored at Oxford, also argued for the retention of much contemporary syllabus content. The roots of some of the later negative reactions to 'modern mathematics' can be discerned in his description of the 'needs' of craftsmen.[62] The university and technical college teachers present, usually themselves working in the area of applied mathematics, supported many of these suggestions for reform although Willmore, a pure mathematician, considered numerical analysis not to be an appropriate school subject. Given the similar locations and subject-segmental interests of most of the speakers from the universities and industry, this similarity with Oxford is unsurprising. When we come to consider the teachers, however, some important differences emerge.

These actors were, generally speaking, from lower status schools than those present at Oxford. This was reflected in the relative lack of discussion of Oxbridge scholarship examinations. It also presumably accounts, in part, for the increased discussion of the teachers 'shortage'. That the publicizing work of the ATCDE, Langford and others, in the context of what was probably an objectively worsening supply situation, was also a factor here is suggested by the amount of time devoted to the problem by the speakers from the Ministry and the Inspectorate.

Again, it was presumably partly as a result of this increased activity and concern over teacher supply, and manpower supply in general, that a more uniformly critical attention was paid here to the school/ university transition in mathematics. Several speakers, Flemming, Rollett and, arguably, Egner, seem to have been using the opportunity provided by the new climate of opinion to raise questions about university entrance and teaching practices. Ironically, it was in this context that Tomkys, willing to see the problem as lying in the schools, and implicitly granting university mathematicians control over both their own and the schools' curricula, raised the possibility of the introduction of some new topics into the sixth form. This apportioning

of the 'blame' for the difficulties undergraduates experienced in studying mathematics was to become, in 1961, a central issue in the debate on
mathematics education and teacher supply.

On curriculum reform in general, Rollett's belief that it would
follow automatically, given 'enlightened teaching', and more mathematics teachers, is in line with the view expressed in Mathematical
Association reports. At this stage then, key members of the HMI were
not giving primacy to this. Furthermore, the lack of welcome any
radical proposals for changes in pedagogy might be expected to receive
amongst selective school teachers in general is suggested by the response, recorded in the minutes, to Scott's suggestions for reformed
examination problems. There is no record of any of the ATAM
members present (including Brookes, Fyfe, Collins and Tammadge)
having entered this discussion. That some of the teachers present were
ready to begin to re-examine their definition of 'mathematics' in the
light of messages from groups outside the school is clear, however, from
the unsigned extracts of letters written after the Conference and
reproduced in the minutes. One, fairly typical of the thirteen quoted,
reads:

> I gained many valuable ideas at the conference and, having heard
> of the many applications of mathematics in industry, am now
> better able to place the subject in a broader perspective. I think
> that the criticism that mathematicians straight from school are
> often unable to translate a practical problem into a mathematical
> form is a valid one. I shall try to stress this 'translation' and to
> place a little less emphasis on the acquisition of isolated techni-
> ques. I had not realised how serious was the shortage of
> mathematicians. I shall certainly see what can be done in this
> school towards increasing supply.[63]

Another, possibly a 'convert', wrote:

> I came up to Liverpool with preconceived but very erroneous
> ideas of what I was going to hear, and the gravity of the problem
> was most forcibly brought home to me. It made me realise how
> cloistered school life really is . . . It has also caused me to look
> very closely at my teaching methods and those of my other
> mathematics masters, and there is room for quite a new outlook.
> It has given me a much needed shake-up.[64]

These letters, taken with that from Quadling *et al* after the Oxford
meeting, can be taken as evidence that the alliance of applied mathematicians and industrial personnel, whether because of their perceived right

to influence the school curriculum and the definition of mathematics or because those in the schools saw possible career opportunities and resources becoming available through the interest of those within 'industry' in the subject, were succeeding in persuading some teachers, including some in the prestigious independent schools, that change in school mathematics was necessary and/or strategically worthwhile.

Conclusion: Movements for Change

Eggleston, in his ideal-typical (and descriptive) nine stage model of the curriculum development process, has argued that curriculum change begins with the 'preliminary identification of the possibility of curriculum change in, or beyond, existing defined areas of the curriculum'.[65] He continues:

> This may be done by teachers, heads, administrators or researchers. It may spring from many sources. Sometimes it may arise from the work of isolated teachers responding to problems of motivation or discipline in their classrooms. It may arise from a desire by enthusiasts to incorporate 'new' knowledge or previously unincorporated knowledge into the school curriculum ... It may spring from responses to external pressure groups.[66]

We are now able to see that, by mid-1959, these processes were well under way in relation to English secondary school mathematics. In the last two chapters we have seen how, at Oxford and Liverpool, pressure groups external to the schools, in the form of an alliance of university mathematicians, representing mainly the applied segment of the subject, and employers of graduate labour invested some of their considerable resources of time, money and status into conveying to teachers from the selective sector (who prepared their students and employees) their 'requirements' of the school curriculum. They legitimized these by reference to the nation's 'needs' for scientific and technological manpower. Judging from the letters received by the organizers of these meetings, we can assume that at least a minority of the teachers present were, in terms of the model employed here, partially resocialized in subject terms. They came, that is, to see mathematics, and potentially school mathematics, as a different reality. It was also clear at Oxford that many teachers in the independent schools, well-placed to compete successfully in the competition for university (especially Oxbridge) scholarships and places, were ready to make curricular changes which would serve to produce more appropriately subject-socialized students. In fact, two of the signatories of the post-Oxford letter to Hammersley, Quadling of Marlborough and Jones of Winchester, were to be founder members of SMP.

Most of the debate at these conferences, reflecting the occupational interests of their organizers, was concerned with applied mathematics. Only briefly, and in relation to the transition of pupils from school to university, was modern algebra discussed. During the same period, however, as was seen in chapter 4, a group within the leadership of the ATAM was beginning, partly under the influence of the ICSITM, and using resources generated by developing the Association's membership in arenas relatively untapped by the Mathematical Association, to argue for the introduction of post-1800 algebraic ideas (recently campaigned for by the Bourbaki group[67]) into school syllabuses. The leadership also continued to campaign for pedagogic changes, partially legitimizing both elements of its mission in terms of improving the child's 'understanding' of mathematics. This grouping, located across universities, training colleges and selective schools, appears to have been mission-based rather than locationally defined. A clearer example of the latter was the grouping of members in the secondary moderns concerned, for a variety of reasons, to introduce GCE mathematics into their schools.

Individual teachers were also beginning to work to introduce newer mathematics into their school courses. Mansfield, for example, at Holloway School, later to be briefly associated with SMP, had begun to develop a pre-'O' level textbook which included 'modern mathematics'.[68]

By mid-1959, therefore, there existed, scattered throughout the selective schools, partly as a result of the activities of Hammersley and his allies and partly as a result of the work of ATAM activists, a number of teachers, partly in contact with one another through the associations and conferences, interested in the possibility of changing the nature of school mathematics and aware of possible sources of support for this mission. Others, less directly committed to change or worried as to how their institutions would cope with its demands, would, nevertheless, have been finding it increasingly difficult to regard school mathematics as fixed and unchangeable. In Berger's terms, plausibility structures (i.e., 'social definitions of reality, social relations that take these for granted, as well as the supporting ... legitimations'[69]) supporting reform were being gradually constructed. Within the Mathematical Association, those actors favouring some re-examination of school mathematics (some of whom were university-based but some of whom, like Cundy, were in the schools) could now expect to find more allies both inside and outside of the Association.

Griffith and Mullins have argued, in relation to the creation of new research areas within university disciplines, that:

> The difficulties of the conceptual re-organization required by major advances preclude mass conversion to any new points of view. An idea must gradually recruit adherents, such recruitment usually being expedited by active proselytizing; this process requires high degrees of communication and social organization to succeed.[70]

In examining a number of cases of such change, they have also demonstrated the importance of organizational and intellectual leaders in this process. In the case of school mathematics, Hammersley and Hope (and others in the ATAM) can be seen to have been important figures, both in the construction of what Griffith and Mullins term 'coherent activist groups' and in the transforming of the normally 'loose network' of subject practitioners into a temporarily denser network. As a result of their activities, by mid-1959, Eggleston's second stage had been entered. Here, he claims, we find:

> The establishment of a pressure group within the system consisting of teachers and other personnel who have come to identify the changes as being not only desirable, but also feasible and in accord with an ideological perspective to which they subscribe. At this point the communication networks of the system — the educational press, conferences, the Inspectorate and advisers, who pass between schools — may play an important part. By this stage a *de facto* commitment to a restructuring perspective will have been reached; there will also be at least an implied professional consensus about the desirability of the change promoted so that significant challenges from other teachers can rest either unsaid or at least be discounted. Some informal work along the new lines will already have begun in a number of schools as part of the establishment of a preparatory case.[71]

In the case under examination here, while 'consensus' was certainly somewhat lacking, we have seen that such a pressure group, deriving from the ATAM, and whose activities would lead to the founding of MME, existed within the lower status institutions of the selective sector and some post-school institutions. Furthermore, as a result partly of the

activities of Hammersley et al, the processes of formation of such a
pressure group within the more prestigious and highly resourced
independent schools, to culminate in the founding of SMP, were
beginning to unfold. Thwaites, the organizational leader of SMP, also
locates the origin of his mission in the Oxford meeting.[72]

In the next three chapters I shall consider a number of further
developments between mid-1959 and 1961 which might be seen as part
of Eggleston's third stage, in which pressure groups, 'having established
the area of proposed development and partially legitimated it', search
for 'institutional support' to realize their mission, and which culminates
with small groups being ready to seek funds to launch curriculum
projects (his fourth stage).[73]

More generally, it is important to stress that the active interest
developed by major companies in the 1950s in mathematical and
scientific education and, in particular, the involvement of a number of
them in the Oxford and Liverpool conferences, represented a major
shift in the resources potentially available to those promoting various
missions within mathematics. Not only was money now possibly
available, but, as a result of the conferences, 'authoritative' statements
supporting curriculum reform had become available from an influential
source. Given this change, it might be useful to view the overall
sequence of events leading to the subject redefinition described in this
study in terms of two main periods or stages, less descriptively based
than those of Eggleston.

In the first, an external group, in alliance with members of one
university-based segment of the subject, raises the question of possible
change. At this stage, since important resources are at stake, its demands
are treated with some respect by subject members. In particular, groups
within the subject are likely to play down their differences and promote
their common interest in securing resources for the subject. A second
period is quickly moved into, however, in which, once the resources
seem fairly secure, various groupings within the subject, perceiving
opportunities for the development of their missions and careers,
struggle to win a share. Here, competing groups promote specific
versions of possible change. In this period the intensity and complexity
of the debate tend to increase and, given the increasing range of interests
involved as more actors perceive the opportunities available, it becomes
possible that the original instigators of the events, notwithstanding their
control over important resources, will become relatively marginalized.
Timing, furthermore, will become critical. All other things being equal,
those groups which promote their claims soon after the 'need for
change' is recognized by resource-holders will tend to be seen as the

main movers of change, with all the reputational consequences this implies.

It is the working out of such general processes that will be examined in the following four chapters. Although it would be futile to attempt to precisely date the hypothesized shift from the first to the second of the ideal-typical periods described above, it will be seen in chapters 9 and 10 that, after mid-1961, a decisive shift towards a more competitive period does seem to have occurred.

Notes

1 DAVIES (1973), p. 324.
2 MINISTRY OF EDUCATION (1958), p. 147.
3 *Ibid.*, p. 153.
4 See, for example, WOOTON (1965), pp. 1–16.
5 See KLINE (1966).
6 See KUHN (1963), and chapter 2 above.
7 See WOOTON (1965), p. 8, and HUGHES (1962), pp. 12–14.
8 See WOOTON (1965), pp. 9–16.
9 See HUGHES (1962), pp. 27–8.
10 *Ibid.*, pp. 16–17.
11 *Ibid.*, pp. 16–17 and WOOTON (1965), p. 7.
12 *The Times* 11 April 1958.
13 See 'Contemporary problems in mathematical teaching and staffing', *Nature*, 182, pp. 1064–5.
14 *Mathematics, Education and Industry* (1960).
15 Tables Eleven to Fifteen are compiled from the Conference Register published in *Mathematics, Education and Industry* (1960), p. 2 and pp. 152–6.
16 *Ibid.*, p. 2, for the information on which this table is based.
17 WARING (1975), pp. 160–2.
18 *Mathematics, Education and Industry* (1960), p. 7.
19 *Ibid.*, p. 9.
20 *Ibid.*, pp. 50–3.
21 *Ibid.*, p. 145.
22 *Ibid.*, pp. 17–18, pp. 14–15, and pp. 83–4.
23 *Ibid.*, pp. 16–19.
24 *Ibid.*, for example pp. 66–7 and pp. 84–5.
25 *Ibid.*, for example pp. 14–15.
26 *Ibid.*, p. 71.
27 *Ibid.*, pp. 29–30.
28 *Ibid.*, p. 31.
29 *Ibid.*, p. 31.
30 *Ibid.*, pp. 22–5.
31 *Ibid.*, p. 79.
32 *Ibid.*, pp. 79–81.

33 See BERNSTEIN (1971), p. 47.
34 *Mathematics, Education and Industry* (1960), p. 118.
35 *Ibid.*, p. 122.
36 On which subject, see the remarks of Rollett later in this chapter.
37 *Mathematics, Education and Industry* (1960), p. 123.
38 *Ibid.*, p. 122.
39 *Ibid.*, pp. 28–9.
40 *Ibid.*, pp. 44–7.
41 *Ibid.*, pp. 89–92.
42 *Ibid.*, pp. 19–22.
43 *Ibid.*, p. 27.
44 *Ibid.*, pp. 129–131.
45 *Ibid.*, p. 130.
46 *Ibid.*, p. 131.
47 *Ibid.*, pp. 131–3.
48 *Ibid.*, p. 133.
49 *Ibid.*, p. 134.
50 *Ibid.*, pp. 82–3.
51 *Ibid.*, p. 16.
52 See Table Six above.
53 *Mathematics, Education and Industry* (1960), pp. 124–8.
54 *Ibid.*, pp. 106–9.
55 *Ibid.*, p. 109.
56 See chapter 3 above on differentiation by sex.
57 MINISTRY OF EDUCATION (1958).
58 *Mathematics, Education and Industry* (1960), p. 111.
59 *Ibid.*, p. 115.
60 *Ibid.*, p. 113.
61 *Ibid.*, p. 115.
62 See chapter 10 below.
63 *Mathematics, Education and Industry* (1960), p. 150.
64 *Ibid.*, pp. 150–1.
65 EGGLESTON (1977), p. 125.
66 *Ibid.*, pp. 125–6.
67 See HALMOS (1968).
68 See MANSFIELD and THOMPSON (1962).
69 BERGER (1970), p. 52.
70 GRIFFITH and MULLINS (1972), p. 963.
71 EGGLESTON (1977), p. 126.
72 See THWAITES (1972), p. viii.
73 EGGLESTON (1977), pp. 126–7.

7   Developments: The OEEC, 'The Times' And Mathematics

I have shown that, by mid-1959, various individuals and groups were beginning to argue publicly, with varying degrees of commitment and for a variety of motives and reasons, for some redefinition of school mathematics. In the next three chapters, I shall examine, in differing degrees of detail, those events and activities which led to the situation where, by late 1961, a number of groupings of mathematics teachers began to conceive of 'curriculum projects' as vehicles through which to realize their mission of reform. It will also be shown how these missions came to be developed and modified in this period of increasing competition for resources and for control of the nature of possible change.

This chapter has two sections. In the first, I examine how modern algebraists came to have a major influence in these debates, especially by capturing the opportunity represented by the decision of the OEEC's Office of Scientific and Technical Personnel to produce reports on school mathematics. Although the focus here will be on the OEEC seminars and publications, I shall also consider the responses of members of the ATAM and the Mathematical Association to these developments up to April 1961, especially the diffusion of the message of the OEEC seminar by ATAM activists. In the second section, I shall briefly discuss the coverage of mathematics education by *The Times* during this period. This will serve to demonstrate how successful academic entrepreneurs were in using various resources, especially that provided by the climate of concern over scientific and technological manpower and the nation's economic competitiveness, to bring the debate on mathematics education into extra-subject arenas where considerable resources were controlled by, for example, politicians and industrialists.

In chapter 8, I shall examine three conferences of April 1961 which might be seen as representing a significant watershed in the events leading to reform. I shall concentrate on one of these, convened by Thwaites, then Professor of Theoretical Mechanics at the University of Southampton and previously a teacher at Winchester College, because (i) it had present representatives of all the groupings so far discussed; and (ii) unlike the others — the annual meetings of the ATAM and the Mathematical Association — it produced and published a set of specific proposals for curriculum reform. This outcome represented a major success for Thwaites' entrepreneurial activities, first, because the proposals had come from what could be claimed to be a 'representative' meeting and, secondly, because they appeared early in what was to become a period of competition for resources.

Chapter 9 has two sections. In the first, I continue my analysis of Thwaites' activities and their results by examining the use he made of his inaugural lecture in May 1961. Given the media's developing interest in mathematics education, his discussion of its 'problems', when reported in *The Times*, was, through generating a long debate in the correspondence columns of the paper of the 'decision-making class', to lead to discussions in Parliament of the 'crisis'.[1] In terms of the model employed here, he successfully persuaded actors outside of his subject to argue for further resources to be provided which subject practitioners could use to resolve internal conflicts and problems. In the second section, I shall analyze a conference, sponsored by BP in November 1961, at which the debates, in terms of my model, can be seen to have been as much about which of the two Associations, the ATAM or the Mathematical Association, was to gain control of a potentially resource-generating, and hence powerful, Committee, as about the perspectives of the actors involved. It will also be seen to have been an arena in which the claims of the modern algebraists for their subject were further diffused, in particular by members of the ATAM. By the end of chapter 9, I hope, therefore, to have shown both how modern algebra came to be seen as a necessary feature of school mathematics and how the political climate of opinion had been manipulated by various entrepreneurs in such a way as to ensure that further resources would be available, from 1961 onwards, to groups intending, through the medium of 'curriculum projects', to reform school mathematics.

Modern Algebra: The Royaumont Meeting

Davies has noted that, in analyzing disciplinary change, it is necessary to consider both the national and international levels of content and paradigm.[2] I have already briefly referred to American developments which were to have some influence in England. Here I shall follow this up by considering the results of the activities of the international network of university mathematicians favouring modern algebraic approaches. These actors, by successfully capturing, in Bucher and Strauss' terms, the resource generated by the decision of the Office of Scientific and Technical Personnel of the OEEC to support a seminar and the publication of a Report on school mathematics, managed to insert their perspective into the ongoing debate on the subject in a number of societies, including England.

This meeting, the Royaumont Seminar, took place in the autumn of 1959 in France.[3] Together with an associated survey of current practice, it had been conceived within the OEEC earlier in 1959 for 'the purpose of improving mathematics education' for 'university-capable' pupils.[4] English participants were Maxwell, of the University of Cambridge, Hope, of the ATAM, Wall, of the NFER, and Land, Vice-Chairman of the Liverpool Conference. The overall President of the Seminar was Dr. M.H. Stone of the University of Chicago, Chairman of the International Commission on Mathematical Instruction of the International Union of Mathematicians, a university mathematicians' body. He had previously been involved in the Chicago-based 'Conference on Training and Research Potential in Mathematics' in February 1958 at which school mathematics in the USA was agreed, by university mathematicians, to be in need of reform.[5] The three sections of the Seminar were chaired by Professor J. Dieudonné, one of the French Bourbaki group of modern algebraists, Professor H. Fehr of Columbia, a member of the SMSG Advisory Committee, and Monsieur P. Théron, of the French Ministry of Education. Although the participants were drawn fairly equally from higher education and the schools, it was to be the claims and interests of university mathematicians, especially pure mathematicians, that were represented in the published conclusions, which I shall now describe.

Stress was laid on the discontinuity that now existed in most countries between school and university mathematics:

> In the 1880s college and university study was mainly concerned with calculus and analytical geometry. Since that time, university study has undergone great change, incorporating new developments in analysis of both theoretical and practical importance. This study has been made more compact, concise and unified through the use of topology and modern algebra. This change was necessary to keep students abreast of the greatly expanding knowledge of mathematics.

The secondary school programme, to the contrary, has not changed much since 1880, when it was reasonably satisfactory. Today it is totally inadequate and outmoded.[6]

It was school mathematics that had to be changed, taking its direction from university practice:

Since there is no turning back, nor hope of lengthening the years of study devoted to mathematics, there is a 'squeeze' in the course of this study. The only solution is for the secondary school to take on some of the burden now resting on the university, perhaps as much as is compatible with the intellectual ability of secondary school pupils'.[7]

The following summary of the 'case for reform' was provided:

(a) The new developments in graduate and research mathematics imply a necessary shift in emphasis for secondary school mathematics. New topics such as abstract algebra, vector spaces, theory of sets, etc., will enter the school programme, bringing a changed point of view on what mathematics is today.

(b) The new applications of mathematics suggest new problem material. Probability, statistical inference, finite mathematical structures, linear programming, numerical analysis — all indicate expansion in useful applications of mathematics.

(c) The development of new standards of accuracy and clarity of statements and the emphasis on mathematical structures indicate a need for reconsideration of the concepts embedded in our classical treatment of mathematics.

(d) The tremendous increase in knowledge in the various branches of mathematics demands a synthesis and broader base for teaching at the pre-university level. To learn mathematics today requires more efficient and more general approaches.

(e) The changes in cultural, industrial and economic patterns of many nations call for a basic change in educational patterns. More people must be better trained in scientific knowledge. Even laymen must come to understand science; today, knowing mathematics is basic to understanding science.[8]

Clearly, at this seminar, the dominant participants (there is evidence in the Report that not all participants accepted the radical position of

Dieudonné and his allies[9]) took it for granted that 'mathematics' meant 'university mathematics'. Furthermore, it was this 'mathematics' that school pupils should necessarily study. The conclusions, as well as arguing for the inclusion of modern algebra in school courses, also included arguments for the unification of traditional branches of elementary mathematics, possibly through a vector approach or 'motion geometry' (introduced into most West German schools in 1957, according to the survey results), for increased use of 'modern symbolism', for removing much of traditional school geometry and algebra, for ending the separate study of trigonometry, for introducing probability and statistics, and for more attention to be paid to preparing pupils for axiomatic approaches.[10]

Quite clearly, the aim of the dominant coalition at this Seminar was to change the conditions of subject socialization in the schools for their future students. Kuhn's discussion of the consequences of paradigm change within disciplines suggests that the textbook has been a crucial device for realizing such strategies and, here, in the discussion of 'problems of implementation', the 'need' for new textbooks was given great emphasis:

> The present textbooks for secondary school mathematics are traditional in spirit. They tell pupils how to do their mathematics, but they seldom give the underlying theory and, if they do, it is sometimes mathematically inaccurate and not in harmony with improved concepts. The uses of variable and function can be cited as examples.
>
> It is necessary, therefore, that new books be written, contemporary in mathematical exposition, pedagogically sound, and interesting and stimulating to the pupils. This calls for cooperative experimenting and writing by university professors of mathematics, professional educators and qualified secondary school teachers.[11]

One specific recommendation intended to facilitate this was that a group of mathematicians, educators and teachers be convened to meet in August/September 1960 to 'work out detailed syllabi for which courses can be planned and textbooks produced' to carry out the reform 'required'.[12] The final proposals of the latter group (which included Hope), as well as the official account of the Royaumont Seminar, were to be published in the second half of 1961. These *Synopses for Modern Secondary School Mathematics*,[13] reflecting, as had the conclusions of the original Seminar, the French and American university mathematicians' interests in abstract algebras and geometries, might be seen as a manual for those wishing to reform school mathematics in this direction.

The syllabus for eleven to fifteen year-olds for 'Arithmetic and Algebra', for example, stresses 'operations' and their 'properties', i.e., structure, as against skills in manipulation. Nearly all the associated Commentary is devoted to set theory.[14] For geometry, for the same age range, stress is laid on 'transformations' (i.e., rotations, reflections, translations, etc.), simple coordinate geometry, and vectors, i.e., approaches which allow the early integration of algebra and geometry.[15] Reflecting, however, the presence of Hope, Choquet and Servais, i.e., carriers of the ICSITM perspective, the commentary favours the pedagogical strategy of initial approaches through apparatus and physical models, i.e., an intuitive approach.[16]

In the post-fifteen recommendations, more modern algebraic concepts (groups, rings, fields, ...) are suggested for the syllabus, alongside an increasingly algebraic, abstract study of geometry. No major changes are suggested in the study of the calculus.[17]

Proposals are also made for the study of probability and statistics throughout the secondary school. Again an intuitive, experimental start is recommended but, after fifteen years of age, the study should become more axiomatic.[18]

It can be seen that, taken overall, these documents represented authoritative support, i.e. legitimation, for the introduction of modern algebra into schools, at least for the most 'able'. While the Royaumont Seminar had included a contribution from Professor Tucker of Princeton, associated with the American reform movement as Chairman of the Commission on Mathematics since 1955, on modern applications of mathematics, the *Synopses* and the original report were primarily concerned with pure algebra and geometry. It was therefore the interests of university pure mathematicians (a sub-discipline in England but more nearly the discipline of mathematics in France and the USA where much of what counted as applied mathematics in England was taught and researched by 'physicists') in receiving suitably socialized students that was represented in these publications.

Although these documents were not to be published until 1961 (they received a favourable review from Wheeler in *Mathematics Teaching* in late 1961, and an unfavourable review in the *Mathematical Gazette* from Goodstein in February 1962[19]), Hope and others (T.J. Fletcher, for example, who had attended the meeting of the ICSITM which preceded, in August 1959, the Royaumont Seminar and who replied to Goodstein's review in 1962[20]) were to do much to diffuse these ideas to members of the ATAM after 1959. As a result, the shift towards a concern with content as well as pedagogy amongst the Association's activists continued further.

In the March 1960 issue of *Mathematics Teaching*, for example, attention was focused on the transition from school to university, an issue raised at Liverpool, and which had also been the central topic at the August 1959 meeting of the ICSITM mentioned above.[21] Fletcher, President of the Association in 1960, discussing Bourbaki in his account of the meeting in the journal, argued for the inclusion of modern algebra in school curricula, appealing to both the national interest and psychology to legitimate this:

> This corporate body of mathematicians — virtually a secret society — has published over the years a series of textbooks relaying the presentation of mathematics at university level on new foundations. These changes must be carried into the schools and must become part of our general culture. This task seems impossible if one fails to see that these changes are not increasing complications of old ways of thought which are already too difficult for many pupils, they are a thorough-going simplification, a complete reorientation of the whole pattern which develops mathematics in a way which is not only better by its own internal standards, but which also is in far greater sympathy with the known experimental facts of psychology concerning the formation of mathematical concepts in the mind of the child.
>
> When these facts are understood it need cause no surprise to find that the elements of algebra may be taught with success before the elements of arithmetic (which is a more complicated system), or that fifteen year-old students at a Froebel Training College in Belgium have been doing creative work in a part of topology which only a few decades ago was at the very frontiers of mathematical knowledge. The Commission is preparing a complete series of school texts inspired by these ideals, and their appearance is awaited with keen interest. England is being far slower than some other countries to study these new ideas, and in this field of mathematics teaching, in spite of the high technical standards achieved by our very best pupils, we are by no means a leading country. A generation from now we may find ourselves outdistanced by countries which seek new ideas with greater vitality.[22]

In the same issue Wheeler reported the results of a survey of the heads of mathematics departments of English universities, carried out by the London Study Group for the thirteenth conference of the ICSITM.[23]

This produced some evidence of dissatisfaction with school mathematics, especially its perceived emphasis on tricks and 'empirical skills' rather than 'logic' and 'fundamental principles'. There is also evidence in the Report that some mathematicians in the universities wanted some 'modern mathematics' to be taught in the schools.

Further diffusion amongst school teachers of the ideas of those dominant at Royaumont occurred at the Easter 1960 annual conference of the Association, reported in *Mathematics Teaching* in July.[24] Hope, now being described as the 'self-styled Public Relations Officer for the New Mathematics', argued for some 'modern' ideas to be experimented with at school level, and against Euclidean geometry. Trivett spoke on statistics, Wheeler on sets, and Collins on non-Euclidean geometries.[25] (All this occurred alongside the continuing debate on the place of the GCE and mathematics in the secondary modern schools, of which it was reported that 'some members ... felt that to take GCE examinations in a school gave a certain amount of prestige to the school, both inside and out'.[26]) This issue also contained a warm review of Felix' axiomatic *Exposé moderne des mathématiques élémentaires*, a key text in the European 'modern mathematics' movement, which Fletcher recommended for training college students.[27]

The November 1960 issue included a translation of an article by Choquet, Professor at the University of Paris, then President of the ICSITM and a key figure at Royaumont, on 'modern mathematics and teaching'. This both presented an introduction to modern algebraic structures and argued for their study in school (through an experimental beginning for the pupil, moving gradually to an abstract approach).[28] The issue also included a list of recommended 'foreign publications' including Lesieur and Revuz' *Le langage simple et précis des mathématiques modernes*, a book containing talks to French teachers on set theory and elementary algebraic structures.[29]

The last issue, in March 1961, to appear before the round of annual conferences to be discussed in chapter 8 contained a Report by Fletcher of the 1960 ICSITM meeting in Poland whose theme had been 'mathématiques de base' (i.e., modern mathematics of the pure variety).[30] He described a talk by Papy, then Vice-President, which argued for the basing of the teaching of elementary mathematics on set theory, and a series of demonstration lessons to children which had included such topics as 'relations' (Papy), groups and symmetry (Tumau), and residue classes (Felix). He repeated his argument of the previous year:

> The six lessons illustrated aspects of the central theme of the Vice-President's discourse. Many of the parts of mathematics

that are considered modern and advanced can be understood by much younger pupils, they are basic in the part they play in the structure of mathematics as a logical discipline, and basic in the psychological development of the mathematician. These ideas must be better appreciated, and become part of everyday classroom practice.[31]

The issue also contained articles by Hope on 'Stage A' statistics, Sillitto on new approaches to geometry teaching (referring to Felix' work), and a positive review of an introduction to set theory alongside a blistering attack by Hope on the book by Morgan discussed in chapter 3 of this study.[32]

Clearly then, by 1961, under the influence of European and American algebraists felt through the ICSITM and Royaumont, some members of the ATAM leadership had further modified their mission, putting a much greater emphasis on introducing 'modern mathematics' into schools. Evidence that the general membership were not always happy about this will be discussed in chapter 8.

Notwithstanding the activities of some individual members, including those also active within the ATAM, no parallel sense of mission is apparent in the pages of the *Mathematical Gazette*, the journal of the Mathematical Association, in this period. After 1956, under the editorship of Professor Goodstein, a pure mathematician from the University of Leicester, and Dr. Cundy of Sherborne School, a future founder member of SMP, the work of reformers was more or less reviewed as it appeared, but it was not given the special attention it received in *Mathematics Teaching*. Goodstein, for example, in 1957, described a major publication from the ICSITM as 'important' and of 'special interest' to members of the Mathematical Association.[33] This had included Dieudonné, Choquet and Piaget amongst its authors. In 1959, he recommended that teachers read Beberman's *An Emerging Programme of Secondary School Mathematics*.[34] He very briefly reviewed the reports of the Oxford and Liverpool Conferences (the former had previously received coverage of three pages from a participant).[35] Cundy, between 1958 and 1961, also reviewed, mainly positively, several books by reform-orientated researchers such as Dienes.[36] He also recommended Birkhoff and Beatley's 'modern' *Basic Geometry* to teachers as required reading (although he added that it 'could not be used in a normal English classroom').[37] Nevertheless, at least until 1961, no special concern about the place of 'modern mathematics' in schools is expressed in the non-review sections of the journal. There is no sign here, as there was in the case of the ATAM, of a significant campaigning group within the leadership of the Association committed to a consideration of the place of modern ideas in schools. Furthermore, the Report of the 1958 annual meeting at which the Report, *The Teaching of Algebra in Sixth Forms*, was discussed, demonstrates that only a small minority of those present criticized its lack of concern with this issue. A Mr. Donnellan, described as the 'chief critic', had 'felt that an opportunity had been missed of rethinking school algebra in the light of modern developments in linear algebra and group theory'.[38] Furthermore, Flemming, in reviewing the HMI's *Teaching Mathematics in Secondary Schools* in the *Gazette*, described it as the 'fitting climax to the present round of activity' concerned with mathematics teaching, i.e., to the series of reports of the Association and the IAAM discussed in chapter 3.[39] In addition to the fact of these documents in which 'modern mathematics' received only the briefest of mentions being both partially produced and well-reviewed by representatives of the dominant coalition within the Association, further evidence of a lack of concern with moving 'modern mathematics' into schools is provided by the content of the presidential addresses between 1958 and 1961. None of these four Presidents, including, in 1961, Maxwell, who had attended Royaumont, made use of their addresses to argue for major curricular reform or experiment in this area. Langford, who was later to support SMP, although noting in his address of 1958 the increasing discontinuity between school and university mathematics, actually stressed the 'great revolution in secondary teaching methods' in mathematics that had, in his opinion, already been achieved in England, before concentrating in his conclusion on the issue of teacher 'shortage'.[40] Newman, in 1959, in his discussion of the nature of mathematics, including 'modern mathematics', mentioned Beberman's American work with schoolchildren, but mainly to criticize its pedagogical assumptions.[41] It is probably accurate to summarize this evidence by saying that, at this time, the Association's leadership, as far as the issue of 'modern mathematics' and school teaching was concerned, responded to events elsewhere (as in a different sense the ATAM activists also did) rather than initiated them. In fact, it was eventually under the pressure of having to produce a report on the place of 'modern mathematics' in the school curriculum for the International Congress of Mathematicians to be held at Stockholm in 1962 that a Sub-committee of the Teaching Committee, under the chairmanship of Newman and with Hope as a member, was formed to investigate 'modern mathematics'.[42] Until this event, and to some extent after it, the leadership seemed more concerned with the issue of teacher supply than that of 'modern mathematics'.

I have shown in this section that, by the time of the conferences of

1961 to be discussed in chapter 8, European and American 'modern' university mathematicians had, by capturing the Royaumont Seminar and, to some extent, the ICSITM, succeeded in diffusing their version of 'mathematics', via the ATAM, to some English school teachers. It will be seen that, partly as a result of this, the discussion at the key Southampton Conference of April 1961 was to be concerned much more equally with both pure and applied mathematics than that at either Oxford or Liverpool had been.

'The Times' And Mathematics: 1959-Early 1961

The development of an editorial interest by *The Times* in mathematics and science education represented a crucial resource for those involved in academic politics within the subject. It enabled actors with the requisite status, such as Hammersley, Langford and Thwaites, to use the occasion of addressing subject practitioners' meetings to transmit messages to decision-makers and resource-holders outside of the subject. They further facilitated this by referring their claims for mathematics to the concern of politicians and commentators, shared by some staff of *The Times*, with the economic value of educated manpower. In fact, a process analogous to media-induced deviance amplification may have occurred.[43] As politicians and others, receiving messages of gloom from within the mathematics and science communities, came to talk more and more of the 'problems' of these subjects and their economic implications, editors and journalists may have paid yet more attention to such messages.

I shall now discuss the coverage of mathematics over these two years by the paper likely to have been read by most politicians and major employers. It will be seen that the central feature of this coverage was that members of the Inspectorate and other subject members with various official positions (in associations, for example) were able to present claims for and about mathematics to extra-subject, resource-controlling audiences.

In September 1959, a discussion of mathematics at the annual meeting of the British Association was reported. Space was given to the remarks of Dr. Laybourn, Chief Inspector of Schools for Bristol. He had concentrated his talk on the 'shortage' of science and mathematics teachers which, in his opinion, was threatening the production of the 'scientists and technologists of tomorrow'. A new suggestion, as far as the pages of *The Times* were concerned, was that there was a need for the rewriting of 'out-of-date' textbooks.[44] A further report of the meeting, four days later, also raised the issue of the nature of school mathematics in recording an adviser's claim that primary school mathematics must be reformed to emphasize 'understanding' rather than getting sums right.[45]

In a December 1959 leader, following the publication of the Crowther Report, the paper argued, in relation to the raising of the school-leaving age:

> It is clear, too, that this added schooling would supply technical education with a firmer base. Potential technicians and skilled craftsmen are now lost for want of a finer polish to those mathematical studies which are a necessary key to success in technical college courses. Here the case that the price of reform would be money well-spent stands firmly on its feet.[46]

In January 1960, it reported the presidential address of Adams to the Mathematical Association, emphasizing her desire for mathematics to be acquired as 'a by-product of use and the servant of need'.[47] In May, coverage was given to a speech by Eccles, the Minister of Education, in which he bemoaned the 'shortage' of mathematics and science teachers and, as Flemming and Rollett had done at Liverpool, accused the universities of not providing enough 'help'.[48] In August, it publicized a report by the British Employers' Confederation which, supporting the raising of the school-leaving age, expressed dissatisfaction with the standards in elementary English and mathematics of boys and girls entering industry.[49] In September, it again gave space to those discussing mathematics at the annual meeting of the British Association. Reporting the address of Sir A. Pugsley, Professor of Civil Engineering at the University of Bristol, it gave wider publicity to the criticisms of the teaching of applied mathematics previously voiced at Oxford and Liverpool.[50]

The reporting of the TUC Conference, in the same month, gave space to arguments linking the 'shortage' of mathematics and science teachers to the standard of living.[51] And, also in September, the meeting of the Headmasters' Conference was reported thus:

> In view of the national demand for scientists, the headmasters felt that the severe shortage of mathematics teachers was creating something like a national emergency. Mr. T.E.C. Woodford, Leeds Grammar School, said mathematics was the language of science and without this foundation advanced scientific studies were impossible. At present this foundation was disappearing from the schools.[52]

There is evidence here that those factors tending to make graduate mathematics teachers relatively scarce were beginning to have an effect on the most prestigious and well-resourced schools in the secondary sector. The HMC was now to add its voice to those arguing for action in this area.

It was noted earlier that Rollett and other members of the HMI had attended the Oxford and Liverpool meetings. Rollett had also replied, for the United Kingdom, to the questionnaire distributed in parallel with the Royaumont Seminar.[53] The results of these involvements can possibly be seen in *The Times'* report of a speech by Wilson, Senior Chief Inspector, to the AAM in January 1961. This first stressed his having argued for the importance of more girls continuing their study of mathematics, but then moved on to the nature of school mathematics. Having referred to the imminent 'nation-wide campaign' to 'improve' primary school mathematics, he was reported to have continued: 'do not drive these children back at the age of twelve on antiquated material or regimented methods as sometimes has happened with English language and literature in the past'. The 'good teacher' of 'willing and intelligent pupils' needed to make changes 'to keep up with the frontiers of mathematical knowledge and with the mathematical needs of the world as it would be ten years from now'.[54]

The Times continued to promote messages questioning the nature of current school knowledge when, a month later, it reported that Lockwood of Birkbeck College, a classicist and Chairman of the Secondary Schools Examination Council, was, along with the Council, very worried about the 'syllabus problem'. He wanted the cooperation of the examination boards in a study of the structure of courses up to 'A' level, and had argued:

> I am sure we can take a substantial step forward in assisting schools if we can begin by a wide reconstruction of 'A' level syllabuses by the removal of deadwood and remoulding some to the requirements of science teaching. A new approach to the syllabus can go a very long way to developing a more general education.[55]

This must be seen as partly reflecting the contemporary concern amongst some headteachers and educationists with 'over-specialisation'. The SSEC report of 1960, for example, had argued against 'excessive' specialization; Peterson was running a campaign against it from Oxford; Crowther discussed it at length.[56] It also, however, indicated an increased readiness on the part of the SSEC to encourage or accept syllabus reform, arguments for which were being increasingly diffused by *The Times*.

In February 1961, a working party of the Incorporated Association of Headmasters had met at Churchill College, Cambridge, under the chairmanship of Egner, a Head of a technical grammar school who had spoken at Liverpool, to review the position in relation to the supply of mathematics teachers. Their report argued that, in the light of 'modern trends in mathematics' and the 'need of science, engineering, industry and education for mathematicians', more and better mathematics teachers were needed in schools.[57] They supported the suggestion, previously made by Jones at Oxford, that an Institute of Mathematics be set up to give professional status to mathematicians. They also recommended that a meeting be held between heads of university mathematics departments and headmasters to consider ways of expanding numbers. To publicize their arguments, a letter was sent to *The Times*, jointly signed by Goddard, President of the IAH, and Smith, Chairman of the HMC. It continued the attack now under way from the schools on university entrance procedures and teaching practices in mathematics, legitimating its arguments by reference to the national interest:

> We should like to take this opportunity to emphasize the very serious shortage in one department, that of mathematics. Mathematics is, of course, a key subject in modern life and is basic for the survival of our technological civilisation. A very considerable percentage of grammar and public schools are already suffering seriously through insufficient or inadequate teachers. Nor are the prospects of getting more men from the universities increased by the very high standard required for an honours course in mathematics and the consequent exclusion of many men who would be of immense value in the schools.
>
> One thing is to us quite clear. Unless there is in the immediate future a substantial increase of highly competent teachers of mathematics in the schools, a position which is already disturbing will become disastrous.[58]

By early 1961 therefore, as a result of the mediating by *The Times* of the messages of 'primary definers',[59] i.e., actors with appropriate credentials from the communities of mathematics and education (i.e., those concerned with selective secondary education in the main and holding positions in associations and the Inspectorate), readers of this paper will have become aware of various 'needs', especially to improve the supply of mathematics teachers and to bring secondary school mathematics 'up to date'. During 1961 this awareness would represent a considerable resource for those attempting to realize various missions of reform. Furthermore, partly as a result of the activities of ATAM activists following Royaumont and the increased discussion of mathematics in *The Times*, the conferences of 1961 — to be discussed in the next chapter — were to be held in a climate of opinion markedly different from that in which those at Oxford and Liverpool took place. There was now to be an increased sense of urgency about the proceedings, as well as much more of a concern with the claims of modern algebraists.

Notes

1 See THWAITES (1961a).
2 DAVIES (1973), p. 324.
3 See OECD (1961a).
4 *Ibid.*, p. 7 and p. 105.
5 See WOOTON (1965), pp. 9–10.
6 OECD (1961a), pp. 105–6.
7 *Ibid.*, p. 106.
8 *Ibid.*, p. 107.
9 *Ibid.*, p. 47 and p. 73.
10 *Ibid.*, pp. 105–25.
11 *Ibid.*, p. 119.
12 *Ibid.*, p. 122.
13 OECD (1961b).
14 *Ibid.*, chapter I, especially pp. 13–16.
15 *Ibid.*, chapter II, especially p. 83.
16 *Ibid.*, p. 85.
17 *Ibid.*, chapters III and IV.
18 *Ibid.*, p. 263 and p. 271.
19 GOODSTEIN (1962) and WHEELER (1961d).
20 FLETCHER (1962).
21 See immediately above.
22 FLETCHER (1960a), pp. 34–5.
23 WHEELER (1960), pp. 29–31.
24 ELLIS (1960).
25 *Ibid.*, pp. 20–9.
26 *Ibid.*, p. 26.
27 FLETCHER (1960b), pp. 65–6.
28 CHOQUET (1960).
29 *Ibid.*, p. 66.
30 FLETCHER (1961), pp. 23–8.
31 *Ibid.*, p. 27.
32 See HOPE (1961a), HOPE (1961b), HOPE (1961c) and SILLITTO (1961).
33 GOODSTEIN (1957).

34 GOODSTEIN (1959).
35 See the *Mathematical Gazette* (1958), p. 242, and (1961), p. 64, for Goodstein's reviews of the publications arising from the Oxford and Liverpool meetings respectively. For the earlier account of the Oxford meeting see PARKES (1957).
36 CUNDY (1960).
37 See the *Mathematical Gazette* (1959), Vol. 43, p. 134.
38 See the *Mathematical Gazette* (1958), Vol. 42, p. 196.
39 See above, chapter 3.
40 LANGFORD (1958).
41 NEWMAN (1959).
42 See NEWMAN (1961) and HUGHES (1962), pp. 29–30.
43 On the amplification of deviance, see COHEN (1972).
44 *The Times* 4 September 1959.
45 *The Times* 8 September 1959.
46 *The Times* 11 December 1959.
47 *The Times* 7 January 1960.
48 *The Times* 23 May 1960.
49 *The Times* 12 August 1960.
50 *The Times* 2 September 1960.
51 *The Times* 9 September 1960.
52 *The Times* 29 September 1960.
53 OECD (1961a), p. 241.
54 *The Times* 4 January 1961.
55 *The Times* 27 February 1961.
56 See MONTGOMERY (1965), pp. 159–61.
57 See HUGHES (1962), pp. 33–4.
58 *The Times* 7 February 1961.
59 The term is that of HALL et al (1978).

8   The Conferences of April 1961 And 'Modern Mathematics'

In this chapter I shall discuss three conferences of mathematicians that took place around Easter 1961. The first to be discussed, organized by Thwaites, might best be seen as the third in the series begun at Oxford in 1957, while the second and third were the normal annual events of the ATAM and the Mathematical Association. The issue of 'modern mathematics' and schooling was to be discussed at all these meetings. I shall concentrate on the particularly influential Southampton Conference.

Thwaites and the Southampton Conference

It was in the climate of concern over mathematics education described in the last chapter that Bryan Thwaites, Professor of Theoretical Mechanics at the University of Southampton and later to be prime founder of SMP, entered centrally into the debate on mathematics education. Thwaites, in his late thirties, had already had a varied career and, like Hammersley, had straddled occupational boundaries, an experience always likely to relativize perspectives.[1] After an education at Dulwich, Winchester and Cambridge, he had worked, from 1944–1947, as a Scientific Officer at the National Physical Laboratory. For the next four years he lectured at Imperial College. He then taught at Winchester until 1959, but maintained a commitment at Imperial. In 1959, he had been appointed to the chair at Southampton. Throughout his career he had sat on a wide range of committees including, for example, the Aeronautical Research Council, Dulwich College Mission (Honorary Secretary and Treasurer), and the Hampshire County Council Approved School Committee. In 1960 he had edited *Incompressible Aerodynamics*.[2] He was well-endowed then, by virtue of his having been educated and having worked in prestigious locations, and by his committee and publishing experience, to enter the round of academic politics initiated at Oxford.

Looking back in 1972, by which time the project he was to initiate had become an enormous 'success', he argued that his concern with reforming school mathematics dated from 1957. The Oxford Conference had been an 'eye-opener':

> It was clear to me that the gap between the two kinds of participants at this . . . conference was far too wide for comfort. So, on becoming a Professor of Mathematics at Southampton University, I sought to carry things a stage further, first by following up the Oxford meeting (and a similar conference in Liverpool in 1959) by one aimed specifically at producing an 'ideal' school mathematics syllabus; and second by devoting my Inaugural Lecture to an attempt at a definitive statement concerning the vital dependence of good mathematics on the supply of good teachers.[3]

When I interviewed him in 1977 and asked him to account for his interest in reform he emphasized his having been a professional mathematician and, for some time, a schoolmaster, in the context of the changes that had occurred in applied mathematics with the development of the computer. School mathematics had become irrelevant to 'life-in-the-large'. Many teachers were in a rut; the Mathematical Association had become an 'extremely "trad" organization'. He had also been convinced, he said, that the quality of mathematics teachers was likely to continue to decline into the 1970s if no action were to be taken. The 'authorities at the time', he felt, had been unwilling to admit this.[4]

A number of features of the manner in which he organized the Southampton Conference might have been expected to make its debates more widely influential than those of Oxford and Liverpool. First, the Organizing Committee was such that continuity was maintained with the earlier conferences, giving the meeting the status of the third in a series. In particular, the chairmen of both previous meetings were included which, as well as helping to ensure that Thwaites did not offend Hammersley and Rosenhead, would allow him to draw on the extra-subject resources they had previously tapped (see Table 17).[5] Secondly, all the major groupings involved in the developing conflict over the nature of selective school mathematics were represented. In particular, the alliance of applied mathematicians and employers and the groups favouring 'modern' algebras were both present in strength. This might, of course, have led to dissension rather than agreement on what

Table 17:   Southampton Conference Advisory Committee

Professor B. Thwaites	University of Southampton
Professor E.T. Davies	University of Southampton
Dr. J.M. Hammersley	University of Oxford
Sir W. Jackson, FRS	Associated Electrical Industries
M.J. Lighthill	Royal Aircraft Establishment
A.P. Rollett	HMI
Professor L. Rosenhead	University of Liverpool
Professor F.W. Wagner	University of Southampton

should be done but Thwaites tried to avoid the possibility of this becoming public by arranging the Conference in such a way that disagreements were minimized. A number of committees were created, each having the task of producing a draft report on some specific aspect of the agenda. These were then discussed at plenary sessions and finally went to make up the book *On Teaching Mathematics*.[6] Since specific proposals for syllabus reform were included, legitimated by the 'representative' nature of the meeting, Thwaites had done much to ensure that this Conference, especially in the widespread climate of 'crisis', would lead to — or at least serve to legitimate — action.

As in my discussions of the earlier conferences, I shall begin my account with an analysis of participation. I shall not be able, however, to provide an analysis of debates since, because of the organization of the meeting, the available record is not in the form of verbatim minutes. I shall instead discuss the reports of the various committees, and consider the relationship between their recommendations and their membership.

Participation

It can be seen from Table 18 that the majority of participants were from the universities, boys' independent schools and other selective schools.[7] (I shall delay my analysis of the various writing committees, discussing each later in relation to its respective report. Thwaites, however, chaired the Central Committee and sat on five others.)

The Mathematical Association and the ATAM both had active

Table 18: Occupational locations of participants at Southampton

University	34
College of technology	1
College of education	1
Private industry	15
Government research	3
HMI	1
Schools: Independent boys	26
Independent girls	1
Direct grant boys	7
Direct grant girls	3
Mixed grammar	8
Boys' grammar	12
Girls' grammar	8
Mixed technical grammar	1
Boys' technical grammar	1
Mixed bilateral	2
Mixed comprehensive	1
Boys' comprehensive	3
Uncoded	2
Total	130

members present. Maxwell, then President of the former, sat on the University Mathematics Committee, and Rollett of the HMI, a member of its Council, also attended. Members of the ATAM present included Brookes, Tammadge (to join SMP), and Morris (amongst the founders of SMP). Of these, Brookes acted as Secretary to the Mathematics in School Committee and Morris and Tammadge chaired two of its sub-committees.

A number of other future SMP writers were also present. Overall, including Thwaites, Tammadge and Morris, they numbered eight. Of these, three were from independent schools, two from universities, two from direct grant schools and one from a mixed grammar school. Between them, they chaired five committees. In this sense at least, this meeting led into one curriculum project.

Table 19: Individuals attending both the Oxford and Southampton conferences

J. Crank	Courtaulds, then Brunel College of Technology
R.H. Cobb	Malvern College
Dr. J.M. Hammersley	University of Oxford and AERE (Harwell)
T.L. Kermode	Lancing College
Dr. E.A. Maxwell	University of Cambridge, and Oxford and Cambridge Examination Board
J.A. Oriel	Shell
A.P. Rollett	HMI
J.Y. Rushbrooke	King's School, Macclesfield
W.E. Scott	English Electric
W.G. Sherman	British Thomson-Houston, then Associated Electrical Industries
Professor B. Thwaites	Winchester College, then University of Southampton

Eleven individuals attended both the Oxford and Southampton meetings (see Table 19).[8]

Thirteen attended both the Liverpool and the Southampton meetings (see Table 20).

Five attended all three. None of these were from the schools (see Table 21).

Eight private companies, two government research establishments, nine major public schools and six other educational organizations, including the HMI and the Oxford and Cambridge Board, were represented at both Oxford and Southampton (see Table 22).

Represented at both Liverpool and the Southampton meeting were seven private companies, the same two government research establishments and seventeen educational organizations, including six independent schools, five universities and the HMI (see Table 23).

Six private companies, the two government establishments, three

Table 20: Individuals attending both the Liverpool and Southampton conferences

M.E. Aassi	Cairo Teachers' College, then University of Southampton
W.B. Brookes	Maghull Grammar School, then University of Southampton
J. Crank	Brunel College of Technology
V.W.D. Hale	University of Hull
Dr. J.M. Hammersley	University of Oxford and AERE (Harwell)
T.A.S. Jackson	University of Liverpool
J. Kiely	Blundell's School
A.P. Rollett	HMI
Professor L. Rosenhead	University of Liverpool
W.E. Scott	English Electric
J. Sharatt	Hindley and Abram Grammar School, then Samuel King's School
W.G. Sherman	British Thomson-Houston, then Associated Electrical Industries
A.R. Tammadge	Abingdon School

Table 21: Individuals attending the Oxford, Liverpool and Southampton conferences

J. Crank	Courtaulds, then Brunel College of Technology
Dr. J.M. Hammersley	University of Oxford and AERE (Harwell)
A.P. Rollett	HMI
W.E. Scott	English Electric
W.G. Sherman	British Thomson-Houston, then Associated Electrical Industries

Table 22:   Organisations represented at both the Oxford and Southampton conferences

Private industry
Ferranti
Shell
Rolls-Royce
Vickers-Armstrong
British Iron and Steel Federation
ICI
Mullard
English Electric

Governmental
Atomic Energy Authority
Royal Aircraft Establishment

Educational
Marlborough College
Malvern College
Clifton College
Christ's Hospital
St. Paul's School
Winchester College
King's School, Macclesfield
Warwick School
Lancing College
Taunton School
University of Oxford
University of Cambridge
University of Liverpool
HMI
Oxford and Cambridge Examination Board

Table 23:   Organisations represented at both the Liverpool and
Southampton conferences

Private industry
English Electric
Ferranti
Shell
Dunlop
Rolls-Royce
British Iron and Steel Federation
ICI

Governmental
Atomic Energy Authority
Royal Aircraft Establishment

Educational
Malvern College
Blundell's School
Marlborough College
Christ's Hospital
St. Dunstan's College
Durham School
Imperial College
Brunel College of Technology
University of Hull
University College, Swansea
University of Liverpool
University of Sheffield
Alsager Training College
Manchester Grammar School
South Shields Technical Grammar School
Blyth Grammar School
HMI

Table 24: Organisations represented at the Oxford, Liverpool and Southampton conferences

Private industry
Ferranti
Shell
English Electric
Rolls-Royce
British Iron and Steel Federation
ICI

Governmental
Atomic Energy Authority
Royal Aircraft Establishment

Educational
HMI
Malvern College
Marlborough College
Christ's Hospital
University of Liverpool

independent schools, one university and the HMI were involved in all three (see Table 24).

Five of these centrally concerned companies and about a dozen others, plus the National Science Foundation of the USA (involved in funding SMSG in the USA), funded the meeting (see Table 25).[9] Thwaites was clearly able to rely, at this time, on industrial support for his activities.

Analysis of the Report of the Proceedings

As well as the Committee proceedings already referred to, the Conference, like those at Oxford and Liverpool, included a series of lectures given by speakers from industry and government research establishments. These speakers had been invited to talk on 'mathematical modelling', the focus of the earlier meetings, because, according to Thwaites, 'it was believed at the time, and the meeting subsequently confirmed, that many schoolmasters [were] insufficiently aware of this all-important component of applied mathematics'.[10] These speakers, whose talks are summarized in *On Teaching Mathematics*,[11] are listed in

Table 25: Financial contributors to the Southampton conference

Associated Electrical Industries Ltd.

Associated Portland Cement Manufacturers Ltd.

British Iron and Steel Federation*

Courtaulds Ltd.*

Distillers Co. Ltd.

Dunlop Rubber Co. Ltd.

English Electric Co. Ltd.*

General Electric Co. Ltd.

Hoover Ltd.

IBM World Trade Laboratories (GB) Ltd.

ICI Ltd.

Mullard Research Laboratory

National Science Foundation of America

Pilkington Bros. Ltd.

Plessey Co. Ltd.

Shell International Petroleum Ltd.*

Unilever Ltd.

Vickers-Armstrong (Aircraft) Ltd.

A group of assurance offices

Ferranti Ltd.*

* supported all three conferences

Table 26: 'Industrial' speakers at Southampton

S. Benjamin	Ferranti Ltd.
P.T. Davies	Shell Research Ltd.
W.S. Elliot	IBM
H. Hitch	Vickers-Armstrong
R.R.P. Jackson	British Iron and Steel Federation
M.J. Lighthill	Royal Aircraft Establishment
H.H. Robertson	ICI
W.E. Scott	English Electric Ltd.
D.M. Tombs	Hoover Ltd.
P.E. Trier	Mullard Ltd.

Table 26. However, not only the alliance of these speakers and the applied mathematicians from the universities was represented amongst the programmed speakers. The 'modern algebra' movement was represented by Professor Begle, of Yale, and Swain, both of whom worked with SMSG in the USA.[12] Their perspective received further support from Papy, influential within the ICSITM, who provided a demonstration lesson.[13] This meeting, therefore, unlike those at Oxford and Liverpool, received major inputs from university pure mathematicians favouring 'modern algebraic' approaches.

I shall discuss below the reports of the main committees. These, of course, represent the views of dominant coalitions within each committee and, presumably to varying degrees, must fail to reflect conflicts of perspective. Thwaites, in his preface to *On Teaching Mathematics*, notes that there was not 'unanimity amongst the members of the conference on the manifold matters which have been discussed', but claims that, since the reports were discussed in plenary sessions, 'it is fair to say . . . that this book does indeed represent the consensus view of the members of the meeting'.[14] It will, in fact, be seen below that the particular emphases of the various contributory reports are significantly related to the nature of the membership of the committees.

Thwaites, however, was clearly concerned to produce 'agreed' proposals for action. Disagreement would threaten this. In his preface, in which he focuses on the 'national crisis' of the 'shortage' of mathematics teachers, the failure of the higher education system to expand supply, and the 'need' for the educational system to be able to change over cycles of time less than the length of a teacher's career, a number of comments lend support to this interpretation. He attacks, for example, the pure/applied distinction.[15] Given the very real differences between these sub-disciplines, this might be seen, in terms of the model employed here, as an attempt to unite mathematicians, at least symbolically, in the search for resources for the subject. Furthermore, and supporting this view, after having identified the 'parentage' of the meeting with those organized by Hammersley and Rosenhead, he stressed the importance of coordinating the efforts of the 'many other associations and individuals' concerned with the 'problems of mathematical teaching', adding that this would require 'substantial financial help'.[16]

Having made these general introductory comments, I shall now analyze the recommendations of the various committees which produced chapters for the book which followed the Conference.

Committee for the Introductory Chapter

The Committee which produced this chapter, after the Conference, consisted of five non-Oxbridge university representatives, including Thwaites and Begle, a teacher from an independent school and a teacher from a direct grant school (see Table 27).[17]

Table 27: *Introductory Chapter Committee Membership*

University	5 (including Chairman)
Independent boys' school	1
Direct grant boys' school	1 (Secretary)

Five of the eight pages were devoted to developing a strong case for an increase in the numbers of mathematics students in universities. Drawing on 'Scientific and Engineering Manpower in Great Britain' (HMSO; 1959), they claimed that industry would require forty per cent more mathematicians in 1962 than it had in 1959, and government establishments another ten per cent more. Of 'necessity', the proposed expansion of higher and further education would also require extra mathematics graduates. An argument was developed which claimed to show that, in grammar schools, there currently existed a shortage of

2,500 mathematics teachers and of 650 honours graduates in particular.[18] This was supported by reference to a recent IAH enquiry which 'revealed' that thirty-nine per cent of vacancies for mathematics masters in over 1000 independent and grammar schools were unsatisfactorily filled in 1960.[19] Here a reference to the curriculum was included:

> It is wrong to suggest that, at these earlier levels, mathematics can be taught adequately by teachers without qualifications who may well be entirely unaware of the changing nature of the subject and who, despite their best intentions, are therefore obliged to present merely the mathematics of their own school-days in exactly the same way as that in which it was first presented to them.[20]

The interests of the university members in both expanding mathematics teaching in the universities, which would possibly bring increased opportunities of career development, and in receiving suitably subject-socialized students are clearly reflected in this chapter. Indeed, the latter concern dominated the remainder of it. Referring to a talk given by Rosenhead to the Mathematical Association, the writers outlined the 'familiar enough' comments made about the 'second category of quality' of students, i.e. the not 'really bright mathematical students', within the universities:

> The students do not understand the mathematical ideas which university teachers consider basic to their subject; they are not skilful in the manipulative processes of even elementary mathematics; they can not grasp new ideas quickly or at all; and, particularly, they have no sense of purpose — i.e., they do not seem to realize that in order to study mathematics intensively they must work hard on their own trying to sort out ideas new and old, trying to solve test problems, and so on.[21]

Clearly, therefore, expansion would be ideally accompanied by changes in the area of subject-socialization:

> Unless the average standard of university entrants can be improved — and this means in practice the provision of more teachers, especially at the sixth form level — the output of graduates may be affected to the extent that it becomes utterly inadequate for the country's essential requirements.[22]

Furthermore, school mathematics must also change:

> There has been, as never before, a rapid evolution in the outlook of mathematics, and a rapid development in its scope, its

contents, its methods, and its applicability to the problems of the everyday world ... If mathematics is to be attractive to boys and girls at school, the committee for chapter IV felt that it must be presented as a lively and expanding subject, exciting both in itself, and in its relevance to the demands of modern society.[23]

School syllabuses and teaching methods, they continued, had escaped being influenced by 'the attitudes of present day mathematics' because of the teacher 'shortage'. This must be remedied by closer contact with the universities, who were 'nearer to the mathematics of the present day'.[24]

Recent graduates do, of course, carry new developments in university disciplines into the schools, and the problems of teacher supply may have hindered this particular channel of university influence on the definition of school mathematics. The Committee clearly intended other channels of influence and control to be developed. For them, the definition of selective school mathematics should certainly, and legitimately, be strongly influenced by university mathematicians, if only because the schools formed their potential students and 'successors'.

The Industrial Committee: 'Mathematics in Use'

The Committee that produced the chapter entitled 'Mathematics in Use' was dominated numerically by actors from industry (see Table 28).

Table 28:   'Mathematics in Use' Committee Membership

Private industry	6
College of technology	1 (Chairman)
Royal Aircraft Establishment	1 (Secretary)
Mixed grammar school	1
Independent boys' school	1

Cotgrove and Box, in their study of scientists in industry, have noted, in somewhat functionalist terms:

An increasing proportion of graduates in science are now employed in industry, government research institutes, [and] teaching. As such, it is less likely that they will either think of themselves, or be defined as being members of the scientific community. In fact, they occupy roles in distinct sub-systems of society, each with specific goals and norms. The primary function of the industrial research laboratory is not the advancement of knowledge as such, but rather the application of knowledge and skills to the development of marketable products'.[25]

This committee's proposals, in fact, clearly reflected the industrial actors' concern that the mathematicians they employed should not have been socialized primarily into the cognitive and technical norms of pure mathematics. Having stressed again the importance of 'modelling' and the application of mathematics to practical problems, they argued for more numerical analysis and statistics, but less abstract algebra and geometry, to be studied in university courses. They argued that their employees must have the 'right attitude of mind', which involved 'an ability to communicate with other industrial personnel' and not the feeling that 'industry should be interested in his mathematics rather than the other way around'.[26]

Because of the growth of computing and 'modelling' in industry, however, these industrial actors remained potential allies of the university mathematicians in promoting expansion. Their differences lay in the area of the nature of the 'mathematics' that was to be expanded.

'School To University' Committee

This chapter was written by a Committee consisting of university mathematicians, including Thwaites, and teachers from a range of selective schools (see Table 29).

In line with Kuhn's emphasis in his analysis of science on the importance to members of the discipline of receiving appropriately

Table 29: 'From School to University' Committee Membership

University		4 (including Chairman)
Schools:	Independent boys	3 (including Secretary)
	Boys' grammar	2
	Girls' grammar	1
	Mixed grammar	1
	Mixed comprehensive	1

socialized potential successors, the concern expressed was very much with changing the nature of the school mathematics studied by potential university students. Reflecting the university members' concerns, the report argues that, if 'provision for a greatly increased number of mathematical students' is to be made at the university level then the 'attitude' developed to mathematics in the schools must be changed:

> About the less tangible question of the pupil's attitude to the subject we do not make such specific suggestions, but indicate some possible lines of approach. From their work on elementary geometry they should have acquired the concept of proof, and the teacher should emphasize the logical need for deduction of results from axioms, even when those results are obvious from a physical point of view ... They should have developed the power to visualize in three dimensions, and understand the idea of a function. Without learning formal theorems on convergence they should understand what is meant by the sum to infinity of certain simple series, and that not all series possess such a sum. The power of generalisation of mathematics should be learnt from the examples of the laws of fractional and negative indices, and from the properties of complex numbers. Finally, they should appreciate how mathematics can be applied to the physical world by abstracting certain entities from it ... and representing them by a symbolic model ... These attitudes are much needed for further progress in the subject, and it is a common criticism of new students at the university that they lack them.[27]

The preferences of both pure and applied university mathematicians for certain cognitive and technical norms are represented here, and in the subsequent suggestions. The report wanted to see 'mathematical ways of thought' rather than 'extensive knowledge of facts and techniques' developed, since the former were 'more important for future progress in the university'.[28] Some traditional topics, such as Euclidean geometry, might well be removed from the sixth form course to make room for new topics such as numerical methods and probability. 'Genuine' problems should be set in applied mathematics.[29]

Mechanisms for 'up-dating' school teachers' knowledge, i.e., for resocializing them subject-wise, were also discussed. Conferences and courses, and, possibly for political reasons, the reports of the Mathematical Association, were recommended. Examining arrangements were also considered. The Oxbridge scholarship examinations, possibly because of the lack of Oxbridge faculty and the presence of grammar school teachers on the Committee, were said to 'overload' pupils by introducing too many 'advanced topics' (i.e., topics that took traditional mathematics further than 'A' level). Arrangements for university entrance examinations in general were attacked, perhaps because, in terms of the model used here, they produced unevenly socialized recruits:

> It appeared that several advantages would follow from amalgamations between the examining boards. If the number of distinct 'A' level papers set each year were reduced it would be easier to achieve from year to year the highest standards in them [and] the highest common factor of knowledge in first year university courses would be enhanced.[30]

Taken overall, therefore, this report seems, in its major recommendations, to have reflected the concerns of the university members. Remembering how ready some teachers in the independent sector were, at Oxford, to respond to the claims of university knowledge definition, it is probably safe to infer that the conclusions represented some sort of agreement between the seven members of the Committee from these two high status sectors. The criticism of Oxbridge may have come from the members based in state selective schools, but it may have received support too from the non-Oxbridge university members. Certainly Thwaites, when interviewed in 1977, said he had always deplored the influence of the Oxbridge scholarships on the schools.[31]

'Mathematics in Schools' Committee

The main Committee here was again dominated by university mathematicians, including Thwaites, and the independent schools (see Table 30). The Committee also included, as well as Swain of the SMSG, Tammadge, Brookes and Morris of the ATAM. (Four of its nine members were to work with SMP in the future.) Given this composi-

Table 30: 'Mathematics in School' Committee Membership

University		3	(including Secretary)
Schools:	Independent boys	2	
	Direct grant boys	1	
	Direct grant girls	1	(Chairman)
	Mixed grammar	1	
Uncoded		1	

tion, it is not surprising that, having noted that school mathematics had remained unchanged since the turn of the century, they argued that there was an urgent need to rethink its content and, probably reflecting the ATAM presence, its 'treatment':

> It was evident that there was ready acceptance for the suggestion that some modern mathematics and a modern approach towards the teaching of traditional mathematics should be introduced, as soon and as generally as possible ... Almost without exception those concerned with this chapter felt that there is a need for a critical re-appraisal of our syllabi at all levels, that there is a very real need, despite criticism on the score of overloading, for the introduction of 'modern' mathematics and for a radical change in the treatment of, and attitude towards, the content whether old or new.[32]

And, in the first two 'vital' years of grammar school mathematics:

> There are certain concepts, the understanding and appreciation of which are essential to the proper development of a mathematical education from the earliest stage. These should be deliberately stressed on every appropriate occasion throughout the school course, so that the attitude towards mathematics is in keeping with the modern spirit within the subject. The most important appear to be:

> 1 Introduction and use of a correct mathematical language.
> 2 Symbolism and equality.
> 3 Set, relation and function.
> 4 Equivalence relation, order relation.
> 5 Symmetry, similarity and congruence.
> 6 Inductive discovery, and deductive proof.
> 7 The converse of a statement.
> 8 Importance of 'if and only if' as opposed to 'if ... then'.
> 9 Meaning of a definition and postulate.
> 10 Idea of an axiomatic system.
> 11 Equations as 'mathematical models'.
> 12 Solutions of equations and inequalities.
> 13 Simple dimensional analysis.[33]

Alongside the references here to the preferences of university applied mathematicians, the (partially) alternative perspective dominant at

Royaumont and within the SMSG, that of the modern algebraists tempered by the pedagogical perspective of the ICSITM, is clearly apparent; as it also is in the following remarks:

> Meaning and insight are achieved by a gradual process in which old principles or techniques are met in new situations, where familiar ideas are seen to be special cases of more general ones; in which apparently totally unrelated phenomena are seen to be but different manifestations of a single phenomenon ... For example, since the distributive law is a recurrent fundamental concept, even its simplest applications, such as finding the cost of three articles at 2s 1d each or of multiplying three by twenty-one should have attention drawn to them as being examples of the same fundamental idea ... Many of these concepts have been taught in this way by some teachers, but there is much more that could be done in this direction and, in order that it should be done, mathematics teachers themselves must be fully aware of the structure of the subject.[34]

These views were shared by the two joint sub-committees on the general school course (i.e., the 'O' level course), one of which was chaired by Morris of the ATAM, later to help found SMP, and on which no university personnel sat (see Table 31). In spite of the absence of the latter, however, and the claim that the sub-committees had 'dealt with mathematics as part of a general education and not merely as a specialised subject to be studied primarily to satisfy the requirements of external examining bodies', the dominant coalition within these groups had clearly looked to the universities for knowledge definition:

> In view of the great changes that have taken place in recent years in mathematics at university level, including those changes that

Table 31: Subcommittees for the general school course: membership by school

Chaired by Lloyd		Chaired by Morris	
Independent boys	1	Independent boys	5
Direct grant boys	1	Independent girls	1
Direct grant girls	1	Mixed grammar	2
Mixed grammar	3	Girls' grammar	1
Boys' grammar	2	Boys' comprehensive	1
Mixed technical grammar	1	Mixed bilateral	1
Boys' comprehensive	2		
Mixed bilateral	1		

are often considered collectively under the term 'modern mathematics', there is a prima facie case for a critical look at the content of present school syllabi.[35]

No specific references are made here to uses or applications. They continued:

> Research should be instituted without delay to ascertain which parts, if any, of traditional syllabi should be omitted as of doubtful value, and what might more profitably be included. During the time that this research is taking place, there is a clear need for examining the way in which the traditional content of the syllabus is taught, with a view to inspiring in children something of the modern attitude towards the structure, pattern and beauty of mathematics.[36]

The nature of this 'research' is not explored. Also seen as needed, were 'specialist mathematics teachers', from the earliest stages upwards, and, in line with the Royaumont proposals, textbooks:

> There is an urgent need for textbooks which present the subject from a modern point of view, and no single member of the conference was able to name a single British school textbook which does so ... Such books must be written as soon as possible.[37]

They also wanted the universities to provide courses for teachers on 'modern mathematics'.

Their conclusions included suggestions that set theory should be used as a 'common language' throughout the course, that greater emphasis should be laid on the structure of algebra as against techniques, that the concept of 'function' should receive more emphasis, that heavy manipulation should be avoided, that more statistics should be taught, and, finally, reflecting the concerns of applied mathematicians and 'industry', that 'models' of situations should be set up more frequently. The potential tension between the axiomatic basis of modern algebra and the ATAM's pedagogical perspective can be seen in the remark that, while 'clarity of thought and precise use of mathematical language' should be encouraged, this must not be allowed to 'stultify mathematical experience'.[38]

The above discussion clearly suggests that the diffusion of the modern algebraists' perspective on 'mathematics', whether through the ATAM by Hope and Fletcher, or actually during the Conference by Begle, Swain, Papy and others, was beginning to result in more 'converts' amongst school teachers.

On the two sub-committees for double-subject 'A' level the universities were represented by Hammersley. Again, one was chaired by an ATAM member, Tammadge, who was to become involved with SMP (and who had been at school with Thwaites). The locations of the other members are shown in Table 32.

In their report three principles were stated: (i) that all potential mathematics, science and engineering students should have some acquaintance with 'modern mathematical ideas and methods'; (ii) that they must be 'well-grounded and fluent' in their mathematics in order to be able to cope with new situations; and (iii) that applied mathematics must be considered as 'consisting largely' of the building of mathematical models:

> Indeed, many present courses in applied mathematics can be vigorously criticised as being, in essence and spirit, pure mathematics.[39]

The influence of Hammersley, and the series of conferences promoting this message, is apparent here.

Then, after a discussion of pedagogy similar to that of the general course sub-committees, they presented a model syllabus, the effect of which was 'to reduce substantially the geometrical content and the complexity of the manipulation ... to make room for one or more topics of modern mathematics'.[40] In particular, referring to the Gulbenkian Report,[41] they suggested the inclusion of simple set theory or matrix algebra, arguing that it would be advantageous for pupils to experience algebras based on axioms different from those of 'ordinary school algebra'. Furthermore:

(a) they introduce the idea of operations with entities which are not ordinary numbers, so helping to bridge the gap between school and university;

(b) they assume no large body of mathematical knowledge.[42]

Table 32: Subcommittees for the double-subject 'A' level: membership

Chaired by Nobbs			Chaired by Tammadge		
University		1	Schools:	Independent boys	4
Schools:	Independent boys	5		Direct grant boys	1
	Direct grant boys	2		Direct grant girls	1
	Boys' grammar	4		Mixed grammar	1
	Girls' grammar	2		Boys' grammar	2
	Boys' technical grammar	1		Girls' grammar	4

The concerns of ordinary teachers were reflected, however, in the possible disadvantages noted:

(a)   they are not easy to examine satisfactorily;
(b)   there is a lack of suitable textbooks for schools.[43]

For these reasons, they argued:

> We are of the opinion that immediate steps should be taken to prepare suitable school textbooks, to be used in the first place experimentally. The topics should not be used in examinations until such a book is available ...[44]

Again, courses on 'modern mathematics' for teachers were requested.

All of these suggestions were seen as providing potential help for their pupils with the transition to university mathematics. Various suggestions were also made as to how the sixth form curricular arrangements might be modified so as to improve the supply of mathematicians.[45]

The overall content of the reports forming chapter 4 of *On Teaching Mathematics* suggests that, by this time, the messages from extra-school groups within university mathematics and industry, concerning both pure and applied mathematics, had been successfully diffused by their respective promoting movements to significant numbers of teachers in the schools who, because of the sources of the messages, were apparently willing to regard them as making legitimate claims on school mathematics. This willingness would presumably have been strengthened by their strategic concern to satisfy those in the universities who, by controlling entrance to degree courses, effectively controlled the relative academic status of their schools.

University Mathematics Committee

This Committee, dominated by actors from the universities and independent schools, included Thwaites, Maxwell, who had attended Royaumont, and Hilton, a university pure mathematician who was to run courses on 'modern mathematics' for teachers in 1961/62 (see Table 33). They could, therefore, be expected to concern themselves with the 'transition' problem. They argued:

> Many students find that it is extremely difficult to bridge the gap which at present exists between school and university mathematics, both in content and presentation, and as a result become disappointed and disillusioned and lose interest in the subject.[46]

Table 33: *University Mathematics Committee: membership*

University		11 (including Chairman and Secretary)
Schools:	Independent boys	5
	Direct grant boys	1
Uncoded		1

They saw this as resulting from the 'acute shortage of mathematics teachers' which was 'rapidly assuming the proportions of a national disaster'. This reference to the nation served to partially legitimate their subsequent claim for more students:

> It should be made quite clear to potential students that a training in mathematics provides a basis for a first-rate education (the classical scholars ought to support this view), quite apart from any narrow interpretation of usefulness ... A training in mathematics is a good training to be an efficient member of society ...[47]

To prevent students losing their 'appetite' for the subject, they proposed that there should be three types of university mathematics course 'to cater for the widely different abilities and outlooks of students'. To some extent, this already occurred, but they recommended that there should be:

> standard nomenclature for comparable courses and that there should be some kind of parity of esteem between them so that students will be more easily persuaded to take the courses best suited to them than be selected on the 'kicked-down-stairs' principle.[48]

In describing these X, Y and Z courses they assumed a double-subject 'A' level 'which will provide a reasonably reliable guide both to the general mathematical maturity of the candidate and to his knowledge and ability'. This sixth form course would, they hoped, following the Gulbenkian Report, include 'modern mathematics'. In this respect, they deplored 'the difficulties presented to reformers by those members of examination boards who are unwilling to see the necessity of change'.[49] Pupils who obtained good results on such a sixth form course would be potential students for the X course; those with poorer results, or single subject mathematics, for Y and Z.

The X course would consider a 'wide range' of mathematical subjects, both pure and applied, in 'considerable depth'. The Y and Z courses, beginning as one, would be 'wider in scope' in the first year, but would treat topics 'less deeply'. There would be 'greater emphasis on practical mathematical techniques'. Both would continue, after diverging, to 'convey something of the ideas of modern mathematics'. This was especially desirable because these courses would supply most graduate school teachers. The Y and Z courses, but not the X, would have subsidiary subjects.[50]

It can be readily seen that 'parity of esteem' was not likely to arise from these arrangements: the Y and Z courses being more 'practical' and less like traditional single honours courses, and receiving the less 'able' students. In fact, the suggestion for three types of course might be seen as a strategy for expanding numbers without having to change traditional curricular practices for the most 'able' students. The inclusion of 'modern mathematics' in the Y and Z courses, seen as the producers of graduate mathematics teachers, would, furthermore, help achieve some subject resocialization of the teaching profession, and hence of their potential students.

Further reasons why 'parity of esteem' might best be seen as well-intentioned rhetoric can be found in their discussion of teaching arrangements in the universities:

> We are of the opinion that the only way to improve the teaching position in the university departments is to appoint lecturers whose prime duty will be to teach. The consequences of this, for example on promotion, which at present is based largely on successful research, will have to be faced.[51]

This, they argued, would allow exchanges of staff between school and university. They continued by arguing that the Oxbridge supervision system had much to recommend it, but that, 'in view of staffing difficulties probably the best compromise is a combination of lectures and supervision for the X course, and of lectures and examples classes for the YZ group'.[52] The less 'able', that is, would receive less teaching of Oxbridge 'quality'.

The Committee also made yet another suggestion that 'refresher courses for schoolmasters' should be provided. These should be 'coordinated by the organization charged with dealing with the crises in the mathematical profession'. They also suggested that university mathematicians should meet regularly to 'discuss, and hence improve, university teaching'.[53]

Considered overall, it can be seen that, in this report, the university mathematicians effectively protected their high status single honours course, which had been attacked at Liverpool, by suggesting new routes through university mathematics. These would, as well as protecting the X course from criticism, allow expansion of mathematics departments, an associated improvement in career opportunities, and make some contribution to the 'resocialisation' problem (and, eventually, to the 'transition' problem). It can also be seen, however, that 'parity of esteem' was not likely to be a realizable feature of the proposed arrangements.

Committee for the Concluding Chapter

It can be seen from the discussion so far that different committees, representing different sets of missions and interests, produced differing proposals for change in mathematics education. The actors from industry, arguing for less abstract mathematics, were confined to one of these, although the presence of applied mathematicians such as Thwaites and Hammersley ensured that their shared views on 'modelling' were carried into other reports.

In the reports of the educationally-based committees, however, it was the content and spirit of 'modern mathematics' which, presumably under the combined influence of the ATAM, SMSG and university pure mathematicians such as Hilton, received most discussion. This emphasis was grounded in the concern with the 'transition' problem. That much of what was written by the Central Committee in the conclusion to *On Teaching Mathematics* did not reflect this might be understood partly in terms of its membership (see Table 34), which included Thwaites and Hammersley, and partly in terms of strategic considerations, given that the conclusion represented an appeal for resources from extra-subject groups more likely to respond to the claims of 'modelling' than 'set theory'. The concluding chapter opens thus:

> From the days of the Armada it has been a national failing, or perhaps a pastime fed by temperament and climate, to continue the game in the face of the gathering storm. The dangers of such

Table 34:   Central Committee Membership

University		4 (including Chairman)
Schools:	Independent boys	1
	Boys' grammar	1 (Secretary)
	Direct grant girls	1

conduct mount directly with the time it takes to put on armour. In recent years many have come to see and agree that our national economy, indeed the survival of our standard of living, hangs upon our technological skills. These are the prime raw material of this tiny crowded island. There is no raw material known to man which takes a longer time to win and fashion. There is no weapon less readily forged and buckled on than a mathematical education; and mathematics is crucial for science and technology.[54]

It went on to describe the overall purpose of the book. It was concerned, not with the 'higher flights of mathematics or of pure mathematical research for its own sake', but with 'the mathematical side of the means of production of bread and butter technologists' and the 'methods of bestowing a general mathematical understanding, or numeracy . . ., upon the whole population.'[55]

This seems a highly selective summarizing of the earlier chapters, which concerned themselves specifically with grammar school pupils likely to study mathematics to 'A' level and, in discussing the X course, with future mathematical scholars. This may be partly explicable in terms of the underlying concern with problems of teacher supply. As Esland, however, has argued, in relation to different 'publics', differing elements of perspectives will tend to be suppressed or emphasized.[56] This selection process also seems to have been operating here.

Having legitimated their mission by reference to officially recognized national 'needs', they presented proposals and appeals for resources to realize them. They wanted a doubling of the 'mathematical intake' to universities from 1962, 'changes in syllabus and some very considerable changes in outlook' in school mathematics, new types of free textbook to bring 'new material' to the teaching profession, periodic study leave for teachers, exchange schemes to help 'cement the work of schools, university and industry', the co-opting of industrial representatives on to GCE boards, and conferences and study groups aimed at improving university teaching.[57]

The major resource sought was modelled on the National Science Foundation of the USA, the body funding the work of Begle and others in SMSG. They argued that a 'task force', similar to the NSF, should be set up by the government without delay. It should be drawn from the schools, universities, technical colleges, industry and research establishments. This plea was again legitimated by reference to the nation's 'needs':

> The use of mathematics in the community and the teaching of mathematics in the schools has a national importance and requires a national policy coordinated by a vigorous central effort. Delay in public and government recognition of this may be catastrophic.[58]

Furthermore, in relation to the 'urgent need' for syllabus reform, they claimed that:

> This business of moulding and remoulding the syllabus to meet developments, and of producing suitable textbooks both for schoolchildren and school teachers, calls for substantial full-time (and part-time) work by a largish body of well-qualified people as a national responsibility.[59]

By April 1961 therefore, as a result of the importation of the notion of curriculum development from the USA, via the SMSG and similar projects, the possibility of developing similar structures, with their associated career opportunities, was beginning to be canvassed within the mathematics community in England.

The degree of success of Hammersley, Thwaites and the other 'entrepreneurs' within mathematics in persuading extra-subject actors of the importance of their mission is indicated by the willingness of Eccles, then Minister of Education, who may himself have been seeking resources for his Ministry, to contribute a foreword to the book:

> The schools and industry are both short of mathematicians. The fact of the shortage and its gravity has been recognized in the educational world for some time. We know that the quality of mathematics teaching could and should be improved, the curricula brought up to date, and above all the number of mathematicians with good qualification increased. Much is being done already. The doubling of the number of places in teacher training colleges and the introduction of the three year course; the provision of special courses for serving teachers; and the expansion of the universities — all these will have their effect. But they are not enough. These developments serve to make this conference timely. I am glad to commend the constructive proposals made at the conference by mathematicians from the schools, the universities and industry.[60]

This suggests that the would-be reformers might now have expected some official support for their activities.

Other Conferences in April 1961: The Associations

During the same month 'modern mathematics' was to be discussed at the annual meetings of both the associations to which school teachers of mathematics belonged.

At the London meeting of the ATAM the development of the original pedagogic mission to include the promotion of 'modern mathematics' continued, but was to meet with some resistance from non-converted members. Major speakers were Papy, Vice-President of the ICSITM, who also attended the Southampton meeting, Hope, then President of the ATAM, and Dr. Ruth Beard, who spoke on Piaget.[61]

Hope began with references to the original mission, emphasizing the Association's 'child-centred approach', but adding, significantly, that the 'mathematics we hoped to teach' had not received equal attention. He then argued that children's 'perceptions' may often 'lie outside the realm of traditional school syllabuses and may form the basis for topics of "modern" mathematics'. Having argued that these perceptions should guide teaching, he went on to reproduce some of the claims made at Royaumont, thus further diffusing them:

> Mathematics today has a different structure from that which obtained fifty years ago in the traditional courses, so much so, that we require almost a complete refit to understand the situation. Modern algebra with its axioms and logical structure replaces the geometrical one which persisted from the Greeks although much of the terminology has a geometrical flavour. Algebra provides a rigorous basis reaching back to the theory of sets and of the natural numbers. Generalisations are easier algebraically than geometrically. Algebra brings precision, conciseness and mechanism to thought processes.
>
> The algebra syllabuses must include theory of sets; consideration of number systems, groups, rings and fields; vector algebra, transformations; matrices; homomorphisms and isomorphisms.[62]

He described some of this mathematics, with a special emphasis on vectors, which he favoured as the 'structure best fitted to our present age'. He concluded by arguing that the transition to university would become easier for 'our pupils' (temporarily forgetting the secondary moderns?) if these topics were to be studied at school. The Association therefore had a number of tasks. Primarily, it must encourage experiments in the teaching of the new mathematics in line with the pedagogical assumptions of the Association.[63] In this talk, a further shift in Hope's thinking towards a concern with the introduction of 'modern' content into schools can be detected.

Papy concentrated on describing his work on set theory with pupils aged from eight years upwards. He then gave a demonstration lesson on 'relations'.[64] Beard gave a general account of Piaget's work, stressing that, pedagogically, his findings suggested that children needed practical work and experience before they could grasp ideas. Other experiments, she noted, suggested that geometry, for children, might start with topology, a key branch of 'modern mathematics'.[65]

Alongside these talks, seminars were held on the usual ATAM concerns, but the report by Fielker in *Mathematics Teaching* in July 1961 concentrated on 'modern mathematics' and Piaget. Indeed, he wrote:

> Rather than two complementary themes, one felt that Dr. Beard's lecture on Piaget's work was a supplement to those of Mr. Hope and especially of Professor Papy, in the sense that Piaget's experiments showed that modern mathematics was, to put it simply, the correct and more natural thing to teach. In this almost revolutionary atmosphere the seminar groups with their more familiar topics — aids, first year in the secondary modern school, the sixth form, film-making, methods of teaching this and that, syllabus construction — seemed to hark back to another era.[66]

At the concluding session of the Conference, according to this report, a 'thirst for information and dissatisfaction with the conservatism of existing syllabuses' were expressed.[67] Possible action to remedy this situation was discussed. Various books on modern algebra were recommended (a list was reproduced in the journal) and it was agreed to set up study groups of interested members throughout the country (a list of twelve secretaries of such groups appeared in the journal).[68] Pressure was to be brought to bear on official bodies, especially to demand courses for teachers. It was reported in the journal in July, by Wheeler, that a letter summarizing 'the feeling of the conference and stressing the urgent need for study courses in modern mathematics' had been sent to Rollett (HMI), the secretaries of the Association of Education Officers and the Association of Education Committees, and to the Directors of University Institutes of Education.[69]

At this meeting then, a considerable number of members began to accept, or at least consider, the legitimacy of the definitional message diffused, via Hope, Fletcher and others, from the European and American university pure mathematicians, a message gradually combined by Hope with the original pedagogic mission of the association. Furthermore, these teachers were both asking for courses on 'modern mathematics', i.e., for potential subject resocialization into new cognitive and technical norms, and making organizational arrangements, as a movement, to further this process in other ways. My data do not allow me to judge to what extent their interest represented, in Lacey's terms, 'internalised adjustment' or 'strategic compliance'.[70] But, whichever the mechanism, a social movement now clearly existed which aimed to promote modern algebraists' definitions of mathematics within the school system.

Not all members were ready, however, to become converts to the new cause, as is illustrated by an exchange of letters in the July issue of *Mathematics Teaching*. C.T. Stroud, of Newland Park College, a teacher training institution, had written to attack the growing stress in the journal on modern algebra. He and others at the Conference had not been convinced of the case for the reform of content. Not only was he not convinced of the value of 'modern mathematics' to the pupil, but neither could he see what should be left out to make space for its study, especially as 'conventional work is clearly needed at present for science and technology as well as for exam purposes'. He added:

> Frankly, sir, quite a number of members of the conference were bewildered by what acceptance of Professor Papy's thesis would mean.[71]

Having thus attempted to legitimate traditional content and dismiss modern algebra, he concluded:

> Finally, sir, may I express the hope that the activities of the ATAM and the policy of *Mathematics Teaching* will continue broadly-based, as they always have been? Rank and file members depend on the association and the bulletin for help and it would be a pity to give undue emphasis to any one aspect of the subject, however influential its protagonists may be.[72]

Wheeler, a Lecturer in Education at the University of Leicester, replied on behalf of those accused. He claimed that Papy had illustrated how modern concepts could be 'worked into a scheme for beginners'. While the 'practical value' of Papy's ideas might be debatable, we should go ahead and study them, and test them in our classrooms: 'Mr. Stroud may, as he hints, be speaking for a substantial number of our readers. He is not speaking for all'.[73]

Given the evidence discussed earlier of a secondary modern-based grouping in the Association more concerned with introducing GCE examination courses into their schools than with more general reform, Stroud was probably describing the attitude of many members. The enthusiasts for 'modern mathematics' were not likely to carry the whole membership with them at this time. The Association's concern with anti-formalistic pedagogic approaches would itself have enabled critics to successfully attack Hope and his allies unless the latter had been very careful to stress the possibility of 'modern' abstract ideas being taught in a child-centred, practical fashion. The emphasis put by Collins and others on choosing applicable mathematics for pupils to study might also have raised potential problems for the advocates of modern algebra. In spite of these potential contradictions, however, by mid-1961 a substantial group within the ATAM was committed to experimenting with 'modern' ideas in the classroom. This commitment would eventually result in the publication of *Some Lessons in Mathematics: A Handbook on the Teaching of 'Modern' Mathematics*, published in 1964, but largely compiled by members during a writing week at Leicester in September 1962, and to the Midlands Mathematical Experiment (MME), to be discussed in chapter 10.[74]

At the April annual meeting of the Mathematical Association, Professor Newman spoke on 'modern mathematics and the school curriculum' in the context of the report being prepared for the Stockholm meeting of the International Congress of Mathematicians. Having suggested that the agenda for the Stockholm meeting had led to a 'preliminary airing' of this subject in many countries, and having noted that he would not be either advocating or opposing the introduction of 'such subjects' into schools, he went on to describe some modern algebraic ideas with some reference to their possible relevance in the classroom.[75] He argued that some of the modern algebras, especially the theories of sets and groups, were likely, at school level, to be restricted to somewhat trivial uses. He wanted, from school mathematics, 'substantial calculations with worthwhile results', and these might not be provided by these topics. He felt, furthermore, that the benefits of abstraction and generalization could only come after the pupils had previously studied much usable mathematics. An emphasis on general 'explanation and understanding' should not 'drown out the uses':

> In the presentation of axiomatic theories applications of real substance are also a safeguard against a danger of which I am sure everyone here is well aware: that if concepts of great generality are introduced before pupils have progressed far enough to have in their heads an adequate stock of more elementary mathematics to serve as examples, they may attach no real meaning to these notions.[76]

He concluded by arguing that more experiment was needed before any curricular decisions were made about these topics.

At the same meeting, Rosenhead, the Professor of Applied Mathematics who had chaired the Liverpool Conference, gave a paper critical of English education in general, from which were taken the comments on the not 'really bright' students appearing in *On Teaching Mathematics*.[77] He coupled these comments with an attack on what he regarded as excessive specialization within schools and universities. He hoped the latter would henceforth concern themselves somewhat less with the teaching of specialist material, an approach which suited only the 'very ablest', and more with general education.

Neither of these speakers, both important within the Association, argued strongly for the inclusion of 'modern mathematics' in school curricula as a way of helping to resolve the perceived problems of mathematics education. Neither did the then President, Maxwell, who had attended Royaumont, propose such a course as a way out of the 'crisis' he referred to in his address.[78] As I suggested earlier, others' initiatives were being responded to:

> You will know, too, that many activities of general mathematical interest are taking place with which the association is not directly involved. Members of the association sit, in private capacity, of course, on most of the committees concerned with school mathematics at all levels; and, again, representatives are even now preparing reports for submission to the congress of mathematicians to be held at Stockholm in 1962.[79]

He saw a key role for the Association:

> The crisis in the teaching of mathematics is now upon us, heavily but, as yet, by no means overwhelmingly; and it is to members of the Mathematical Association that the public ought to look for guidance.[80]

There is some support here for the view of some of my pro-reform interviewees[81] that, in terms of what they then saw as necessary, the Mathematical Association had become too 'conservative' a body to work to resolve the 'crisis'. Unlike the ATAM, many of whose activists had joined precisely because of a dissatisfaction with current practice and hence were ready to contemplate radical changes, this Association had become more of a representative body for selective school mathematicians in general. This feature of the Association was reflected in its 'good practice' approach to the writing of reports. The relegation of the axiomatic material to the appendix of the 1957 report on the teaching of algebra, when modern algebraists were sitting on the writing committee, may partially have reflected Newman's views on the appropriateness of modern algebra as a topic for schools, but it also presumably reflected a concern to keep broadly in line with the members' current practice.[82] Furthermore, applied mathematicians also played an important part in managing the Association's affairs, and they tended to have other concerns, as we have seen earlier. There was also a strong current of school-based opinion, represented, for example, by Langford, President in 1958, which felt that the universities, rather than the schools, should make changes in response to the 'transition' problem.[83]

Conclusion

Considering these three meetings together, it can be seen that two clear groupings existed in mid-1961 from which radical proposals for curriculum change were likely to come. One was the network of mainly independent school and university teachers associated with the series of conferences held at Oxford, Liverpool and Southampton. The other was the grouping within the ATAM favouring 'modern mathematics'. In the first group in particular, conflict was likely to occur over the respective importance of applied mathematics, especially 'modelling', and modern algebra, especially 'structure'. It must also be noted that no simple relation seems to have existed between a university teacher's sub-disciplinary commitment and his or her view of appropriate school mathematics for 'university-capable' pupils. Newman, a pure mathematician who had published in topology and, as early as 1937, proposed the study of some linear algebra in schools,[84] tended to argue against introducing abstract modern algebra into schools. Not that this vitiates Kuhn's analysis in its general sense: it clearly mattered a great deal to university pure and applied mathematicians what their potential students studied at school, and how. Furthermore, the results of the Southampton meeting, at which the universities were well-represented, also demonstrated that many in the university mathematics departments did want changes of the sort that Newman feared. In the USA and some European countries, such academics were already dominant figures in the movements to reform school mathematics, and it was their analysis that Hope and others within the ATAM seem to have favoured.

In chapter 9, I shall examine the ways in which the groups and individuals favouring various kinds of redefinition built on the outcome of these conferences of 1961, especially that held at Southampton, to achieve reform.

Notes

1 See, for example, GOLDTHORPE et al (1980), pp. 18–19.
2 The information is from *Who's Who* (1974).
3 THWAITES (1972), pp. viii–ix.
4 Interview with Thwaites (7 March 1977).
5 THWAITES (1961b), p. xxii.
6 *Ibid.*
7 *Ibid.*, pp. xv–xviii for the list of members on which this table is based.
8 *Ibid.*, for the conference register on which Tables Nineteen to Twenty-Four are based.
9 *Ibid.*, section four of the Chairman's Acknowledgements.
10 *Ibid.*, p. 60.
11 *Ibid.*, pp. 61–97 for abstracts of these talks.
12 *Ibid.*, pp. xv–xviii and p. 60.
13 *Ibid.*, p. xvii and p. 60.
14 *Ibid.*, p. xiv.
15 *Ibid.*, p. xii.
16 *Ibid.*, p. xiii.
17 *Ibid.*, the section on 'membership of committees', on which Tables 27 to 34 are based.
18 *Ibid.*, p. 4.
19 *Ibid.*, p. 4.
20 *Ibid.*, pp. 3–4.
21 *Ibid.*, p. 5.
22 *Ibid.*, p. 6.
23 *Ibid.*, p. 7.
24 *Ibid.*, p. 7.
25 COTGROVE and BOX (1970), p. 19.
26 THWAITES (1961b), p. 9 and p. 11.
27 *Ibid.*, p. 19.
28 *Ibid.*, p. 24.
29 *Ibid.*, pp. 18–19.
30 *Ibid.*, pp. 23–4.
31 Interview with THWAITES (7 March 1977).
32 THWAITES (1961b), p. 26 and p. 44.
33 *Ibid.*, p. 28.
34 *Ibid.*, pp. 28–9.
35 *Ibid.*, p. 29.
36 *Ibid.*, pp. 29–30.
37 *Ibid.*, p. 30.
38 *Ibid.*, pp. 30–1.
39 *Ibid.*, p. 32.
40 *Ibid.*, p. 33. For the syllabus, see pp. 36–42.
41 See HUGHES (1962), pp. 27–8, for an account of this report.
42 THWAITES (1961b), p. 34.
43 *Ibid.*, p. 35.
44 *Ibid.*, p. 35.
45 *Ibid.*, pp. 43–4.

46 *Ibid.*, p. 46.
47 *Ibid.*, p. 47.
48 *Ibid.*, p. 48.
49 *Ibid.*, pp. 48–9.
50 *Ibid.*, p. 50. For the course outlines, see pp. 53–4.
51 *Ibid.*, p. 52.
52 *Ibid.*, p. 52.
53 *Ibid.*, p. 55.
54 *Ibid.*, p. 98.
55 *Ibid.*, p. 98.
56 ESLAND (1971), p. 85.
57 THWAITES (1961b), pp. 99–103.
58 *Ibid.*, p. 100.
59 *Ibid.*, p. 101.
60 *Ibid.*, p. ix.
61 See the report of the Easter Conference (1961), *Mathematics Teaching*, No. 16, pp. 32–52.
62 *Ibid.*, p. 44.
63 *Ibid.*, pp. 46–7.
64 *Ibid.*, pp. 47–51.
65 *Ibid.*, pp. 39–43.
66 *Ibid.*, p. 33.
67 *Ibid.*, p. 52.
68 *Ibid.*, p. 52.
69 WHEELER (1961b), p. 55.
70 LACEY (1977), pp. 71–4.
71 STROUD (1961), p. 57.
72 *Ibid.*, p. 58.
73 WHEELER (1961a), pp. 58–9.
74 See FLETCHER (Ed.) (1964).
75 NEWMAN (1961).
76 *Ibid.*, p. 291.
77 ROSENHEAD (1961).
78 MAXWELL (1961).
79 *Ibid.*, p. 173.
80 *Ibid.*, p. 174.
81 HOWSON (26 March 1976) and THWAITES (7 March 1977).
82 See the discussion of this in chapter 3 above.
83 See, for example, Langford's letter to *The Times* (26 May 1961).
84 NEWMAN (1937).

9   The Search For Resources

This chapter has two sections. In the first, I describe the ways in which Thwaites, following the Southampton Conference, worked to publicize the 'crisis' in mathematics in extra-subject arenas in an attempt to legitimate the granting of resources to those arguing for reform. In the second, I examine conflict between members of the ATAM and the Mathematical Association at a Conference held in late 1961 over access to the control of possible changes.

Mathematics Education Becomes A Public Issue

This section, as well as illustrating the conflicting perspectives of school and university mathematicians of the 'crisis' and its causes, will examine those events captured by the third stage of Eggleston's 'interaction map of curriculum development', in which a 'pressure group', 'having established the area of proposed development and partially legitimated it', continues its search for resources to realize its missions.[1] Griffith and Mullins have described, for the six cases of scientific change they analyzed, how activist groups 'ventured actively into the politics of science in order to obtain or protect appointments and research support'.[2] Here, similarly, it will be seen how members of the growing movement for reform in school mathematics, and Thwaites in particular, finally succeeded, after three or four years of campaigning, in making the 'crisis' a public political issue and, in doing so, generated another resource, that of extra-subject political pressure, to be used in their campaign. In fact, Thwaites' activities of persuasion and organization were beginning, by this time, to resemble those of the 'organizational leaders' identified by Griffith and Mullins as having played a crucial role in scientific change. These actors seem to have played a similar role in the sphere of science as Becker's 'moral entrepreneurs' did in the field of deviance.[3] (Thwaites and others might, by analogy, be termed 'curriculum entrepreneurs'.)

Having already organized the Southampton Conference, Thwaites now used the opportunity presented by his inaugural lecture, presumably knowing that *The Times* could be got to report it, to attempt to recruit further extra-subject support for his aims.[4]

He devoted this lecture to the 'crisis'. After a number of introductory remarks, notable for their possibly strategic stress on the increasing integration of previously separate branches of mathematics and his devaluing of the pure/applied distinction, he announced that he would not be discussing his research interests:

> A new professor, however, finds himself all too soon distracted by issues with which he was not appointed to deal, and it was less than six months ago that a situation began to force itself upon my attention and to claim an increasingly large share of my time. As a result, I am now certain that to use this occasion for an exposition, however brilliant, of my own personal interests would be an act of considerable irresponsibility. For the truth is that the whole profession of mathematics is like a very sick man, a man in a high fever and so still restlessly active, but suffering even so from a wasting disease advancing so fast that one hesitates to speak too loudly of recovery. Strong words you may say, even ill-considered words coming, as they do, from a general physician rather than from a specialist consultant. Yet, from my examination of the patient, I am in no doubt at all that his condition is extremely grave. In plainer language, if the present shortage of mathematics teachers at all levels of education is allowed to develop any further, there is the strong possibility that mathematical education, as we have known it in this country and in this century, will have come to an end within twenty years, a possibility of incalculable consequences for the life of the nation as a whole.[5]

He followed this with a series of anecdotes to illustrate the difficulty of staffing schools and universities with what he regarded as adequately qualified staff. He then noted the negative feelings on both sides in the school/university transition debate, and continued:

> I, therefore, attempt two things this evening. First, I propose to convince you that, when headmasters have talked of an impending national catastrophe, they have spoken, not as publicity-

seeking alarmists but as highly experienced and responsible men of affairs. Secondly, in suggesting certain courses of action, I hope to make clear that it comes within the interest of everyone of goodwill in education to help solve a problem which is far beyond the capacity of mathematicians themselves.[6]

He then presented statistics relating to teacher supply in universities and selective schools. Using data collected from a 1961 survey of heads of university departments of mathematics, and making assumptions based on past staffing practices, he concluded that in these institutions:

(i)   the present deficiency equals at least one year's total output of Ph.D.s;
(ii) the maintenance of staffs at their present level requires a doubling of the annual output of Ph.D.s.[7]

For the schools, using data obtained from a recent survey by the IAH, and referring to the Churchill College meeting of February, he stressed problems of 'quality' as well as quantity. He was disturbed by the recently decreasing proportion of graduate mathematicians entering the schools who had first class degrees. Relying on Ministry figures, he noted:

We find that the percentage of first class degrees is eighteen for those over fifty-one years of age, while it is 3.8 per cent of those under thirty.[8]

He also presented the analysis printed in *On Teaching Mathematics*, concluding, on various assumptions, that for 'grammar-type' schools:

(i)   the present deficiency equals at least three years' total output of honours graduate mathematicians;
(ii) the maintenance of staffs requires at least a doubling of graduates in departments of education.[9]

Having established a persuasive argument in this area, he moved on to discuss the 'transition' problem. His perspective here may well have reflected his experience as a mathematician working across the boundaries of school and university:

One often hears talk of university mathematics and school mathematics as if they involve physiological processes requiring entirely distinct parts of the human brain; how often, for example, has one heard a university teacher assuring a sixth-form master that it is best that his pupil should know nothing of this, that, or the other interesting mathematical topic ...

What pernicious nonsense all this sort of thing is. I do not credit for one moment that there should be, or need be, any change of outlook by the student as he passes from school to university. Possibly the prime trouble is the exclusiveness which seems to be practised by each of the two groups of mathematical teachers; and if this is so, then I would like to see a vast increase in the opportunities for interchange, of men and ideas, between the schools and universities.[10]

A greater sense of unity amongst 'all types of mathematicians' was needed, and a new 'professional institution to which they would all naturally belong'.

Moving on to other possible solutions for some of the problems discussed, he stressed the need for more than 'small adjustments to our existing educational system in mathematics'. Because of the 'enormous magnitude of the problem':

Nothing less than measures on the largest scale, prosecuted with great vigour and determination within the next few months, have any chance of restoring mathematics to the essential position which I myself consider it should hold in education. Such measures are bound to involve radical changes of many kinds, but these we must face squarely.[11]

He wished industry to employ fewer mathematicians for a few years. He favoured differentially higher salaries for teachers of mathematics as against other subjects. He wanted more interchange between schools, universities and industry. For all this to become 'practical politics', a 'campaign forcefully presented on a nation-wide scale' was an 'urgent necessity'.

Reproducing the conclusions of the Southampton meeting, he argued that the mathematical entry to the universities should be doubled at once. The universities must cease to take only the very best 'A' level students. New courses — 'general honours courses to distinguish them from the traditional, essential and valuable special honours courses' — must be developed for the new intake. On the content of school mathematics education, he hinted at curriculum change:

I would like to mention the distaste which intelligent young pupils often have for the mechanical problem-solving side of mathematics: they feel that there is so little scope for the imagination, so little elasticity in the intellectual give and take of the subject. There is, I am sure, an enormous field of investigation here in the drawing up of mathematical syllabi which we can not afford to neglect.[12]

He concluded with more dramatic references to the 'crisis':

I feel that it is right to say that mathematics, in May 1961, has quite possibly passed the point of no return, the point beyond which there will be a steady and irretrievable decline, on the average, in the quality of students coming into the universities, in the proportionate numbers of adequately qualified teachers both in schools and universities, and in the overall prestige and standing of mathematics as an academic discipline.[13]

Referring to the National Science Foundation of the USA, 'which receives massive funds from central government', he stressed the need for a 'central coordinating body' to have authority 'over all the processes of education in mathematics (and ... the mathematical sciences too)'.[14]

In this lecture, in which Thwaites played a role very similar to that of one of Becker's 'moral entrepreneurs', the theme of industry's 'needs' which had been so central in the series of conferences was given less emphasis. Indeed, in the short term, they were requested to forsake mathematicians. The emphasis was instead on the adequate reproduction of a body of mathematics teachers for pupils in selective schools and the 'prestige and standing' of the discipline. Thwaites was also clearly beginning to promote curriculum reform as one element of this proposed enhanced production of university mathematics students.

The Times (24 May 1961) carried a very full report of the lecture. It began:

A grave warning that mathematical education as it has been known in Britain this century could come to an end within twenty years was given by Dr. Bryan Thwaites, Professor of Theoretical Mechanics at Southampton University, last night.[15]

It continued in a similar fashion. His various proposals for action, with the exception of curriculum reform, were all reported. Some of the anecdotes (a head had appointed his gardener to teach mathematics, for example) were reproduced.

In the same issue, an editorial described the lecture as especially important since mathematics was 'the central discipline common to all sciences'. It reiterated his conclusions on teacher supply, adding that the 'state of affairs that Dr. Thwaites describes is truly alarming':

Mathematics teaching is in a downward spiral; demand grows while the output threatens to contract. If the declension can not be arrested, deterioration is probable throughout a wide range of scientific education.[16]

Thwaites' proposals on salary differentials were supported, as were his suggestions for a professional institute 'to apply pressure' and for new types of university mathematics courses. *The Times* also argued that unfilled capacity existed in university mathematics departments.

In its article, and in the editorial, *The Times* again, in Hall *et al's* terms, basically reproduced the message of a legitimate 'primary definer' of reality.[17] In doing so it had reproduced Thwaites' emphasis on the need for the universities as well as the schools to take action, and this led to a heated correspondence over the next month. The locations of the twenty-four writers were mainly educational, as can be seen from Table 35.

A number of interest groups, including the universities, the advanced technical colleges and the selective schools, became involved in this debate, and the positions argued for in relation to the resolution of the 'crisis' clearly derived, in many cases, from the writer's occupational interests. A number of individuals involved in the movements aiming to reform curricula also took this opportunity to argue for resources.

The major point at issue became whether the schools or the universities should be seen as the cause of the 'shortage' of mathematicians. While some correspondents, such as Ollerenshaw, stressed the increased demand from industry and the technical colleges, most of those from either schools or universities respectively argued either that university mathematics was unnecessarily abstract and difficult or that school mathematics was an inadequate preparation for university work.[18] The exchanges on this issue began with a letter from J.L.B. Cooper (Mathematics Department, University College of South Wales and Monmouthshire), who legitimated his arguments by international comparison:

> The factors which deter students from entering honours degrees
> in mathematics are largely to be found in schools. One of these

Table 35: Locations of 'The Times' correspondents* after Thwaites' lecture

University:	Oxbridge	5
	Other	5
Schoolsø:	Independent/direct grant	5
	Other	2
Other (non-industrial)		7

* Including three membes of the Council of the Mathematical Association.
ø Including three early members of SMP.

is the advanced level syllabus in mathematics, which has been stripped of a large part of its intellectual interest and turned into a purely manipulative grind in the interests of a short-sightedly utilitarian view of the subject. Another important factor, according to my enquiries, is that schools, in giving advice on careers to pupils with mathematical ability, tell them that mathematics is not worth studying by those aiming at industrial careers. This means that on the whole only those prepared to consider teaching as a career undertake mathematics courses: as our honours graduates have generally found good careers in industry, it is not surprising that the schools are in difficulties ... The charge that university courses in mathematics are unduly abstract will not stand up to a comparison of these courses with those in, say, France or America.[19]

His remarks were quickly challenged from the schools. E.H. Lockwood of Felstead School (Independent) replied:

Professor Cooper should be called upon to justify his astonishing statement ... that the advanced level syllabus in mathematics 'has been stripped of a large part of its intellectual interest and turned into a purely manipulative grind'. I have intimate knowledge of the papers set by two of the boards and in reference to them the statement is entirely untrue. The syllabuses have in fact changed rather little in the last forty years and might better be criticised for that reason. The university courses have changed a great deal, becoming ever more abstract, designed more to produce research students than teachers.[20]

A day later, M.F. Robins of Rugby School (Independent), who had attended the Southampton Conference, replied specifically to the charge that schools warned pupils off mathematics courses, and attacked the universities for what he saw as their exclusive interest in the 'gifted':

I can assure him that we are not so short-sighted. Many of our better pupils go into industry ... But whereas good talent can go where it will, the less gifted but still reliable student is finding great difficulty in being accepted for an honours course in mathematics in many universities. This is the cause of the problem of the shortage of teachers as we see it.[21]

P. Evans, Headmistress of St. Swithuns School (a Winchester Independent) had no doubt about the universities' failings:

> In girls' schools ... there seems no prospect now of ever finding
> the required number of mathematics teachers ... The raising of
> standards by the universities seems certainly to be one of the
> chief causes ... Universities seem to assume that, unless a
> candidate is potentially able to get a first or second class degree
> in mathematics, she ... should not be admitted. While we all
> long for the teacher with a good degree, in the schools we would
> also welcome the teacher with a third class degree ...[22]

F.L. Allan, the Secretary of the IAH, took a similar position:

> The key to the problem lies with the universities ... The very
> high standards of scholarship known to prevail in departments
> of mathematics often have a severely discouraging effect upon
> competent sixth formers who are less than brilliant, when they
> contemplate a university course. There is good philosophy in
> the old Cambridge joke 'God bless the higher mathematics and
> may they never be any use to anyone at all'. Truth should indeed
> be pursued for its own sake on the higher levels of pure thought.
> But the universities also have a functional purpose, at least in the
> broad sense that it is their business to prepare a man for forty
> years of useful work in the world ... They should concern
> themselves with the middle ranges of ability ... If mathematics
> dons thus adjusted their concept of function they could promote
> admissions from the schools on a much larger scale. This in turn
> would mean increased numbers of mathematics graduates ...[23]

These attacks on the universities' teaching and recruitment practices
drew several counter-attacks from those in the universities. Rankin
(Mathematics Department, University of Glasgow), defending the
universities' right to define mathematics, and illustrating the perspective
on mathematics of 'modern mathematicians', wrote, in reply to the
charge that courses were now too difficult and unsuitable for school
leavers:

> It is true that there have been considerable changes over the
> years in the character of the mathematics taught in British
> universities, but this is to be expected of any living subject. The
> main change has been a move away from the mathematical
> 'jugglery' referred to by one of your correspondents to a more
> logical study of mathematical structures and ideas. The type of
> honours examination question now set is in fact easier, in that it
> demands less in the way of memory and manipulative technique
> than the type of question common fifty years ago ... Because of

the use of special terminologies, the newer mathematical subjects may be meaningless to teachers in the schools (or even to some in university mathematics), but this does not necessarily make them harder for the student ... Many of the newer subjects are likely to be of more use to the intending school teacher than the older ones: this is especially true of abstract algebra and set theory, which should help to clarify his understanding of elementary mathematical and logical processes and in this way should improve his skill as a teacher.[24]

One particular reform urged by correspondents from the schools (and also by Lighthill, of the RAE, who was one of four correspondents who had attended the Southampton meeting) was the introduction of less specialized, and less difficult, university mathematics courses for intending teachers. Langford, for example, Head of Battersea Grammar School, who had raised the issue of teacher supply in his presidential address to the Mathematical Association in 1958, argued:

There is plenty of good material in the schools, but it will never reach the universities unless there are drastic changes. We need three things done without delay: double the size of the honours schools in most of the universities ... , create an alternative course for intending teachers in the honours schools (this course would be in no way comparable with that at present in vogue) and extend, on a large scale, the facilities for general honours courses in which mathematics will be read in conjunction with other subjects in Arts or in Science ...[25]

This drew a reply from another recent President of the Mathematical Association, in this case a university mathematician. Here, away from the arenas of the Association, Newman, possibly also taking opportunity of the changed climate of opinion, seems to have taken a more positive view of 'modern mathematics' than he had at the Association's meeting in April described earlier:

Any move to bring in what would be, in effect, university courses especially designed for school teachers, 'in no way comparable with those at present in vogue', ... would lead inevitably to the creation of a separate subject, 'school mathematics', taught only to be retaught, fixed and completely ossified. Never has there been a time when it was more important, even for the most practical reasons, for teachers to have learnt something at least of the extraordinary transformations and developments in mathematics in the quite recent past. Many of the new mathematical concepts have already found their way into physics and engineering, and they are continuing to do so. It is important that there should be in the schools those who will be competent to guide the process, not too fast and not too slow, of bringing these ideas into contact with the school course.[26]

In this correspondence, the selective school and university-based mathematicians were both clearly concerned to absolve themselves from responsibility for the increasingly publicly-acknowledged 'crisis'. Each expected the others' practices to be changed. Most correspondents wrote from within the subculture associated with the selective school/ university route. It fell to two correspondents, based in a technical college and a college of advanced technology, to argue that the less specialised courses referred to already existed in their institutions, but were 'non-U'. They claimed that these already took account of industrial uses of mathematics in a way university courses in mathematics generally did not.[27]

Most correspondents also took the current structure of sixth form study as given. It was correspondents from outside mathematics — A.D.C. Peterson, the Oxford educationalist then running a campaign against 'specialization', R.F. Peel, Professor of Geography at Bristol, and W.A.C. Stewart, Professor of Education at Bristol — who raised the possibility of this being changed to encourage more pupils to study mathematics for longer.[28] Some correspondents, Hammersley and Tammadge especially — both present at Southampton — used the opportunity to continue the search for resources for the subject, legitimating this by reference to the policies of the USA, with its sponsorship of courses and new mathematics textbooks through the NSF. Hammersley, in particular asked:

> Will the public and the government recognize that such an apparently small and sectional issue ['the dearth of mathematicians'] has ... the gravest repercussions upon the future economy of the whole nation?[29]

This correspondence over three weeks in *The Times* resulted in a major breakthrough for the movements wishing to reform mathematics education. Politicians were now to reproduce the mathematicians' definitions of reality in extra-subject arenas. In fact, questions were asked in the House of Commons (13 June 1961) and the House of Lords (7 June 1961). On 7 June, Lord Boothby, reproducing Thwaites' figure of 3000 for the shortage of selective school mathematics teachers, and noting the importance of mathematics in the training of scientists and technologists, wished to know what the government was intending to do 'to avert the incipient disintegration of technical training'.[30] Viscount Hailsham, as Minister of Science, replied that some action had already been taken, this being a 'matter for serious concern', and that:

> The grave shortage of mathematics graduates able and willing to teach has been made known to the university authorities and consultations are taking place with them about how the problem can best be tackled. The Minister of Education has also taken measures to improve the supply of non-graduate teachers in this subject.[31]

The debate then covered the issues of coordination of interested bodies, differential salaries and the anxieties of parents. Hailsham was negative towards the salary proposal, noted the need for coordination, claimed to fear government control of the universities, and continued:

> The anxiety of parents in relation to the teaching of mathematics is not well-founded. The number passing the GCE at 'A' level is probably six times what it was not so long ago. Whereas between the wars practically the whole output of mathematics graduates went into teaching, certain developments in industry, particularly with computers, have meant that a whole new range of opportunity is open to mathematics graduates.[32]

He did not feel that the teaching profession should have the whole supply of graduates in mathematics. Mathematics teaching could be improved to increase the supply. It can be seen that this debate was structured around Thwaites' themes of May.

In the Commons, on 13 June, Mr. Costain (Con) asked the Minister of Education for a White Paper setting out the government's proposals to deal with the 'shortage' of mathematicians, and of mathematics teachers in particular, in 'view of recent widespread anxiety'.[33] Eccles replied that various measures had already been applied, and that those studying mathematics as a main subject in the training colleges had more than doubled in five years. The new three-year course would raise standards. Numbers should continue to rise with the expansion of the colleges. The main problem was a shortage of mathematics graduates, particularly those able and willing to teach. The question was under active discussion in schools and universities. He felt the university side of the problem to be most important, and had made the need for action known to the university authorities, through the Vice-Chancellors' Committee. The Department had also discussed the shortage with the Teacher Advisory Council. An early conference was proposed to discuss the evidence collected and possible courses of action.[34]

The Times followed up this round of discussion with an editorial on 19 June. This noted the tendency of school and university to blame each other for the 'critical state of affairs'.[35] It also noted, however, as a result of the correspondence, the possible inadequacy of the 'A' level syllabus, and the 'failure of school mathematics to incorporate the new concepts of the discipline'. Furthermore, it noted that the 'mathematical crisis' had brought the present arrangements for running education into question. Academics, therefore, must respect their 'freedom' and respond to 'established national needs'. Increased coordination was necessary: 'improvement here should come from the conference called for this autumn by the V.C.'s Committee between university and school teachers of mathematics'.[36]

Thwaites and the letter writers had clearly succeeded in moving issues of mathematical education into the national political arena. Partly, this reflected the increased activities of many groups and individuals in the years from 1957 to 1961, but, more specifically, Thwaites had achieved this by using his prestigious position as a Professor of Mathematics, and the legitimacy he had gained by organizing the Southampton Conference, to gain access to the national media. Here he had successfully embedded his arguments on mathematics education in the climate of concern in political circles over the supply of scientific manpower (which, of course, his activities helped reproduce). Having, in this way, mobilized the support of politicians concerned with this issue, his lecture had, indirectly, led to the setting up of a conference between school and university interests where, under political pressure, mathematicians would discuss ways of resolving the 'shortage' problem. The resulting increase in public awareness of the 'crisis' would, in the next few years, provide a valuable resource for those seeking support to 'improve' curricula.

The effects of these developments were illustrated in the Commons' debate on science of 10 July. Peart (Lab) opened with references to Gagarin's flight in space. The language was that of 'crisis':

> In the end education became the key. After the Gagarin flight in space, the TES, which he read but did not always believe, ... , said 'More than anything else it is a triumph of education'. This was what worried him. Here Britain had fallen down. This was the main defect in their scientific effort. The country faced a crisis in the teaching of mathematics but when the government was prodded they gave a complacent answer. This was not

sufficient. The government must rethink otherwise this crisis
would frustrate scientific effort in schools and productive effort
... Britain faced virtually an industrial Dunkirk.[37]

Eccles, as Hailsham had done the previous month, pointed to the
enormous increases over the last eight years in the numbers passing
mathematics and science 'O' and 'A' levels. This represented progress in
secondary schools and a massive swing to science: 'this was a revolu-
tionary change ... , a silent revolution'. He reiterated his arguments of
June on the training colleges. He stressed the role the colleges of
technology could play. The universities were to be expanded.[38]

Mathematics was to be discussed again on 17 July.[39] It was also to
be raised as an issue at the Tory party conference in October, where one
speaker, reported in *The Times*, argued that Eccles should have the
methods of teaching mathematics, which 'had changed little in recent
years', investigated.[40] Increasingly, in discussion within the educational
and political arenas, curriculum reform was being referred to as one way
of resolving the 'crisis'. This partly reflected the parallel discussion of
science syllabuses, a central issue at the British Association meeting in
September.[41] It was, in fact, in October that the Science Masters'
Association announced their intention of developing new 'updated'
syllabuses which, according to *The Times*' account, would remove
'deadwood' and introduce 'new ideas of the day'.[42]

A point had been reached, therefore, where, as a result of the
activities of various interested groups and individuals, and particularly
because the debate had become articulated with that on science and the
economy, 'mathematics' — at least at school level — was likely to be
subjected to some major redefinition for the first time in many years.
Potential redefiners, such as Thwaites and Hope, were now in a
situation where resources might well be expected to become available
and, furthermore, the climate of opinion was such that those supporting
current definitions would inevitably find themselves on the defensive.
The particulars of redefinition were to be much argued over — we have
already seen the different emphases of industrial actors, a major
potential source of funds, and the university 'modern' mathematicians
and their supporters whose power derived from their partial control of
university entrance criteria. In this situation, groups would increasingly
compete to achieve their own particular missions. Some of these
activities will be discussed in the next chapter. But already, in September, i.e., early enough for them to be well-placed in the competition for
funds, Thwaites had gathered together a small group of public school
teachers to discuss possible curriculum reform strategies.[43] And, in

August, Wheeler of the ATAM contributed a piece to the TES in which he argued that the case for reform, in the light of the 'New Maths', was unanswerable.[44] He legitimated his argument by reference to the OECD's *New Thinking in School Mathematics* and *Synopses* as well as Choquet's article in *Mathematics Teaching*, while worrying that many teachers would not currently be able to understand their contents.[45] In line with the ATAM's original mission, he argued that it was important that groups of teachers try the new topics in their classrooms: this would avoid the inherent danger of overly 'formalistic' approaches. The importance of 'intuition' and 'proper pedagogical principles' were stressed. His fellow members, Hope and Collins, were also discussing what they might do in this area. The move into the period of competition for resources referred to in chapter 6 was underway.

At the beginning of November, the conclusions of the Conference of Professors of Mathematics organized by the V.C.'s Committee were published in *The Times*. According to this report, the original initiative had come, not from the Ministry, but from the Incorporated Associations of Headmasters and Headmistresses, and from Thwaites' lecture.[46] It was chaired by Sir W. Hodge, Professor of Geometry at the University of Cambridge and a previous President of the Mathematical Association, who had argued in his address of 1955 for some 'modern' ideas to be introduced into school mathematics. An observer was also present from the Ministry of Education.

A paper had been presented by the headmasters asking for various measures to be considered to improve the supply of graduate mathematics teachers. These were the introduction of different types of honours courses, the admission to universities of girls who had not studied 'A' level applied mathematics, and one month full-time residential courses at universities to enable teachers to keep up to date with 'modern' developments. Thus, while requesting changes from the university mathematicians, the headmasters effectively accepted the university's right to define the nature of selective school mathematics. The parallel paper from the headmistresses requested a lowering of entrance standards, right back to 'O' level. The conclusions of the meeting included the recommendation that new types of mathematics degrees, of a broader type, should be developed. A Continuation Committee, under Hodge's chairmanship, to help put this into practice, and to liaise closely with the Ministry and the schools, was set up.[47]

At this meeting, the university mathematicians, although under some political pressure, had clearly maintained control of their courses. In particular, they had evaded criticism of their special honours courses by taking up the proposal developed at Southampton for the introduction of other courses of a 'comparable status'. Their ability to channel the most 'able' students into research fields was little affected by the decisions. The Conference had also accepted that courses should be provided for teachers. This would, in terms of my model, allow the universities to begin resocializing teachers subject-wise. That they desired and were ready to do so is illustrated by the fact that many universities provided lectures and courses for teachers on 'modern mathematics' from 1961/62 onwards.[48]

The Continuation Committee was also to work towards setting up a body to coordinate the political activities of mathematicians. Named the Joint Mathematical Council, this was finally set up in July 1962 and included the following amongst its institutional members: the Royal Society, the London Mathematical Society, the Conference of Professors of Mathematics, the Mathematical Association, the ATM (the renamed ATAM), and the mathematical section of the ATCDE.[49] It also included Thwaites as one of three co-opted members, thus recognizing both his contribution to the subject earlier in the year and, presumably, his having by then already been well-advanced in the setting up of SMP. This connection was to prove to be a useful resource for SMP in future years.

Thwaites' activities had led then, not only to the increased political concern noted earlier, but also to the establishment of a body which, in future disputes over mathematics, might be claimed, by whoever controlled it, to speak for all mathematicians, an important potential resource for subject practitioners. Whether, had not Thwaites and others already been successful, by mid-1962, in getting curriculum change underway, this body might itself have organized change, is not a question for which I have the evidence available to attempt an answer. Clearly, however, given that other individuals and groups had initiated changes, the JMC could be expected to be interested in monitoring these on behalf of its constituent interests.

The BP Conference: Intra-Subject Conflict

In this section I shall examine the events at a Conference held in November 1961.[50] These events belonged clearly to the second of the ideal typical periods of subject redefinition which I outlined in chapter 6. In this period, once resources were clearly potentially available from various sources, those within the subject with competing missions and interests began to struggle to capture a share of what was available. More specifically, the events described here will serve to illustrate processes of intra-subject conflict over possible resources and, especially, inter-associational conflict in which members of the ATAM promoting 'modern mathematics' attempted, successfully, to force this Conference to pass resolutions favouring possible reform and, less successfully, to wrest control of a planned committee, which might control considerable industry-derived resources, from the leadership of the Mathematical Association. The analysis is based on the minutes of the meeting (which took the form of a more or less verbatim record of the proceedings).

The meeting, chaired by Combridge, President of the Mathematical Association and a mathematician at King's College, London, was one of three supported by BP, on mathematics, chemistry and arts teaching, in successive weeks. Waring, in her work on science education, has shown that the initiative for these came from within BP, representatives of which approached the relevant subject associations.[51]

As at the earlier conferences involving industry at Oxford, Liverpool and Southampton, speakers were invited from the three sectors of university, industry and the schools (here, apparently in the ratio 3:3:1). The then current issues were focused on by the speakers. Edwards, a Senior Lecturer in Mathematics at King's College, for example, addressed the issue of 'modern mathematics'. He personally did not favour the introduction of 'modern' concepts into school syllabuses: 'my view of mathematics teaching in schools is rather similar to my view on teaching foreign languages — the mechanical techniques of manipulation in mathematics and of grammar in languages are best acquired in the plastic years of school life'.[52] He also reported the recommendations of the September meeting of professors of mathematics. Frankl, a mathematician from the Engineering Department at the University of Cambridge, discussed 'models' and applied mathematics. In discussion of this talk, Coaker, of BP, argued that examinations should be constructed to reflect this aspect of problem-solving, by supplying redundant information, etc.[53]

The meeting then continued in another form, being organized around several discussion groups ('syndicates'), consisting mainly of selective school teachers, each of which reported back to a first plenary session. At this session it became clear that agreement existed on the 'need' for more types of mathematics degrees, but not, at this stage, on the introduction of 'modern mathematics' into schools.[54] After another round of talks, on mathematics in industry, from Sellers and Coaker of BP, another round of discussions followed. At the subsequent plenary session, uncertainty about the place of 'modern mathematics' in schools was again expressed. Perhaps it should be taught but not examined, for example? A similar lack of consensus on the place of less tidy examination problems emerged. Some felt pupils were not 'mature' enough to tackle these.[55] This plenary session was followed by a talk on mathematics teaching by Brookes of the ATAM, now a Lecturer in Education at the University of Southampton, which included a plea that the Mathematical Association should 'work with the teacher in the school'.[56]

Another round of discussion groups followed. This time they had been asked to bring back recommendations to be discussed at a final plenary session. I shall not discuss them all here, but one group suggested the establishment of a committee, from schools and industry, to make recommendations for the content of school mathematics at all levels.[57] A similar idea came from a second group. Other recommendations reflected the presence of Wheeler and Fletcher, both now ardent supporters within the ATAM of 'modern mathematics'. Wheeler's group supported the Southampton Conference's recommendation that 'experiments in the introduction of new subject matter and new methods should be encouraged', and added that mathematics must not be seen solely as a tool for industry.[58] They also wanted BP (another group preferred the Mathematical Association) to approach government and industry for funds to support such experiments. Another group 'requested' the Mathematical Association to consider the claims of those wanting to introduce new mathematics into schools and, in particular, to review the OEEC publications on this matter urgently. They added that they were 'bewildered by the conflict of opinion between the establishment and the protagonists of the new mathematics'.[59] They also wanted the proceedings of the Conference published, and circulated to educational establishments and the press. All the groups seem either to have recommended or accepted the proposals for increased numbers of university mathematics students which had come from the September meeting described earlier in this chapter.

It was during the final plenary session, however, following the reading out of the lists of recommendations, that major conflict occurred. Combridge, introducing this session, summed up some of the recommendations. Having noted, perhaps strategically, that, in his opinion, speakers from BP, unlike other industrial representatives he had worked with in committee, recognized that mathematics must be 'allowed to flourish freely in its own way' if the needs of industry were to be served, and having added that the recommendations concerning the universities would be passed on by him through an 'appropriate channel', he raised the issue of the proposed committee on curriculum content. Should this be a committee of the Mathematical Association or 'separate and independent'?[60]

A Dr. Geary, a polytechnic lecturer who had attended the Oxford Conference, immediately questioned the wisdom of the first alternative:

> The members of Syndicate One are very concerned indeed about the appeal of the Mathematical Association and the *Mathematical Gazette* to teachers in all schools. There were statements from schools with say twelve members on the mathematics staff and only one member of the Mathematics Association, that those outside the association wanted to come into closer contact with industry. Possibly the answer is a committee formed away from the Mathematical Association, as you just outlined, comprising teachers in the schools and representatives from industry. The feeling is that the articles in the *Mathematical Gazette* are mainly addressed these days to people interested in university teaching rather than in teaching mathematics in schools. But we feel that teachers in school rather than members of the Mathematical Association as such should take part in this discussion.[61]

Combridge replied thus:

> One can, of course, in making a committee of this kind, operate in the way in which we operated when the AAM produced a report on the teaching of mathematics. There were enough members of the Mathematical Association on the committee which drew up that report for our association to feel quite happy as to what happened about it. Similarly, in this case, I can well believe that a number of people on the committee proposed would already be members of that association and keep in touch with us, so you needn't be afraid that it would be regarded as a rival organization, though of course one wants to keep duplications to a minimum.[62]

A long discussion followed around this issue. Perhaps, Combridge later suggested, after views for and against had been put, the Mathematical Association should 'sponsor' the committee?[63] This drew a reply from a Mr. Beardwood:

> It was felt [in our group] that it wasn't merely a case of all schools, but also all types of mathematics teachers, and there is a fear that the Mathematical Association consists principally of a highly academic type of mathematics teacher. We have the case in point of a comprehensive school of eighteen mathematics

masters on the staff, of whom only one was a member of the Mathematical Association, and it is frightfully important that this sort of thing should get out to all teachers of mathematics in all types of classes and in all types of school, hence it was felt that if this was done essentially by the Mathematical Association it might not make contact with the ordinary mathematics teacher in school.[64]

Combridge then tried to close the discussion:

We enlarged our editorial board two or three years ago to include someone who would get in material from modern schools and the comprehensive schools and it just does not come in — they will not write it. Everybody thinks that what he does is so normal and natural that everybody else does the same; or else he is the only person doing it, in which case there is no need to say anything about it. As I shall be continuing in close contact with the BP people after this, would everybody be satisfied if it were left to the President of the Mathematical Association and representatives of BP to devise a means of calling this kind of committee to do these things.[65]

At this point Brookes, of the ATAM, claimed that the challenge of Mr. Beardwood had not been answered. Fletcher, also of the ATAM, quickly followed him up:

In another association we already have in existence in different parts of the country twelve groups of teachers who are certainly not high-powered university mathematicians, but ordinary teachers in ordinary schools who are struggling to cope with these problems: I am sure their doors are open to any other members and also any people in industry who would be interested in the problems.[66]

Mr. Fryer, of Charterhouse, agreed with some of these critics:

[In our group] we also had the thought that we would be the teachers who would be the people who would make reappraisals of syllabuses and examinations similar to what has happened on the science side . . . That is I think why we were rather emphatic that we need an organization of the teachers and we want to know what is wanted outside. We do feel there is a danger that the true academic people from the universities will shelve propositions that are of more importance to us than to them.[67]

Combridge again tried to end the discussion:

> I'm only being difficult because I don't want a resolution to go out which leaves no means of carrying it out.[68]

Mr. Dorrington, a previous Secretary of the Mathematical Association's Teaching Committee, supported him:

> I didn't want to say anything at this stage but in view of the fact that there are a number of members of the Mathematical Association here who would have heard what has been said regarding the association, I think they could take it to heart. It seems to me that here we have an association which has the organization in being to contact every school in the country through its own members; they have a clerical staff who can circularize all schools and who could, in fact, put these resolutions into being. I would suggest that this conference should have sufficient confidence in the President of the Mathematical Association and those other members here to ask them to try to do this.[69]

Mr. Penfold, of Battersea Grammar School, whose Head, Langford, was a previous President of the Association, offered his support. He then suggested that the recommendations, of which there were some sixteen or seventeen, be voted on separately, and that the Chairman should then, using these results, draw up a summary later.[70] Combridge took this up, suggesting that this would 'leave us to sort out the execution of them in the best possible way afterwards'. After some brief exchanges on this, a Mr. Parkes tried to finally close the argument:

> The difficulty as I see it is if the Mathematical Association, or if the President of the Mathematical Association, doesn't organize this committee nobody will. I should have thought the President of the Mathematical Association is so shaken by the comments about his association that he will take jolly good care to produce a committee that will suit members of this conference, and I would like to suggest that our chairman should organize this committee.[71]

But, before the resolutions were finally voted on, another attack was launched by a Mr. Waltham:

'As a member of your association may I put the view even more strongly that for the journal of the Mathematical Association to be of any use to me in school I would want about seven-eighths of it altered; that it is occasionally interesting — half a dozen pages perhaps, but it is far too highbrow for general use in the schools. In a school in which there is a lot of mathematical work done, only two of us are in fact members of the association; I couldn't really recommend the others to become members at the present moment.[72]

The meeting then went on to pass most of the resolutions. Extended discussion only occurred in relation to one criticizing the 'excessively high standard' of university, especially Oxbridge, entrance requirements. After the Chairman, himself a university mathematician, had argued that to pass this would bring the other resolutions into 'disrepute' with the universities, and other speakers, including Fryer, had supported current practice, this was finally 'decisively lost'.[73] After a plea by Wheeler, the meeting then supported the proposal of the Southampton Conference for experiments to be instituted on the teaching of 'new mathematics'. Finally, it was agreed that the Mathematical Association should take the initiative in setting up the desired committee, and also that it should review the OEEC publications and 'investigate the claims of the advocates of the teaching of new mathematics'.[74]

It can be seen that, at this meeting, members of the ATAM, who were also key figures in the movement promoting 'modern mathematics', launched an attack on the authority of the Mathematical Association. Although this finally proved unsuccessful as far as control of the proposed committee was concerned, Wheeler and his allies were able to push through resolutions, using the recommendations of the Southampton Conference to legitimate them, favouring consideration of 'modern mathematics' as possible school knowledge.

Conclusion

Becker has written, in relation to deviance:

Rules are not made automatically. Even though a practice may be harmful in an objective sense to the group in which it occurs, the harm needs to be discovered and pointed out. People must be made to feel that something ought to be done about it. Someone must call the public's attention to these matters, supply the push necessary to get things done, and direct such energies as are aroused in the proper direction to get a rule created.[75]

If instead of 'rules', we read beliefs in 'teacher shortages' and the 'out of date' quality of school mathematics, it can be seen that similar considerations must apply in the study of the careers of school subjects. While, for example, there clearly were 'objective' factors tending to cause problems in the supply of graduate mathematics teachers, it nevertheless required the efforts, over several years, of various individuals and associations, using a variety of platforms, and legitimating their claims by reference to other subjects and the past situation of school mathematics in terms of accepted criteria (such as 'firsts') as well as by reference to the economic value of mathematics, to make 'teacher shortage' first an issue of general concern within academic arenas and then, by 1961, a major political issue.

Similarly, while there clearly was an 'objective' discontinuity of subject perspective between selective school mathematics and the practice of some segments, increasingly dominant within some countries, of university mathematics, and had been for some years, it again required interested actors, utilizing the climate of 'crisis' resulting from the campaign on teacher supply as a major resource, to enter various arenas in order to persuade others of the 'need' for change.

The last five chapters have demonstrated that such actors, especially the university pure mathematicians, with their followers in the ATAM, and the applied mathematicians, with their industrial allies, did have considerable success in convincing school teachers of the 'need' for change in school practice, while fending off attacks 'from below' on their own curricular practices. In both cases the success of the university sub-disciplinary segments can be seen as having partly resulted from their having found allies outside of their own organizations. The supporters of modern algebra within the ATAM, who had come into contact with the pure mathematicians in various European-wide meetings, such as Royaumont and the ICSITM conferences, gradually made 'modern mathematics' more acceptable to many school teachers by combining it with those elements of their original mission concerned with Piagetian ideas, and proposing 'intuitive' and 'experiental' approaches to its study. The applied mathematicians found themselves able to claim that 'industry' also approved of 'modelling', numerical methods, and so on, as well as being able to derive resources of personnel and money from companies with which to further the promotion of their version of 'mathematics'.

This crossing of boundaries to achieve support was, in fact, a general feature of the events of these years. The pure mathematicians, by winning converts amongst the ATAM membership, could benefit from this organization's proselytizing powers; the applied mathematicians from industrial support. Thwaites' activities in 1961, however, resulted in a particularly significant success for those seeking resources to realize their various missions. Capitalizing on the success of previous individuals and groups in making mathematics education an issue *The Times* was willing to cover, and having carefully structured the Southampton Conference so as to produce actual proposals, he used his inaugural lecture to move the debate on mathematics into more public extra-subject arenas. His initiative, because it received the boost of a lengthy debate in the correspondence columns of the paper of the 'decision-making class',[76] resulted in mathematics becoming an issue in the parliamentary arena, an important resource for the would-be reformers. It also resulted, directly and indirectly, in various meetings between school and university interests at which the need to resolve the 'crisis' was further explored.

By late 1961, therefore, the 'need' to reform school mathematics was seen as legitimate by actors in a number of arenas, including the industrial and the political. In this climate, various groups of individuals who had been involved in the conferences and activities of the preceding few years were to move into Eggleston's fourth stage, the drawing up of detailed proposals for curriculum development and the search for funds with which to implement these.[77] It will be seen in the next chapter that, in the subsequent competition for resources, some would be much more successful than others.

Notes

1 EGGLESTON (1977), pp. 126–7.
2 GRIFFITH and MULLINS (1972), p. 960.
3 BECKER (1963).
4 THWAITES (1961a).
5 *Ibid.*, p. 6.
6 *Ibid.*, p. 7.
7 *Ibid.*, p. 18.
8 *Ibid.*, p. 17.
9 *Ibid.*, p. 18.
10 *Ibid.*, pp. 19–20.

11 *Ibid.*, p. 21.
12 *Ibid.*, pp. 25–6.
13 *Ibid.*, p. 26.
14 *Ibid.*, pp. 26–7.
15 *The Times* (24 May 1961).
16 *The Times* (24 May 1961).
17 See HALL et al (1978).
18 For Ollerenshaw's letter, see *The Times* (13 June 1961).
19 *The Times* (26 May 1961).
20 *The Times* (6 June 1961).
21 *The Times* (7 June 1961).
22 *The Times* (2 June 1961).
23 *The Times* (27 May 1961).
24 *The Times* (12 June 1961).
25 *The Times* (26 May 1961).
26 *The Times* (1 June 1961).
27 See the letters to *The Times* of Arscott (5 June 1961) of Battersea College of Technology, and Mullineux (15 June 1961) of Birmingham College of Advanced Technology.
28 *The Times* (17 June 1961).
29 *The Times* (26 May 1961). Tammadge's letter was published later (14 June 1961).
30 *The Times* (8 June 1961).
31 *Ibid.*
32 *Ibid.*
33 *The Times* (14 June 1961).
34 *Ibid.*
35 *The Times* (19 June 1961).
36 *Ibid.*
37 *The Times* (11 July 1961).
38 *Ibid.*
39 *The Times* (18 July 1961).
40 *The Times* (14 October 1961).
41 *The Times* (7 September 1961).
42 *The Times* (2 October 1961).
43 THWAITES (1972), p. ix.
44 WHEELER (1961c), p. 145.
45 *Ibid.*
46 *The Times* (3 November 1961).
47 *Ibid.*, and HUGHES (1962), p. 34.
48 See the list in MINISTRY OF EDUCATION (1963). pp. 29–35.
49 See the *Mathematical Gazette* (1963), Vol. 47, pp. 130–1.
50 See *Mathematics Today and Tomorrow* (1961).
51 See WARING (1975), pp. 163–4.
52 *Mathematics Today and Tomorrow* (1961), p. 16.
53 *Ibid.*, p. 24.
54 *Ibid.*, pp. 31–41.
55 *Ibid.*, pp. 73–8.
56 *Ibid.*, p. 88.

57 *Ibid.*, p. 91.
58 *Ibid.*, p. 92.
59 *Ibid.*, p. 95.
60 *Ibid.*, p. 97.
61 *Ibid.*, p. 97.
62 *Ibid.*, pp. 97–8.
63 *Ibid.*, p. 98.
64 *Ibid.*, p. 99.
65 *Ibid.*, p. 99.
66 *Ibid.*, p. 99.
67 *Ibid.*, p. 99.
68 *Ibid.*, p. 99.
69 *Ibid.*, p. 99.
70 *Ibid.*, p. 100.
71 *Ibid.*, p. 100.
72 *Ibid.*, p. 100.
73 *Ibid.*, p. 102.
74 *Ibid.*, pp. 100–1.
75 BECKER (1963), p. 162.
76 HALL et al (1978), p. 120.
77 See EGGLESTON (1977), pp. 126–7.

10   The School Mathematics Project And The
Midlands Mathematical Experiment

It has been shown that, by mid-1961, the climate of opinion in some industrial, political and educational arenas was such that individuals able and willing to promote appropriate sets of proposals for the reform of school mathematics might expect to be able to generate considerable supporting resources. In Berger's terms, a plausibility structure had been created to support change. Resources were especially likely to become available to those individuals promoting missions formed in and by those debates initated by some employers of graduates and some university applied mathematicians in the late 1950s, and described here in earlier chapters.

In the competitive search for support, however, not all the individuals promoting sets of proposals would have equal access to initial resources. Access would depend on both their current occupational locations and positions, and on their previous activities within subject arenas. In particular, groups and individuals would differ in terms of their general status, their academic legitimacy, their access to the media, availability of time and the extent of their relevant relationships across the boundary of the subject. In fact, some individuals and groups were to receive much greater support from extra-subject sources than others.

This chapter, which concludes the empirical body of my study, draws on various project reports, journals, interviews carried out with individuals involved in the movement to reform school mathematics, a questionnaire survey of heads of mathematics departments in the secondary schools of two LEAs, and data collected during two small case studies of mathematics departments using SMP. It has two main sections. In the first I briefly examine, in relation to earlier chapters, the proposals of SMP and MME, two multi-school projects conceived in 1961 to produce new textbooks. I also examine the relationship which seems to have existed between the resources initially available to their respective initiators and the further support they succeeded in generating in the period of competition for resources. In doing so, I shall be focusing on the structural factors involved in SMP's relative success. (The question of the relative quality of the products of SMP and MME will not be treated in any detail here. It can be noted, however, that it would be far from easy to erect any supposedly universal standard in terms of which one could understand the decisions made by actors adopting products. These will have judged 'quality', at least partially, in terms of (i) the source of the products; (ii) the degree of fit between their perspective and those embodied in the materials; and (iii) in a context characterized by 'interested' messages from the competitors, the quantity and 'quality' of which would again, to some extent, reflect availability of resources.) In the second section I shall discuss, in terms of the model outlined in chapter 2, a variety of critical responses to SMP. I shall also, at the end of the section, briefly consider the changes in content, pedagogy and the degree of curricular differentiation that seem to have resulted from reform.

Given this decision to focus on what I see as theoretically relevant aspects of these projects' careers, and given the general focus in this study on the sources of innovation, I shall not be presenting a detailed history of either SMP or MME. For this purpose, another study would be needed. The general sequence of events after 1960, however, will be seen to have had much in common with that described by Griffith and Mullins as characterizing ideational change in scientific disciplines.[1] They write of change within a scientific speciality:

> When challenged, some members of a scientific speciality become organized to work towards certain objectives, voluntarily and self-consciously, as a coherent and activist group.[2]

In their study of six such groups, a number of common features were identified:

> Among these ... are the presence of an acknowledged intellectual and organizational leader or leaders, a geographical centre, and a brief period of comparatively intense activity.[3]

A desire to recruit new members also featured in each case.[4]

SMP and MME: A Comparison

I shall begin, as indicated, by describing the personnel and proposals of the two projects.

SMP: Personnel[5]

The original group convened by Thwaites in September 1961 to discuss action towards curricular change in school mathematics, and which was to conceive SMP, was, apart from Thwaites himself, Dr. H.M. Cundy, T.A. Jones, and D.A. Quadling. They were to be joined soon afterwards by T.D. Morris.[6] Thwaites' career has already been outlined.[7] Jones was then Senior Mathematics Master at Winchester College, where Thwaites had previously taught. Quadling, SMM at Marlborough College, had previously authored 'A' level texts and was a member, in the late 1950s, of the Mathematical Association's Teaching Committee. Cundy, SMM at Sherborne, was Assistant Editor of the *Mathematical Gazette* and co-author, with Rollett, of a book on mathematical models (not 'modelling').[8] Morris, about to become SMM at Charterhouse, had been involved with the ATAM. Three of these, Thwaites, Jones and Quadling, had been directly involved in the series of conferences begun by Hammersley at Oxford. Thwaites, in particular, had convened the Southampton Conference of 1961.

The group was, therefore, both well-connected within the subject and, relative to potential school-based competitors, well-resourced in terms of status and academic legitimacy. The importance of this for their mission was well-understood by Thwaites:

> I and Tom Jones asked ourselves who we might invite. We thought of three other public schools of high repute — to give our work high respectability in the academic world. Also to use the public schools' independence to our advantage.[9]

A similar argument appears in his foreword to *SMP: The First Ten Years*:

> These five saw the opportunity of exploiting first the independence of the four public schools with which they were connected by agreeing to work to a common and radically new syllabus, and second, the procedure whereby the Examining Boards would provide new GCE examinations to match the syllabus.[10]

In doing so, these teachers were to bypass the Mathematical Association, which Thwaites then saw as an 'extremely "trad" organization'.[11]

SMP: Proposals

SMP's early proposals for the redefinition of selective school mathematics reflected the debates of the previous few years, the participants' involvement in them and their willingness to accept university mathematicians' definitions of 'mathematics'. Thwaites, himself a university-based applied mathematician, when interviewed, stressed the discontinuity that had developed between school mathematics and the mathematics practised elsewhere:

> Traditional school mathematics had remained static for decades. Many teachers were in a rut. The content of school mathematics had no relevance to life-in-the-large, no relevance to applications in the world at large and the coming computer revolution. Yet applied mathematics in the universities was changing.[12]

Thwaites' presence ensured that the demands of the applied mathematicians would be represented in SMP's redefinition. The mathematical paradigm of the modern algebraists was also, however, to be imported into school mathematics by the group as a result of Thwaites' involvement with the Southampton proposals and because of its members' occupational interest in the 'problems' of the school/university transition. Howson, to join the group in early 1962, described their original views thus:

> We saw the [school/university misfit] in terms of the abstract approach to algebra, just coming in then in the universities. Bourbaki, etc. One felt that this was the way ahead — structure. Note the particular emphasis on structure in the early SMP books. T4 has isomorphism; the early 'A' level drafts included a topological approach to continuity. We felt this was the maths of the future and wanted to give a Stage B treatment of it. We were, in fact, more successful with matrices. This may even be, more realistically, the maths of the future. The stuff on sets was taken over from American work. We were not so committed on that. Much got dropped. We felt the gap that was opening up between school and university mathematics must be bridged.[13]

He added, on the subject of 'structure':

> Structure was central to our aims. Pupils have always had difficulties with factoring and removing brackets. We felt that if they understood the underlying structure their difficulties would disappear.[14]

The early group also concerned themselves with questions of 'approach'. Morris, who was, according to Howson, a 'strong AT(A)M man', as well as being particularly interested in transformation geometry, was a member, in 1962, of the ATAM writing group that produced what was to become, in 1964, *Some Lessons in Mathematics: A Handbook on the Teaching of 'Modern' Mathematics*.[15] This book, presenting suggested classroom approaches to many 'modern' topics, appeared with a foreword by Thwaites and, according to Howson, 'had a major effect on SMP writing'.[16] A summary of SMP's aims, stressing their concern with modern algebra, newer uses of mathematics and with pedagogy, and very much reflecting the OECD and Southampton proposals, appeared in the SMP report for 1962/63.[17]

The proposed syllabus and textbook contents for 'O' and 'A' level can be seen to have represented a compromise between the demands made for redefinition by the modern algebraists (in, for example, the OECD documents) and the alliance of applied mathematicians and employers (in the conference series begun by Hammersley).[18] At 'O' level, representing the formers' perspective, we find set theory and symbolism, the study of number bases, the linear algebras of vectors and matrices, transformational geometry (replacing the Euclidean variety) and probability theory. Representing the latter, we find statistics, and linear programming with its focus on 'models' of situations.[19] At 'A' level, in the earliest available proposals, we find, representing the former, a stress on algebraic structure and operations, groups, equivalence relations, vectors and matrices, and probability. Representing the latter, we find the omission of 'statics', the introduction of statistics, a greater stress on numerical methods, and, again, a stress on the 'modelling' of physical situations by, for example, differential equations.[20] In both courses, alongside the stress to be placed on structure, went an explicit concern with the concept of 'function' in mathematics. The textbooks were also to include a much greater emphasis than those then in use in the selective schools on Stage A experimental and practical work (in, for example, the study of probability).[21] Recommendations were also made, in the early reports, for the reform of examinations by, for example, the introduction of a multiple choice element and the removal of the pressure of time on candidates.[22]

MME: Personnel[23]

MME was conceived and initiated by two activist members of the ATAM: Hope and Collins. Collins, Headmaster of a newly formed grammar school in Solihull, had approached Hope, Principal Lecturer in Mathematics at Worcester Training College, a member of the OEEC seminars and President of the ATAM in 1961, suggesting that a new mathematics syllabus be designed for his school. Other schools became involved through the interest of members of the Technical Schools Headmasters Association (Midland Region).[24]

MME: Proposals

These had much in common with those of SMP and, in particular, in their emphasis on modern algebraic structures, reflected Hope's involvement in the Royaumont meeting. I have already noted, in chapter 4, however, that Collins favoured an emphasis on the applicability of mathematics in curricular selection and this also influenced Hope's proposals.[25]

In the introduction to the 'O' level syllabus, the OECD reports are acknowledged as a major influence, but only in a broad sense:

> The impetus to reform is due in large part to the two OECD reports: *New Thinking in School Mathematics* and the *Synopses For Modern Secondary School Mathematics*. Both of these reports were compiled and written with something like twenty different educational systems in mind. The *Synopses*, in particular, was never intended as a blueprint but as a guide to people developing new syllabuses taking into account the shape of future needs. The MME syllabus, while acknowledging the inspiration derived from these reports, is an experiment in British education with British schools and school traditions very much in mind.[26]

The proposals were then legitimated through the discussion of changes in mathematics in three areas: in relation to 'our expanding technology', in colleges of technology and in the university.[27] A critique of the traditional school mathematics course followed, concentrating on the inadequacies of geometry teaching, and concluding:

> It is the essential simplicity of modern mathematics which must be emphasized. The torrent of new symbolism involved is often overwhelming to those who meet it late in life but, forget the symbolism, forget the jargon about sets and intersections, and look at it from first principles: it is very simple really. The simple ideas are important because they unify. The principles developed from them are working tools in a research situation; they may be used in a technological context. The dreaded symbolism is just a convenient shorthand.[28]

Then, reproducing many of the elements of the perspectives of the ATAM leadership, the document argued for a 'child-centred' approach in mathematics teaching. For example:

> Modern mathematics must grow from the children's experiences. It is possible that hitherto we have not recognized the mathematics in the experience.[29]

The emphasis on 'experience' was continued in the discussion of the importance of Stage A and Stage B work in schools:

> The last thing we should aim at is a rigorous abstract presentation of abstractions which bear no relation to the world as it is developing in the contemporary scene outside school or have no applications to other studies and experiences in which the pupil is engaged.[30]

This ATAM perspective carried with it a stress on pedagogical reform, and the importance of reforming the approach to teaching traditional content:

> The main emphasis on reform must come in the first place by teaching what is known from a new viewpoint. Abstract axiomatics and the rigour of advanced mathematics is more appropriate to the later stages. Long repetitive sequences of drill-examples must give way to discussion of problems and of alternative solutions.[31]

The influence of the suggestions in the *Synopses* can be seen in the suggested treatment of arithmetic where structure, together with set theory and symbolism, were emphasized. As in SMP's proposals, work with number in bases other than ten was introduced. In the study of equations, an emphasis on 'equivalence', relations and functions was suggested. The 'group structure' of addition was another new topic.[32] The teaching of geometry was to be completely redefined by the introduction of vectors and matrix algebra.[33] Some numerical analysis, probability and calculus were also included.

The influence of Collins' concern with applicability, shared by many in the ATAM, can be seen in the suggestion that the applications of these topics, such as simple statistics, should also be studied. Furthermore, and again illustrating the working out of ATAM ideas, throughout the textbooks, drafted later, there were many suggestions for practical work and pupil activity, both being seen as the basis for teacher-pupil discussion.[34]

A major difference from SMP was the initiators' early concern to reform sub-'O' level syllabuses. This was again a reflection of the range of concerns of the ATAM members involved and, in particular, of Hope's belief that the 'simplicity' of 'modern mathematics' would enable it to be taught to most pupils:

> So much of modern mathematics offers simple direct techniques which make a solution almost inevitable. This has its point for the majority of the population.[35]

A similar concern, coupled with the pedagogical perspective of the ATAM leadership, was expressed in an editorial in the Association's journal on SMP by Birtwistle, whose technical grammar school was soon to join MME. He welcomed SMP, but raised questions about its membership:

> What does one infer from the fact that six out of seven boys' schools taking part in the experiment are members of the Headmasters' Conference (i.e., Public Schools)? Does this lead us to expect a syllabus and treatment in keeping with traditional English 'pure academicism'? And will it lead the general run of secondary schools to conclude that the new syllabus is intended for the 'high flyers' only, and 'not for the likes of us'?[36]

SMP and MME: Some Differences and Their Possible Consequences

The proposals of SMP and MME clearly had much in common. Both were aiming at a redefinition of selective school mathematics, commencing with 'O' level, although MME also began with a concern with secondary modern school mathematics. Both proposed redefinitions embodying the demands of both the pure and applied segments of the subject external to the schools. Both had as organizational leaders, in Thwaites and Hope respectively, individuals who had already played key roles in the processes of subject redefinition. Both groups intended to revise their classroom materials after classroom trials. Both were to be successful in persuading examination boards to accept and examine their syllabuses.

Clearly, however, the two groups differed considerably in terms of their structured access to resources. Such differences, especially those of status, plausibly account, at least in part, for their differential access to funds. Thwaites' group aimed to generate £10,000 per year for seven years.[37] By late 1962, more than half of this was assured.[38] By late 1963,

£30,000 was still required but, by late 1964, partly because of 'gifts' from the Leverhulme Trust and the Industrial Fund (which gave the whole of its balance to SMP), this problem had been solved.[39] The main source of SMP's income had been the industrial companies participating in the series of conferences described earlier, a network of contacts with which Thwaites would have been well-connected by 1961 as a result of the Southampton Conference.[40] Howson, in interview, saw the locations of the group as certainly having been linked to their relative ease of access to funds, explicitly comparing their success with MME's relative failure in generating support:

> The group came from public schools. This made an enormous difference. Bryan was able to collect money by wielding their names to people who often came from those same schools. The Solihull group couldn't do this. This was very important.[41]

Thwaites was apparently so confident of generating funds from industrial sources that he was able, in 1962, to turn down the offer of money from the Nuffield Foundation, who were willing to sponsor a mathematics project parallel to their science schemes, because he wanted the group to retain complete editorial control. Howson remembered this:

> He tried to get money from Nuffield. There was a meeting with Tony Becher. Nuffield were prepared to take on the whole of SMP and link it with their science projects. But they demanded total control, and that we used their administrative pattern, with a consultative committee. This was rejected by the group who wanted the freedom to do their own thing.[42]

Becher, in interview, confirmed this version of these events.[43] The importance of this incident here, however, is that it indicates that, by early 1962, SMP were confident of alternative sources of support. (Later in SMP's career, the offer of a grant from the Schools Council of £30,000 was to be declined for similar reasons.[44])

Hope, on the other hand, had much less initial success in generating support. In fact, his major source of funds until 1968, when the Schools Council provided £24,000 over three years, was a sum of a few thousand pounds from the Nuffield Foundation, which he had approached, and which allowed him to be seconded from his post for the year 1963/64.[45] My interviewees associated with the Foundation and the Ministry at this time made it clear that they felt, very early on, given the 'quality' of the group Thwaites had convened, that it was not worth competing with them.[46] Hope and his lower status collaborators were not, therefore, seen as a potential Nuffield Mathematics Project which might compete with SMP. Retrospectively, Howson also stressed the 'quality' of the SMP group in relation to MME:

> Hope had Collins and Stoker — good teachers but not recog-
> nized writers ... But SMP had some members, especially
> Cundy and Quadling, with a lot of writing experience. They had
> a good standing in the world of maths education and were
> therefore invited to give lots of talks ... It was an enormous
> strength having people competent to attend meetings.[47]

The availability of funds from 1962/63 onwards to appoint 'relief teachers', to allow the school-based members of SMP to devote themselves to writing for various periods of time, also gave this project an advantage over MME.[48] The school-based members of the latter must have found it difficult to devote as much time to writing and other project activities. Their Report for 1963/65 explicitly notes the difficulty of finding enough teachers 'with the necessary self-confidence to face other critical teachers'. It is also noted there that, although some LEAs had allowed MME members occasional leave to attend meetings, they could 'ill be spared from their schools'.[49]

What can be seen here is that SMP's greater success in generating support, arguably a function of both their structural advantages and, presumably, of Thwaites' abilities as organizational leader, will have enabled them to devote greater energy to developing and publicizing their work. Amplification of initial differences between SMP and MME would follow. While both groups received requests for speakers, SMP could be expected to cover a wider geographical area more frequently, partly for resource-related reasons, but partly also because of the relatively scattered nature of the schools initially involved. MME's engagements for 1963/65 were reported as follows:

> Herefordshire Teachers of Mathematics
> Coventry Teachers of Mathematics
> West Riding Education Committee
> Bradford Education Committee
> Bristol Institute of Education
> South Staffordshire Mathematical Association
> Kingston College of Technology
> Cheshire Teachers Refresher Course
> Northumberland Education Committee
> South Birmingham Technical College[50]

During the same years similar meetings were attended throughout England by SMP.[51] The predicted difference perhaps emerges, however, when it is seen that, by 1963, Cundy had also completed a tour of American Summer Institutes and Thwaites had spent three weeks with SMSG in California.[52]

SMP quickly became well-known on a national level. This was partly a result of the above activities, shared with MME, but also of a number of other factors. First, there was major intra-subject publicity available through the *Mathematical Gazette*, of which Cundy was Assistant Editor. In one issue in 1963, Cundy himself contributed a piece on SMP, and a discussion of 'O' level syllabus content.[53] Jones also wrote on 'A' level.[54] Secondly, Thwaites, because of his previous activities, was more or less assured of access to *The Times*, and hence further intra- and extra-subject publicity. In October 1962, relying on 'details of the scheme ... given to *The Times* yesterday by Dr. A.G. Howson, of Southampton University, where it is being directed by Professor B. Thwaites', the paper provided its first account of SMP.[55] The project's aims were reported in detail, with a stress on the 'use of mathematics in the modern world'. The names of the schools involved were also given prominence. A longer report appeared in February 1963.[56] This detailed the new syllabus content and contained quotes from various members of the team, as well as from the Headmaster of Winchester College, Sir Desmond Lee. Thwaites himself was reported as having said that the project was a 'fantastic success'. *The Times* coupled this report with a supportive leader:

> In mathematics the disparity between the modern subject and the kind of work done in school is particularly great. The adult mathematician is not doing a more advanced version of school mathematics: he is doing a different kind of thinking altogether. The principal weakness of the present 'O' level syllabuses is not merely that parts of them are 2,000 years old. The subject that they present is not intellectually coherent enough: it is at once artificial (i.e., obviously unrelated to anything within the pupils' experience) and lacking in rigour. That is one of the things that have led to the extreme unpopularity of the subject, and the shortage of mathematicians. It is also one of the things that have led to the present movements for reform in mathematical education, and, in particular, to the cooperative SMP, in which eight schools have tried out a syllabus of a radically new kind.
>
> The pupil needs to be given a set of powerful conceptual tools, whose full purpose would be apparent later, but which would immediately have some relevance to experience and should form a coherent whole. For this purpose it is possible to

bring down some of the topics and methods of real mathematics from the advanced treatises into the schools. The subject is not more difficult for the pupil, though the notation may look a little unfamiliar to those trained on the earlier syllabuses. By comparison with some developments abroad the Project's syllabus seems a compromise, but it is a good first step.[57]

What can be noted here is the strong emphasis on the nature of mathematics, particularly on the need for school mathematics — not 'real mathematics' itself — to be redefined to bring it into line with the 'real mathematics' of the university. From SMP's point of view it was, of course, primarily good publicity. Furthermore, at this stage of a project's career, potential critics (even if provided with any support from the general climate of opinion, which they were not in this case) have no published materials to criticize, only proposals and drafts. A certain space is available, therefore, for a limited time, in which it is possible for a project team to advance their reputation in a relatively unhindered fashion.

Notwithstanding Birtwistle's negative comments on the origins of SMP, a further factor supporting the rapid diffusion of SMP's ideas and materials into the selective schools was their high status source. The eight 'central schools', whose SMMs formed the SMP Committee, were listed in the 1963/64 report as:

> Abingdon School (having replaced Holloway School)
> Battersea Grammar School
> Charterhouse
> Exeter School
> Marlborough College
> Sherborne School
> Winchester College
> Winchester County High School For Girls[58]

They thus comprised four independent schools for boys, two direct grant grammar schools for boys, and two grammar schools, one for boys and one for girls, one of whose heads, Langford, was prominent within the Mathematical Association and had done much to publicize the 'shortage' of mathematics teachers.

In comparison, the 'Phase I' MME schools were:

> Harold Cartwright/Malley, Solihull
> Bournville Boys' Technical, Birmingham
> Turves Green Girls', Birmingham
> Lordswood Boys', Birmingham

> Marsh Hill Boys', Birmingham
> Marsh Hill Girls', Birmingham
> Park Hall Girls', Castle Bromwich
> Biddulph Grammar School[59]

Thus, not only were they not so spread geographically, but, comprising two grammar, four technical and two modern schools, they were, in terms of the criteria of everyday and professional evaluation, of much lower status than the SMP schools. SMP's Director was, furthermore, a university professor, MME's a college of education principal lecturer. Bell, as I have noted earlier, has pointed to the tendency, in stratified educational systems, for lower status institutions to emulate the practices of those of higher status.[60] In the particular case of mathematics, schools in the selective sector turned to SMP's 'O' level materials in quickly increasing numbers in the 1960s. Already, in 1963/64, SMP's materials were spreading, relative to those of MME, into the higher status schools within the state secondary sector, those that, historically, had defined the curriculum that others often attempted to emulate. This is clearly demonstrated in Table 36.[61]

Furthermore, it will be seen later in this chapter that, as would be expected if Bell's argument were correct, it was eventually SMP, not MME, that became the 'new orthodoxy' for GCE 'O' level mathematics. This may have resulted partly from the perceived intrinsic 'quality' of SMP's materials (although many teachers were to complain of the linguistic difficulty of the texts and of a lack of exercises — in spite, often, of continuing to use the materials), but, I would suggest, may, with some plausibility, be accounted for, at least partly, in terms of differences of prestige between these competitors in an academic marketplace. Further research would be needed to assess the separate contributions of such causes, but their combined result was to allow SMP to eventually become self-supporting financially through sales of textbooks in England and abroad. Hence, within the limits set by the market place, SMP became relatively autonomous as an organization.[62]

Initially available resources have, of course, to be creatively used by

Table 36:   SMP and MME schools (1963/64)

	Independent	Direct Grant	Grammar	Technical	Comprehensive	Secondary Modern
SMP	10	3	24	2	1	1
MME	—	—	4	4	1	14

actors if they are to achieve their goals. Griffith and Mullins, discussing the careers of their six activist groups in science, have noted that each had to seek out further resources, including able recruits, and hence that:

> These groups often ventured actively into the politics of science in order to obtain and protect appointments and research support.[63]

Comparable activities, of which Thwaites was, it seems, a master, characterized the career of SMP. Not only did Thwaites, as had Hope, put his efforts into gaining the early cooperation of the examination boards (presumably available both because of the climate of opinion in educational arenas and because of the presence of university mathematicians on key committees) and use his university connections to set up a formidable university-based 'A' level advisory group,[64] but he also used various other strategies to legitimate and protect SMP's definition of school mathematics. He effectively co-opted Langford, an influential previous President of the Mathematical Association, by inviting his school to join the central team.[65] He gained membership of the Joint Mathematical Council of the UK from its beginning as an independent member (later as a representative of the Institute of Mathematics and its Applications), presumably as a consequence of his activities on behalf of the subject in 1961.[66] As a result, when, at the end of the decade, by which time Thwaites had become the Principal of Westfield College, this body produced a report on the 'present state of change in mathematics at secondary level', under his editorship, it represented no threat to SMP.[67] He also ran, in 1963, a survey of heads of mathematics departments in universities and heads of Oxbridge colleges on SMP's early 'A' level proposals which both enabled the group's eventual syllabus proposals to be well-informed and provided potential ammunition against critics.[68]

It was, however, in the area of 'A' level mathematics that SMP received its one major setback. The team had agreed to propose a single subject rather than the traditional double mathematics 'A' level as being sufficient preparation for entrance to single subject honours courses in mathematics in the universities. Under pressure, however, from some universities who made it clear that they would prefer double subject candidates, SMP produced a 'further mathematics' syllabus.[69] Clearly therefore, some university mathematicians, by using the power inherent in their control of entry requirements, had been able to successfully protect themselves from potentially having to re-examine or reorganize their introductory courses. This occurred in spite of Thwaites' efforts to persuade the universities to re-examine their entry procedures (see, for example, his contribution to the Cauis' meeting on this 'problem', in 1963.[70]) In fact, the 'A' level texts were never to be as successful, in terms of diffusion, as were those at 'O' level. Thwaites himself sees this as related to the early problems discussed above:

> I wish now we hadn't got into that argument, although we were fundamentally right. It involved an enormous diplomatic effort. Our judgement was wrong on that issue. I still think it's wrong that just one subject should have a double 'A' structure. I think more candidates would be taking SMP 'A' level now if we'd kept to the usual expectations of a double 'A' level.[71]

Hope, of course, could use his position within the ATAM to diffuse knowledge of MME. He also sought university advice, in the person of Professor H.B. Griffiths of Birmingham.[72] His chances of achieving the degree of nation-wide visibility attained by SMP were presumably, however, considerably reduced by the low status locations of his group's members, its originally localized nature and lack of funds. While, for example, MME ran mainly local self-help conferences as well as, eventually, an annual summer conference at Worcester,[73] SMP gradually succeeded in developing a larger nation-wide programme of proselytizing and resocializing events as more personnel and, eventually, funds became available (see Table 37).[74] This expanding programme, together with the gradual move of SMP personnel from schools into teacher education,[75] a resource to which MME also had some access, ensured that SMP, with its other competitive advantages, would continue to spread throughout the schools. Although it is not nationally representative, my survey of secondary schools in two southern LEAs, carried out in 1976, with a response rate of sixty-five per cent, illustrates the eventual domination of secondary school mathematics by SMP (see Table 38).

Only one of the nine schools using modern textbooks not produced by SMP was using MME materials. These findings must, of course, be carefully interpreted. In one of the two schools, for example, in which I carried out case studies — a comprehensive reporting a 'modern' SMP-based mathematics curriculum, the curriculum was in

Table 37:   SMP teacher training conferences

1962	1963	1964	1965	1966	1967	1968	1969	1970
1	1	1	1	4	5	9	7	8

Table 38: Main school (11–16) mathematics curriculum in two LEAs
(1976)

	Traditional	Mixed	Modern (not SMP)	SMP
Grammar	2	1	1	3
Secondary Modern	3	1	0	11
Comprehensive	4	4	1	28
Independent and direct grant	3	2	7	12

fact clearly differentiated, with the 'less able' receiving little 'modern' content. Furthermore, in both, SMP materials were much 'adapted'. These figures are probably, therefore, best seen as providing information about which textbooks were being used with examination classes.

On a national level, the recent Schools Council Impact and Take-Up Project found SMP materials and ideas to be the most often used of those produced by any mathematics project concerned with the secondary curriculum. In particular, they reported that SMP materials and/or ideas were being used by at least one teacher in seventy-six per cent of the schools in their sample while the comparable figure for MME was twenty-eight per cent.[76] Similarly, while the percentage of 'appropriate' teachers in their sample using SMP was found to be sixty-one per cent, for MME the figure dropped to ten per cent.

Through SMP therefore, mathematics teachers in the independent schools, who had, in some earlier periods, mediated university mathematicians' preferred definitions of school mathematics for the 'able' through the Teaching Committee of the Mathematical Association, seem to have effectively continued this process by another means.

It is also important to note, in concluding this section, that although SMP's success eventually freed them from dependence on such external sources of support as 'industry', they became instead dependent on sales of materials in the market place. They could therefore be expected to respond to changes in the climate of opinion in relation to mathematics education. Some results of this always precarious position will be seen in the following section.

Critical Reactions to SMP

I have argued earlier that, in terms of the model outlined in chapter 2, curricular proposals, i.e., proposals for the redefinition of school knowledge, must be considered as political compromises.[77] In the particular case discussed here, SMP can be seen as a compromise, mediated by public school mathematics teachers, between the demands for redefinition of several extra-school groups interested in the socialization of their successors and/or employees and the demands of some school-based pedagogic 'radicals'. If this is, indeed, an adequate view of subject definition, then we should expect the reactions to the proposals from various groups and individuals to be comprehensible in similar terms. In this section I shall show, in an illustrative manner, that, for SMP, this seems to have been the case.

Members of the SMP team seem to have regarded university mathematics as a legitimate source of definition of school mathematics and, as a result, their proposals, as described above, responded to both pure and applied segments' demands. Given this, and the real differences existing between the two sub-disciplines with respect to 'cognitive and technical norms' and purpose, SMP was always likely to be criticized for not adequately embodying either major sub-disciplinary perspective. That this was so can be illustrated by reference to the report of SMP's own 'A' level survey of 1963.[78] A professor of pure mathematics, for example, commenting on their 'A' level proposals, argued:

> The syllabus looks like the work of someone interested in applied mathematics; there are a number of interesting novelties on that side, but on the pure side it appears to be a way behind what are likely to be the views of the examining board.[79]

Another professor of pure mathematics wrote that the syllabus, in spite of contrary claims, did not 'reflect the present nature of mathematics and its usages':

> This your syllabus does not do. There is no geometrical subject or topic in the whole course.[80]

The definition of geometry intended by the writer is unavailable but was possibly different from that employed by the professor of applied mathematics who wrote:

> It is absolutely essential for anyone who is going to apply his mathematics in such divergent fields as nuclear physics, aeronautics, meterology, crystallography, astronomy or geophysics, to acquire a geometrical sense. This can not be acquired by pretending that geometry is a part of algebra, as your syllabus appears to do. It can be acquired only by some form of exercise in which people are forced to think in geometric terms.[81]

Other respondents seemed dissatisfied with the extent to which SMP were intending to reform the cognitive and technical norms of selective school mathematics:

> [The] new syllabus does not really help us at all and I suspect that its students will come up with the same bad habits and wrong ideas as the rest. I was hoping that your team was going to introduce a new and proper way of thinking about pure mathematics but I see that they are back on the old familiar treadmill.[82]

Others, against this, supported the group's belief that school mathematics should not be characterized by Stage C rigour.[83]

This intra-subject dissension can be further illustrated by Hammersley's comments on 'modern mathematics' in general and SMP in particular, made in 1967. I have two reasons for considering these at some length. First, they demonstrate the reaction of an academic entrepreneur who, having partially initiated the movement to reform school mathematics in England in 1957, from the perspective of an applied mathematician, had seen the French and American modern algebraists gradually colonize the movement on an international level and, through the OEEC seminars and reports, gradually insert key elements of their perspectives into those of activist teachers. Secondly, his reaction is clearly explicable in terms of the model of chapter 2, derived from the work of Kuhn, and Bucher and Strauss.

Hammersley launched his attack on SMP in 1967, by which time several SMP texts had been published and hence were freely available to critics, in his address to the AGM of the Institute of Mathematics and its Applications. It was revised and published in the Bulletin of the IMA under the title 'On the enfeeblement of mathematical skills by "modern maths" and by similar soft intellectual trash in schools and universities'.[84] In this he directly attacked the modern algebraists:

> My reason for including schools [in my title] is my impression that some school teachers accept modern mathematics for the schools, not for any inherent merits which they themselves perceive in it, but because they have been led to understand that it is highly regarded by university mathematicians who (so the argument runs) ought to know best. I wish to counter this line of thought by stating quite categorically that not all university mathematicians approve of modern mathematics and that, even if they did, they are in no special position to know best what is suitable for schools. Certainly an influential subsection of

university mathematicians do support modern mathematics; but this subsection consists mainly of pure mathematicians with little direct personal experience of using mathematics for practical ends. There is no reason to suppose them especially qualified to pronounce on school syllabuses or to discern which types of mathematical skill are most important for industry, or engineering, or scientific research, or for the more general needs of society as a whole.[85]

He then criticized the 'jargon and verbiage' in 'modern syllabuses', especially rife, he argued, in their treatment of set theory, the number system, abstract algebra and vector spaces. Of the latter topics, he wrote:

In moderation this is acceptable; for instance, an early introduction to the use of matrices is fine. But it can very easily be overdone, especially if the emphasis is on algebraic structure rather than on manipulation and applications.[86]

SMP, because it had had 'most prominence and success', and the OECD's *Synopses* received particular attack. The critique was legitimated in terms of the 'extrinsic' criterion of utility[87] that had operated as an organizing principle during the series of conferences begun at Oxford:

I should like to venture one or two remarks about hard and soft mathematics, because my central theme lies very much in that distinction. As I see it, the distinction between hard and soft is not that between difficult and easy, despite any positive correlation; instead it resides in a commitment to achieve prescribed goals, to solve a stated problem, and not to be diverted by the attractions of incidental generalities or circumambient atmosphere. Hard mathematics typically involves the focusing of interest and the marshalling of resources for a solution; soft mathematics the contemplation, the rearrangement, and the reinterpretation of the general panorama of what is already solved. There is a tendency for pure mathematics to be soft and applied mathematics hard ...[88]

He went on to describe himself as 'unexcited' by the subject matter of Smithie's article 'What is modern mathematics?' (which had appeared in the special issue of the *Mathematical Gazette* in 1963 already referred to[89]), however lucidly it had been presented:

> We must accept that what Dr. Smithie describes is indeed the
> language and mode of thought of a considerable body of
> accomplished contemporary pure mathematicians. This fact we
> can not escape. We can not deny the existence of scholars of
> Anglo-Saxon and Old High German, or dispute their right to
> study their subjects to the limit of their fibre. On the other hand,
> we may reasonably enquire to what extent the man-in-the-
> street, whose wont and pleasure it is to read Shakespeare, needs
> to be first conversant with medieval literature.[90]

He added direct attacks on the achievements of some supporters of
'modern mathematics':

> Bernard Shaw said that those who can, do; those who can't,
> teach. In mathematics, those who can't, expound; and what they
> expound is usually soft mathematics.[91]

And:

> A section of the mathematical community is just plugged into
> the sounds of the Bourbaki bandwagon ... If you check up on
> the mathematical qualifications of those who have been active in
> preaching modern mathematics to school teachers ... to see
> what they have published, you will discover that (with only a
> few interesting exceptions) they have published little, or more
> usually nothing. Those who can't, expound.[92]

Hammersley's attack on SMP, which echoed many points made in a
similar piece by Kline on developments in the USA, was to be the first
of several from applied mathematicians and scientists.[93]

Thus far I have concentrated on the reactions of those located
within university mathematics to some aspects of proposals which
would affect the subject socialization of their students. The reactions of
others, however, similarly illustrate the extent to which SMP, both as a
compromise between competing sub-disciplinary demands and as a
project located in the public schools, was to be basically an unstable
compromise, and hence always likely to be attacked from a variety of
directions. The comments of the ATAM activist, Birtwistle, have
already been described. In 1969, foreshadowing later attacks, Lyness,
an HMI since 1946, who had been present at both Oxford and
Liverpool (though not Southampton), legitimated a critique of 'modern'
syllabuses in *Trends* by reference to the problems 'ordinary' teachers
had experienced:

> Too many innovations for the ordinary teacher have been

introduced and he has been expected to change content at too great a pace. It is better to teach well what one knows and has found to be of value, than to fall a victim to 'modernisation' and teach badly what is unfamiliar and of doubtful value.[94]

As will be shown below, such criticism of SMP was to come from within the schools, both from those to whom 'modern maths' represented an occupational threat, and from those ideationally opposed to both 'modern maths' and the general educational perspectives of some of its supporters. To some extent, like the criticism of 'modern maths' from within industry in the early 1970s, which I shall also briefly describe below, this gradual shift towards other sources of criticism of SMP was a reflection of the project's move in the late 1960s, in the context of increasing comprehensive reform, from a concern solely with selective school mathematics to one with the mathematics of the majority of children of secondary school age. According to interviewed members of the group, they were following demand from the schools in moving in this direction. Thwaites, for example, gave this account of the origins of the A-H CSE series:

> Our initial objective was to rewrite just the 'O' and 'A' levels. But 1–5 (the 'O' level series) were being used for sub-'O' level ability pupils. This was a bad thing — perhaps positively harmful — since they were not written for such less able pupils. We had to decide whether to put this right, and decided to try to cope with the demand for SMP from lower down. Then A-H were used right across the board! Therefore, the 7–13 developments were decided on, to cover the whole ability range.[95]

Howson agreed:

> People were already using Books 1–5 lower down. They needed stopping; the books weren't right for this ability range. We were following consumer demand.[96]

As a result of these 'demands', presumably partly a reflection of the moves by some heads and teachers to develop a more common curriculum in the comprehensives and partly of the tendency for lower status actors to imitate higher status actors described by Bell,[97] a committee was formed and the CSE series, basically a rewrite of the 'O' level books by teachers experienced with 'less able' children, was begun in 1967.[98] This new series soon began to be used in comprehensive schools across the country.[99] Subsequently, as 'modern maths' became increasingly salient in the secondary school curriculum for publicly examined pupils after 1970, various extra-school interest groups, dissatisfied with the mathematical and behavioural 'skills' of school leavers, began to attack the newer curricula.

In February 1974, for example, the TES reported a number of such criticisms.[100] These came from the Engineering Industry Training Board, the Shipbuilding ITB, the Air Transport ITB, Huddersfield Technical College, and the Director of Education at the CBI. All concentrated on the 'inadequate' skills, as they saw them, of potential apprentices. Longbottom, of the SITB, for example, argued:

> We have a constant complaint from our craft training managers that we need the old maths for drawing plans, and for develop-ment work.[101]

This particular reaction to the spread of 'modern maths' might have been predicted from the remarks of Langdale at the Liverpool Confer-ence on the mathematical needs of craft employees, described in chapter 6.[102] Simultaneously, scientists were beginning to critically examine mathematical training in schools.[103]

It is no purpose of my study to attempt any 'objective' comment on the validity of some of these implied causal claims. Whether SMP or other projects were producing less well-prepared apprentices than 'traditional' courses, whether the 'quality' of apprentices had fallen, whether employers were merely continuing their normal practice of criticizing educational processes and products,[104] or whether political and media personnel were searching for scapegoats to account for the increasing economic 'crisis', it is probably, anyway, almost impossible to determine. What is clear, however, is that, as a result of the various projects' materials having moved 'downwards', so that some 'average' and 'less able' pupils were studying partially redefined school mathema-tics, various interest groups began to blame 'modern maths' for a variety of perceived ills. Such reactions put SMP, and reformers in general, under considerable pressure, weakening the plausibility of their per-spectives in various arenas and, since SMP was now primarily depen-dent on income from sales of texts, must have posed a potential threat to its ultimate survival as an independent organization.

As I have already mentioned, these moves 'downwards' also gave rise to another source of dissatisfaction — within the schools. This resulted from the perspectival clash between older teachers in the comprehensives, often previously experienced in secondary modern teaching, and often supporting elements of the arithmetic-based tradi-tion described in chapter 3, and the proponents, often younger, of SMP. I shall illustrate this by reference to the comments of three teachers in a boys' comprehensive using SMP materials, in which I carried out one of my case studies in 1977. All three had previously taught in the secondary modern which had recently been merged into the new school.

The first, a fifty-seven year old general subjects teacher who had begun to specialize in mathematics teaching a dozen years earlier, was convinced both that curricula should be differentiated (as they were in this school) and that SMP was unsuitable for many children:

> It all depends on ability levels. With the average pupil and downwards, maths is all about getting a job ... I avoid the modern sort of rubbish. I prefer traditional maths as it has been in syllabuses up till now. CSE is far too wide. Most of the modern topics should go. There aren't a lot of applications for reflections, or whatever they call them now ... Modern maths is an attempt to teach maths to kids who shouldn't be doing maths anyway. It's too time-consuming ... Arithmetic is enough for those with IQs of less than one hundred, and the more formal the better.[105]

The second, about sixty years of age, and emergency-trained, shared a similar perspective:

> I'm not favourably impressed by the SMP books. They're too wordy. There's too much reading, and not enough exercises ... It's all unrelated to real life. We should talk about things like car cylinders. SMP is only suitable for brighter children. Women tend to go for it ... as it's soft.[106]

The third, whose comments may have been coloured by his having lost his head of department's post in the reorganization to a much younger man who had introduced SMP, was no less clear in his view. Again an emergency-trained, ex-secondary modern teacher, he operated within psychometric assumptions and favoured extrinsic criteria of utility:

> Half a person's life is spent calculating. It's an everyday activity. This is surely the main reason for maths for most children — not those in the grammar stream though. But even of those only a few will go on to do maths. Most will just need calculating. Most kids now can't use maths after school, especially with the modern syllabuses. Modern maths is not very relevant, except perhaps for the top grammar school pupils. Sets we used to call factors. It's all just name-changing except for matrices and

graphs. The kids usually ask me what's the point of it? For them there is no point.[107]

And, on SMP:

'I've no time for the SMP books at all. A crowd of people got on the bandwagon. A fiddle ... SMP doesn't have enough examples for ordinary kids ... Practical work, like with dice, is really science ... The average kid isn't interested in mathematical principles.[108]

In these remarks, we see the perspectives of the post-war secondary modern subculture being applied in a critique of SMP. The stress on differentiating the curriculum — common to both selective and non-selective teachers' subcultures in that period — was, however, shared by the thirty year old head of department, a graduate with experience in both secondary modern and grammar schools. (Curriculum differentiation, coupled with careful timetabling, actually enabled members of the department to teach more or less the content they preferred.) He argued that his 'aims' were as follows:

Well, for the top thirty per cent, the same philosophy as the old grammar schools: appreciation of the subject for its own sake, elegance. We don't do totally modern but we can do as much as we want with the top groups. They're the sort of kids receptive to the philosophy behind the modern maths ... The middle forty per cent, the CSE candidates, the good to moderate: maths is a subject like any other for them ... They must be able to do the basics and know something of the rest. I develop a few things in depth, that's all they can take. We're preparing them for apprenticeships. I carefully select topics from modern maths. I wouldn't do matrix algebra with them. Nor topology — not for the average school leaver and technical apprentice ... Mostly we do pragmatic maths ... The bottom thirty per cent: my concern here is to give them a lot of optimism and enjoyment ... We must give them success, stuff they can get right ... They have a limited span of concentration ... Number work, money, metric units, some appreciation of what you can do with fractions and decimals ... Any modern topics are strictly for entertainment value only ... Optimism and confidence-boosting are critical, and accepting that their level of performance will be limited, even in arithmetic.[109]

The head of department in my other case study school (a girls' comprehensive), who was a fifty year old ex-grammar school teacher whose degree had been in chemistry with a mathematics subsidiary, shared these views. Although her department was in the middle of changing to SMP, she felt:

> I believe a lot of what is done is really a waste of time, trying to teach the less able a lot of what we teach them. They should know basic arithmetic to cope with everyday life, plus some maths — measuring, drawing — for physical coordination ... We use *World of Maths* for the less able, not SMP ... I believe all children should have some real maths, not just basic arithmetic. But with the less able, in the last two years, I should say you can forget algebra, trigonometry and geometry, and just do arithmetic topics that will help them when they leave school.[110]

Some elements of such teachers' criticisms of the 'modernisation' and extension of sub-'O' level syllabuses had received support at the level of debate within subject associations when, in 1975, Margaret Hayman, of Putney High School (GPDST), delivered her presidential address 'To each according to his needs' to the Mathematical Association.[111] She argued, at length, in the context of a growing debate about the effectiveness of comprehensive schools, for a return to a greater degree of curricular differentiation in mathematics. Before the War, she claimed, education and work had been well-related for most children:

> For the majority of children mathematics was interpreted rather narrowly as arithmetic but in this field they were competent, confident and could tackle the numerical work involved in their subsequent jobs. Many pupils went from school to apprenticeships of some kind, where the work they had done at school was seen to be relevant and an adequate base from which to develop technical skills ...[112]

But, after the War, Labour Party philosophy had encouraged the moves towards the comprehensive school, and:

> Unfortunately the doctrine of an equal opportunity for a suitable education became confused with an equal opportunity for the same education, and I think that it is here that we find the major cause of many of the educational problems of today ... Because a highly academic abstract education had been seen to

be economically profitable for a few, it was assumed that it was a desirable thing for everybody. And so the old grammar school course was taken over — learned more slowly, watered down, pepped-up with practical illustrations, subjected to new classroom techniques — but no one had the courage to ask if this was basically what the majority of children were capable of enjoying or would find satisfying either in their future work or for its own sake.[113]

She then related this to SMP:

In the early 1960s there was a feeling that a new approach to mathematics would be helpful and the School Mathematics Project in England, together with similar experiments in other countries, was started. This developed from a very academic base, among pupils where the previous system had been most, rather than least, successful. The writers produced some very interesting textbooks suitable for the top ten per cent of the ability range and, by replacing Euclidean geometry by motion geometry, removed one of the harder, but in some ways most rewarding, parts of the traditonal syllabuses. This of course did nothing towards solving the real problem. To quote again from the bulletin of the CBI: 'Many arguments have been put forward to explain this lowering of standards, and the one that is most often heard is that mathematics teaching in schools, particularly in modern mathematics courses as taught at present, does not include enough arithmetic to give young people the necessary grounding in basic computerized skills upon which industry heavily relies'. I think this is fair criticism in so far as many modern syllabuses stress ideas rather than techniques. Much later SMP started to modify its courses for less able pupils, but they remain essentially academic. They are pursuing the myth that if you speak a foreign language sufficiently slowly you will be understood; that the difficulties in the subject are due to the speed at which it is taught, rather than the nature of the mathematical concepts involved.[114]

SMP and other new curricula had not tackled 'basic problems':

Understanding number bonds is very important if you can do it, but learning tables by rote gives a feeling of security to the many pupils for whom the formal concepts are too abstract and provides a firmer foundation for future work.[115]

She partially legitimated her arguments by referring to research (by Brown) on children's ability to 'abstract', arguing that this showed that many children were 'incapable of understanding the mathematical principles involved once these are divorced from practical situations from which they arose'.[116] Furthermore, if such pupils were forced to study 'abstract' mathematics, then indiscipline — 'anti-social behaviour' resulting from 'mathematical frustration' — would follow.[117] Mixed-ability teaching was similarly attacked: 'in a class of thirty there may only be one really mathematical child'.[118] In conclusion, after more references to employers' views, she recommended a well-differentiated mathematics curriculum for the comprehensives:

> The satisfaction of achievement and the intrinsic beauty of mathematical relationships is sufficient justification for the course for more able pupils. For the rest of secondary school pupils we need a new and different approach, but not the same for all. The next twenty per cent of the ability range have some capacity for abstraction, and a course similar to some of the present CSE courses with an emphasis on the practical rather than the abstract mathematics would be suitable. Again, much more practice of basic arithmetic and some simple algebra would add to the pupils' confidence and their capacity to cope with work after school ... For the rest of the secondary school pupils I think we must differentiate between the first three years, when the subject can be taught in the context of the classroom, and the other two years when I think there must be a much closer integration between the school and the outside world.[119]

And:

> To summarize, I think that much of the disorder in schools is because children are being asked to do work in all subjects, but particularly in mathematics, which is beyond their inherent capabilities, and this will continue until we recognize that different children need basically different courses. Even the leaders of SMP admit that they have moved too far away from manipulative skills ... We must stop trying to teach abstract mathematics to all pupils, and concentrate on mathematics for some pupils and competence in arithmetic as a first priority for the majority.[120]

Ironically, SMP, as a group, had developed their early materials in the terms of these psychometric, and differentiation-legitimating, assumptions. Thwaites himself sees mixed-ability teaching as a 'waste of resources'.[121] Their activities in the 1960s, although they may have resulted in an eventual broadening of CSE mathematics courses,[122] had not represented a basic challenge to dominant assumptions in this area of educational thinking.

Under the combined onslaught of extra-school and intra-school criticism, and in the context of a competitive market place for school textbooks, Thwaites and the SMP team began to partially redefine their redefinition of school mathematics in the early to mid-1970s. Howson, in interview, argued that they had gradually come to realize the need for 'practice':

> We didn't originally realize the need for practice, after the concept had been understood, to get the understanding to be second nature.[123]

And, although Thwaites attempted to answer many of the criticisms publicly,[124] SMP had responded to the developing wave of criticism (i.e., the change in the plausibility of 'modern maths') by producing a booklet, *Manipulative Skills in School Mathematics* (1974), which included the following comment:

> Looking back, therefore, we can see that the early SMP books — especially the two 'O' level series . . . were short of revision and drill exercises.[125]

Supplements would, therefore, they announced, be produced which would contain extra examples for practice and revision.[126]

In this context, for the sake of completeness, some very brief comments on the degree of pedagogic change which seems to have resulted from the diffusion of SMP and other projects' materials throughout the state system should perhaps be made. I have previously reported findings on pedagogic strategies and emphases in mathematics and science lessons in a mixed comprehensive school where SMP texts were being used.[127] In this school the stress was very much on teaching children in all bands standardized solutions to standardized problems through repetitive practice, with little attention being paid to 'structure'. Although I have no space to present comparable accounts of pedagogy for the two case study comprehensive mathematics departments, they would be similar to that presented for the mixed school. The comments of the two heads of department on 'practical' work might, however, be taken as illustrative of the extent to which those reformers interested in promoting pedagogic reform have, through SMP, MME and other projects not dicussed here, achieved this aspect of their missions. First, the head of department in the boys' school:

[Practical work] is important to a limited extent. For example, drawing and measuring triangles before trigonometry, and dice in probability. But they will have done a good bit in middle schools with the extra year. I do some models, but I don't automatically do practical work with a new topic.[128]

And, the head of mathematics in the girls' school:

Practical work must be done at home. There isn't time here, and with more difficult classes it's much easier. It's very time-consuming, and I like results to be available for working on. I'm very traditional on teaching methods. I like children to be moving together.[129]

It can at least be hypothesized from such comments, taken together with the results of my earlier study, that, in the majority of schools, the major consequences of the activities of the 1960s reformers, whose perspectives often involved a partial critique of 'transmission' pedagogies, have been changes in content.[130] The findings of the recent HMI survey of secondary education certainly lend some support to this view, especially for the case of examination classes. They report on 'practical' work, for example:

The use of realistic source material such as timetables, catalogues, newspapers, magazines, plans, maps, or instructional manuals was very limited. Material of this kind, and an experimental or practical approach to some of the topics in the course, were found in some ten per cent of GCE courses, in twenty to twenty-four per cent of CSE courses and in some thirty to forty per cent of non-examination courses.[131]

And, more generally, on pedagogy:

The work was predominantly teacher controlled: teachers explained, illustrated, demonstrated, and perhaps gave notes on procedures and examples. The pupils were led deductively through small steps and closed questions to the principle being considered. A common pattern, particularly with low ability pupils, was to show a few examples on the board at the start of the lesson and then set similar exercises for the pupils to work on their own. There were few questions encouraging wider speculation or independent initiative.[132]

On the other hand, some idea of the projects' success in changing content can be gained from other findings of the same survey, reproduced in Table 39.[133] These findings also give some indication of the extent to which the mathematics curriculum, after both its own reform and comprehensive reform, remained differentiated by 'ability'. Some change clearly had occurred in this respect, however, especially for CSE pupils.

Since these results were published the Report of the Cockcroft Committee on mathematics education, set up after the second post-war 'crisis' of confidence in mathematics education described earlier, has also become available.[134] In this document, views of the sort expressed by Hayman are dominant and it is argued that a more differentiated mathematics curriculum should be established in secondary schools.[135] This is legitimated in terms similar to those described in chapter 3 of this study, although the concept of 'attainment' tends to have replaced that of 'ability'.[136] In particular, a 'foundation list' of topics is set out which should form 'by far the greatest part' of the syllabus for the 'lowest forty per cent of the range of attainment in mathematics'.[137] Except that logarithms are replaced by the use of electronic calculators, the list is remarkably similar to that set out for the senior elementary school in the 1930s, described here in chapter 3. Furthermore, as then, the approach is to be 'practical' and 'relevant' for these pupils. It appears, therefore, that curricular differentiation by category membership is destined to survive the period of reform in mathematics. (I have discussed this issue at greater length elsewhere.[138])

Table 39:   Type of course and examination target of pupils in years four and five in full-range comprehensive schools

Course Type	Percentage of schools: course objective		
	GCE 'O' Level	CSE	Non-exam
Modern only	32	22	7
Compromise only	27	36	31
Traditional only	32	27	53
Modern + compromise	2	4	2
Modern + traditional	3	6	1
Compromise + traditional	4	6	5
Total*	100	100	100

*   The entries are rounded to whole numbers in the table.

Conclusion

I have shown that both SMP and MME produced proposals for the redefinition of school mathematics that were clearly orientated to the demands of various powerful, i.e., resource-controlling, extra-school groups. Hence, they might both have expected to receive considerable support from such sources. In fact, initially, SMP received major, and MME only minor, financial backing. Accounts of SMP's 'success' from within the subject have tended to underplay this difference, stressing instead individual and organizational factors. Rogerson, for example, associated with SMP in the early 1970s, argues, in his brief account of SMP's career, that:

> The fact that no other project has achieved anything like the present SMP adoption in schools is because they lacked the combination of strong leadership, extensive cooperative effort and administrative flair shown by SMP.[139]

Flemming, in his similarly brief account, stresses the 'outstandingly able ... management of its affairs'.[140] But, notwithstanding the obvious ability and energy of Thwaites and his collaborators (though also noting that Hope and Collins were among those who had successfully built a rival association to the Mathematical Association), these accounts seem to ignore the major locational and other differences between SMP and what was probably, in 1961 and 1962, its major competitor for resources.[141] In the first part of this chapter I have described some of these differences, and have suggested that SMP's 'success' relative to such projects as MME must be understood, at least partially, in terms of the differential availability of such resources as status, academic legitimacy and finance, and not merely in terms of such factors as 'flair', something SMP members themselves seem to have well understood.

In the second section, I have tried to show that the model outlined in chapter 2, in which curricular proposals and textbooks to be used in the selective sector are seen as the object of conflict between groups with various interests in the socialization of pupils, taken together with elements of the analysis of mathematical educational subcultures presented in chapter 3, can be used in making sense of the critical reactions to SMP which occurred after the late 1960s. The very success of SMP, in ensuring its diffusion 'downwards', brought a curricular selection originally developed within the prestigious independent sector of the selective subculture, and only modified by teacher-writers experienced with 'less able' children, into contact with many teachers whose subject and pedagogical perspectives derived from within the non-selective subculture in which criteria for selecting mathematical content differed considerably. This, together with the dissatisfaction of members of various university disciplines and sub-disciplines ensured that SMP would be continuously subject to criticism. I have drawn on various sources and two case studies to illustrate this.

Furthermore, since SMP then depended on income from sales, some of this criticism could be expected to be heeded. The example of the supplementary booklets was mentioned but, if space allowed, other developments in SMP's work could probably also be related to changes in the market demand for various educational products.

The case study data from interviews, taken together with observational evidence on SMP reported elsewhere, suggested that SMP's materials, when used in comprehensive schools, might often be used within a well-differentiated curricular framework and that, pedagogically, there may have been little change in secondary mathematics education since the 1950s. This suggestion was supported by reference to the recent HMI survey of secondary education. Finally, the main thrust of the Cockcroft Report — for increased curricular differentiation — was also briefly discussed.

Notes

1 See GRIFFITH and MULLINS (1972).
2 *Ibid.*, p. 959.
3 *Ibid.*, p. 960.
4 *Ibid.*, p. 962.
5 See THWAITES (1972), pp. 225–8.
6 *Ibid.*, p. ix.
7 See chapter 9 above.
8 CUNDY and ROLLETT (1961).
9 Interview (7 March 1977).
10 THWAITES (1972), p. ix.
11 Interview (7 March 1977).
12 *Ibid.*
13 Interview (26 March 1976).
14 *Ibid.*
15 FLETCHER (Ed.) (1964).
16 Interview (26 March 1976).
17 See THWAITES (1972), pp. 16–20.
18 *Ibid.*, pp. 20–34, pp. 64–8, pp. 80–8.
19 *Ibid.*
20 *Ibid.*
21 See, for example, the references to 'experiments with coins, dice, beads in a box, etc.' under this heading in THWAITES (1972), p. 26.

22 *Ibid.*, pp. 203–6.
23 My source here is the Midlands Mathematical Experiment (1964).
24 *Ibid.*, p. 5.
25 See, for example, Collins (1958).
26 Midlands Mathematical Experiment (1964), p. 9.
27 *Ibid.*, pp. 9–11.
28 *Ibid.*, p. 11.
29 *Ibid.*, p. 12.
30 *Ibid.*, p. 18.
31 *Ibid.*, p. 18.
32 *Ibid.*, p. 21.
33 *Ibid.*, pp. 21–3.
34 See Midlands Mathematical Experiment (1963).
35 MME (1964), p. 11.
36 Birtwistle (1962), p. 3.
37 Thwaites (1972), p. 12.
38 *Ibid.*, p. 12.
39 *Ibid.*, p. 50.
40 See chapter 8 above.
41 Interview (26 March 1976).
42 *Ibid.*
43 Interview (18 January 1977).
44 Thwaites (1972), pp. 214–5, and interview with Howson (26 March 1976).
45 For the early grant see MME (1964), p. 43. This was for £2,500. For the School Council's grant, see Schools Council (1971), pp. 46–7.
46 Interviews with R.A. Becher (18 January 1977) and R. Morris (16 December 1976).
47 Interview (26 March 1976).
48 Thwaites (1972), pp. 8–9 and passim.
49 MME (1967), p. 11.
50 *Ibid.*, p. 11.
51 Thwaites (1972), passim.
52 *Ibid.*, p. 13.
53 See the *Mathematical Gazette* (1963), Vol. 47, pp. 328–33.
54 See the *Mathematical Gazette* (1963), Vol. 47, pp. 322–7.
55 *The Times* (1 October 1962).
56 *The Times* (20 February 1963).
57 *Ibid.*
58 Thwaites (1972), p. 51.
59 MME (1967), p. 298.
60 Bell (1971).
61 Compiled from Thwaites (1972) and MME (1967).
62 See Thwaites (1972), pp. 164–5, on the conversion of SMP to a charitable trust in 1967.
63 Griffith and Mullins (1972), p. 960.
64 See Thwaites (1972), p. 5. This group included Maxwell, President of the Mathematical Association in 1961, and H. Bondi.
65 *Ibid.*, p. 51.

66 See the *Mathematical Gazette* (1963), Vol. 47, pp. 130–1.
67 See THWAITES (1972), pp. 239–44. The reprinting of the report as an appendix to this book is perhaps itself significant in this respect.
68 *Ibid.*, pp. 71–2 and pp. 53–64.
69 *Ibid.*, p. 64.
70 See DAVID (1963), p. 370.
71 Interview (7 March 1977).
72 MME (1964), p. 8.
73 See MATHEMATICAL ASSOCIATION (1968), p. 9.
74 THWAITES (1972), pp. 245–9.
75 *Ibid.*, pp. 225–8.
76 STEADMAN et al (1980), p. A74 and p. A69.
77 See chapter 2 above.
78 THWAITES (1972), pp. 53–64.
79 *Ibid.*, p. 57.
80 *Ibid.*, p. 59.
81 *Ibid.*, p. 59.
82 *Ibid.*, p. 58.
83 *Ibid.*, p. 58.
84 HAMMERSLEY (1968).
85 *Ibid.*, p. 66.
86 *Ibid.*, p. 67.
87 ESLAND (1971), p. 86.
88 HAMMERSLEY (1968), p. 70.
89 See the *Mathematical Gazette* (1963), Vol. 47, pp. 278–98.
90 HAMMERSLEY (1968), p. 70.
91 *Ibid.*, p. 70.
92 *Ibid.*, p. 77.
93 See KLINE (1966) and BURLEY (1975), for example.
94 LYNESS (1969), p. 8.
95 Interview (7 March 1977).
96 Interview (26 March 1976).
97 BELL (1971).
98 THWAITES (1972), p. 121, and interview with K. Lewis, one of the team (10 December 1976).
99 Four of the proposed CSE series (of eight) were published by the time the SMP report for 1968/69 was written. See THWAITES (1972), p. 205. According to Lewis (see footnote 98), it was because of their immediate popularity that an extension of the series to 'O' level standard was eventually conceived (interview: 10 December 1976).
100 *The Times Educational Supplement* (1 February 1974) p. 3.
101 *Ibid.*
102 See chapter 6 above.
103 See, for example, 'Mathematics and school chemistry', an interim report from a study group set up by the British Committee on Chemical Education in 1973. This appeared in *Education in Science* in January 1974.
104 See, for example, REEDER (1979).
105 Interview (4 July 1977).

106 Interview (4 July 1977).
107 Interview (5 July 1977).
108 *Ibid.*
109 Interview (14 July 1977).
110 Interview (27 September 1977).
111 HAYMAN (1975).
112 *Ibid.*, p. 138.
113 *Ibid.*, p. 138.
114 *Ibid.*, p. 139.
115 *Ibid.*, p. 140.
116 *Ibid.*, p. 142.
117 *Ibid.*, p. 143.
118 *Ibid.*, p. 144.
119 *Ibid.*, pp. 147–8.
120 *Ibid.*, p. 153.
121 Interview (7 March 1977).
122 See, for example, COCKCROFT (1982) and DEPARTMENT OF EDUCATION and SCIENCE (1980), pp. 20–4.
123 Interview (26 March 1976).
124 See THWAITES (1975) and (1969).
125 SMP (1974), p. 10.
126 *Ibid.*, p. 15.
127 See COOPER (1976), pp. 22–36.
128 Interview (14 July 1977).
129 Interview (27 September 1977).
130 On 'transmission', see BARNES and SHEMILT (1974).
131 DES (1979), p. 132.
132 *Ibid.*, p. 136.
133 *Ibid.*, p. 125, for the table on which Table 39 is based.
134 COCKCROFT (1982).
135 *Ibid.*, chapter nine.
136 *Ibid.*, p. 130 for example.
137 *Ibid.*, p. 134.
138 See COOPER (1985).
139 ROGERSON (1975), p. 10.
140 FLEMMING (1980), p. 29.
141 The other major potential competitor at this time was the Contemporary School Mathematics (or St. Dunstan's) project, initiated by G. Mathews (whom Thwaites had apparently tried to involve in SMP: see MATHEMA-TICAL ASSOCIATION (1968), p. 1). This project had the advantages, like SMP, of being based in the independent sector and of having been initiated early in the period of competition for resources, but it had the disadvantage of originally having been based in one school. It apparently received no initial financial support (see MATHEMATICAL ASSOCIATION (1968), p. 2). Another potential competitor, the Mathematics in Education and Industry project, had the advantages of an independent school setting (Highgate) and a commitment to taking industrial 'needs' seriously, but the disadvantage of a 1962, as opposed to a 1961, date of initiation. This

project did, however, receive some financial help from BP (see MATHEMA-
TICAL ASSOCIATION (1968), p. 6). Unfortunately, a lack of space has
prevented me from incorporating these (and later projects) in my analysis.
Clearly, attention to the careers of these projects might well lead to
modifications of my current analysis.

11   Conclusion

Bernbaum, in his review of the sociology of education in general, and of Young's work in particular, in which he argues that assertions about the nature of knowledge should be separated from observations about how people use knowledge, concluded:

> None of this means abandoning the sociology of knowledge . . . Instead it should enable the sociologist to concentrate on studies of the way in which knowledge is produced, distributed and legitimated . . . It should encourage a concern for the ways in which such processes are interpenetrated by social phenomena. Thus it should be possible to develop a real sociology of the curriculum which would enable us to improve our understanding of the distribution of knowledge along with the relationship between the knowledge of subjects which teachers choose to employ and that which other practitioners of a subject might have. Such an approach would manifestly call for a significant sociology of examinations and assessment. We might come to an understanding of how, over time, subjects have been institutionalised in various types of schools, the processes by which, within subjects, certain knowledge is defined as 'important', and the consequences of those definitions for 'teacher' and 'taught'. The whole perspective would give an historical dimension to the sociology of education which it currently lacks.[1]

It is with some of these issues, especially those of the legitimation and redefinition of subject knowledge for schools, that this study has been concerned.

In the conclusion I shall not attempt to precis the preceding chapters. Their account of how one definition of school mathematics was partially de-legitimated, another made (temporarily) legitimate in some arenas and eventually implemented in materials, has already been summarized in the conclusions to earlier chapters. It was shown that the new definition embraced — as the displaced definition once had — the contemporary paradigms of university pure and applied mathematics, themselves taken-for-granted rather than explained in this study. The ways in which the achievement of this redefinition of selective school mathematics depended on the actions of various individuals and groups, working with various resources and missions, in a context offering both constraints and opportunities, have already been discussed in some detail. Here, therefore, rather than merely rework that material, I wish to use my limited space to discuss a number of theoretical and substantive issues in the light of the earlier material. These are, in the order in which I shall deal with them: structure and action in the explanation of curriculum change, the nature of the subject, the process of redefinition, the nature of the redefinition and, lastly, the control of redefinition.

Structure and Action

Many recent writers, both of empirically-based studies in the sociology of education and of more general theoretical work in sociology, have stressed the explanatory inadequacy of any approach which ignores either pole of the couple: structure and action. Bernstein, for example, in his review of the sociology of education, criticized the tendency of writers in this field to overemphasize either structure or action at the expense of their necessary relationship, and argued:

> It is a matter of some importance that we develop forms of analysis that can provide a dynamic relationship between 'situated activities of negotiated meanings' and the 'structural' relationships which the former presuppose. Indeed it is precisely what is taken as given in social action approaches which allows the analysis to proceed in the first place. Neither can the relationships between structural and interactional aspects be created by metasociological arguments as in the case of Berger ... The levels, if they are to be usefully linked, must be linked at the substantive level by an explanation whose conceptual structure directs empirical exploration of the relationships between the levels.[2]

Young argued a similar case, in 1972, in criticizing functionalist models of educational change. Any alternative must, he claimed:

incorporate the way those involved in 'education' give meaning to their activities and to the curricular material that they construct or that is made available. These meanings will vary with the context ... However, this is not enough; classrooms, staff meetings, union conferences and [Schools] Council committees as contexts of interaction, all in part take their meaning from the wider social and economic structure. How these 'levels' and 'contexts' of explanation are linked is a central question to any sociological enquiry and can only be guessed at prior to research. Suggestions about these links are more likely to arise out of research into particular problems with both 'levels' in mind.[3]

I suggested in chapter 2 that, in fact, neither Young nor Bernstein had followed their own suggestions. In particular, I claimed that neither had paid adequate attention to the complexity of the actual processes leading to stability and change, or to the details of social structure — as a context of relationships and resources — within which such processes occur. I argued that Archer, in her *Social Origins of Educational Systems* and elsewhere, has presented a conceptualization of processes of change which has the advantage, for my purposes, of being particularly concerned with educational issues.[4] Her conceptualization of the 'structural conditioning of educational interaction', her analytic cycles of structural conditioning, social interaction and structural elaboration leading to a new structural conditioning of interaction, usefully direct the sociologist to a concern with both structure and action.[5] I have also argued that her stress on understanding power in terms of the resources available to actors, especially if these are seen as partly a function of those actors' locations in some structure, allows a successful articulation of structure and action in the theorizing of change.

Following this approach I began, in my study, by outlining some aspects of the nature of school mathematics in the 1950s, treating the subject as a set of subject and pedagogical perspectives, contexts and relationships, i.e., examining the distribution of resources, the relationships and definitions of 'mathematics' constituting the subject at this time. I also paid some attention to relationships with other arenas of mathematical practice: the universities (chapter 3) and 'industry' (chapters 5 and 6). This account focused on the differentially prestigious subject subcultures, with their respective definitions of 'mathematics', existing within the secondary sector, their origins in what Lawton has termed the public school and elementary traditions, the unequal distribution of valued resources to their members, the discontinuity between selective school 'mathematics' and some varieties of university 'mathematics', the discontinuity between the subject perspectives of many mathematicians in educational institutions and some 'users' of 'mathematics' in industrial and commercial contexts, and the increasing extra-subject concern with scientific manpower in general and the supply of mathematicians in particular at this time. These features of the subject and its social context might best be seen as having represented possible constraints and opportunities for subject members with particular missions (themselves deriving from definitions of subject and interest located in various settings).

Drawing on this somewhat static account, presented mainly in chapter 3, and linking it with the more dynamic analyses of professional conflict provided by Bucher and Strauss and of subjects provided by Kuhn and others, I could then make some sense of various aspects of the redefinition of school mathematics. These included: the sources of the definition of change, rooted in the discontinuities described; the relative success of some subject members in publicizing their missions, rooted in their being able to articulate their missions with the concerns of extra-subject resource-holders; the disputes within the ATAM, rooted in the disputants' different locations and occupational interests; the eventual success of SMP, rooted in the initial resources available to this group; and the nature of the eventual reactions to SMP, grounded to some extent in the distinctive missions and perceived interests of those reacting.

In summary, I believe the usefulness of attempting to articulate issues of structure and process in terms of a resource-based concept of power has been demonstrated by the ability of such an approach to provide plausible accounts of a variety of features of the social process of subject redefinition. I shall now consider other issues in similar terms.

The Subject

In this section I shall briefly comment on the nature of the academic subject in the light of this study. I shall relate my comments to issues raised in chapter 2 and above. In particular, I shall consider both vertical and horizontal differentiation within the subject, and the relationship of this to potential conflicts between subject members.

This study clearly shows that any equation of the subject, in the case of university mathematics, with a single paradigm is not empirically justifiable. As Goodson has shown for geography, Lacey and Ball for English, and many for sociology, a subject consists, ideationally, of a multiplicity of paradigms or, relationally, of sets of competing actors who, while claiming allegiance to a common label, actually work within substantially differing sets of cognitive and technical norms.[6] This conclusion clearly lends support to my earlier criticism, made in the light of work in the sociology of science, of Bernstein and Young's somewhat monolithic conceptualizations of the subject. It also suggests that Kuhn's comments on the role of the textbook in academic life need some reconsideration, and that a more adequate view of the nature of such socializing devices must include attention to possible conflicts of paradigm both within and between them. In particular, the texts produced by both SMP and MME are more adequately seen as compromises, embracing the various paradigms of both pure and applied mathematics as well as elements of 'traditional' school mathematics, than as representing any single new logically coherent paradigm. This view of texts as compromises or, more accurately, since conditions and alliances change, as unstable compromises, allows the sociologist to make sense of the reactions of various actors to them in terms of practitioners' and users' continuing attempts to promote their particular definition of the subject.

A similar vertical differentiation of perspectives was shown to exist within the school subject subcultures. This related, however, not so much to disputes as to the nature of mathematics but, perhaps reflecting teachers' primary concern with the transmission of knowledge, more to disputes over pedagogy. This was illustrated by the dispute within the ATAM between selective school teachers over the role of practical work in mathematics. In the light of such disputes at school and university level, it can be seen that Esland's approach is clearly better able to capture the realities of school subjects than that of Bernstein.

In respect of school mathematics, however, it was horizontal rather than vertical differentiation which seemed the central stratifying feature. Two major subcultures were shown to exist within secondary school mathematics in the 1950s. These involved different versions of 'mathematics' or, more accurately perhaps, drew different selections of content from the corpus 'mathematics'. That of the selective school, of higher prestige, looked forward to the further study of mathematics and science, while that located in the secondary modern sector looked to the workplace and the home for the legitimation of its selection (and was, therefore, further differentiated by sex for many pupils). The first subculture, if we accept Young's (1971) listing of criteria for status, was of higher prestige because of its individualism, abstractness and unre-latedness to everyday life but, and Young himself hints at this, its prestige might with equal plausibility be understood, in a less idealist manner, in terms of the higher social origins and destinations of its pupils, and their immediate location in a sector of higher social status.[7] Those teaching the two versions of 'mathematics' were only broadly speaking, however, located respectively in the different sectors since, during the 1950s, more and more secondary modern pupils were entered for GCE examinations in mathematics. Since it was mainly teachers in the selective schools who were organized within the Mathematical Association, a rival association, the ATAM, was able to grow rapidly by drawing many of its members from such lower status locations. Within this new Association, differences of occupational interest between members from the different sectors motivated a certain amount of dispute over aims.

These vertical and horizontal differentiations within the subject can be seen to have structurally conditioned various aspects of the process of redefinition. The eventual domination of redefinition by university and public school teachers might, for example, be understood, not only in terms of SMP's greater access to resources than that of MME, but also, possibly, partly in terms of the original relative absence of lower status teachers from the conferences organized by Hammersley *et al*, an absence presumably conditioned by their relative irrelevance to the supply of graduate manpower as much as by their status itself. The disputes within the ATAM, referred to earlier, and those between it and the Mathematical Association, as well as those between modern alge-braists and applied mathematicians for control of redefinition provide other illustrations of this structural conditioning of action. Clearly, in the light of such evidence of intra-subject differentiation and conflict within mathematics, often thought of as a subject embodying a defini-tional consensus, it can be seen that any sociological analysis of subject redefinition will demand a theoretical model (for which Bucher and Strauss' model of intra-professional conflict provides one exemplar) capable of capturing processes of conflict. The over-integrated concep-tions of the subject worked with by such writers as Bernstein must, in the light of this study, be rejected on empirical grounds.

Before leaving this section, it might also be noted that Davies was correct to stress, in his programme for a sociology of educational knowledge, the international nature of academic communities and their politics.[8] In this study, the reality of this was clearly demonstrated by the influence of American and European mathematicians on events in England.

The Process of Redefinition

Structural conditioning should not, however, be seen as equivalent to structural determination. Social interaction is not merely some one-to-one reflection of social structural relations. While 'discontinuities', for example, may objectively exist irrespective of whether they are perceived by other members of a society, their effects have to be mediated by members' actions. 'Discontinuities' and 'crises', if resolved at all, are not resolved by the type of 'unconsciously evolved device' referred to by Davis and Moore, in their account of stratification,[9] but through social interaction. Having been identified as a problem by actors, their resolution typically involves their being successfully related to the concerns of the powerful in various arenas, the articulation of possible remedies and, lastly, the implementation of these against structurally conditioned resistance. In this particular case, it was shown how various academic and curriculum entrepreneurs, analogous to Becker's moral entrepreneurs, used their available resources to achieve this (often generating extra resources in the very process). The issue of 'teacher shortage' can be taken as an illustration. This had to be demonstrated to the satisfaction of media and political personnel before, in one sense, it could be said to exist. To achieve this, reference was made by subject members to acceptable criteria (the percentage of 'firsts', for example), while they also attempted to forge a link between the 'shortage' and other 'issues', such as the economic future of the nation. All this required considerable political work. While it was structured, i.e., made more likely and more possible, by such real events as the increasing employment of graduate mathematicians in industry, and the effects of this on teacher supply, this alone ensured no particular outcomes. The possibilities had to be taken up by subject members, motivated by a variety of concerns, as part of a general search for resources for their subject.

Similarly, the opportunity offered by the increasing political concern with potential shortages of scientific manpower had to be successfully mobilized in the interests of a subject whose members' perspectives (especially those of the modern algebraists) often seem to have emphasized not extrinsic, but intrinsic, criteria of utility. The capturing by the modern algebraists of the opportunity offered by the Royaumont meeting and the OECD reports on mathematics well illustrates how, in a sphere of social life where relative 'non-experts' supply resources to 'experts', organized groups can succeed in presenting their missions as being more in line with others' requirements than they might 'objectively' appear.

The bypassing of the Mathematical Association by SMP also illustrates the ways in which relatively powerful groups, i.e., groups with adequate resources available to them, can evade apparent structural constraints. In this case the Association representing university and selective school mathematicians from which, to a large extent, previous definitions of selective school mathematics had originated, did not, as might have been expected, dominate the initial attempts to resolve the 'problems' of the school/university transition. This relative lack of a coordinated response is probably explicable in terms of the variety of interests represented in the Association, including those of many who had built their careers in terms of earlier definitions. Thwaites and his co-actors did not, however, find it necessary to work mainly through the structures of the Association. They could succeed, nevertheless, because they were able to offer a potential redefinition, at a critical point in time, which various extra-school interests would support and because of their structurally conditioned status and academic legitimacy. Had their redefinition been a different one, or come much later, or had they been located in lower status institutions, the outcome may have been very different. A similar relation of action to structural conditioning can be seen in their successful diffusion of their materials. While their proselytizing activities demonstrate the important part played in the diffusion of some innovations by such work, their success was conditioned by both the academic and social status of those involved, by their structurally conditioned access to resources, and by the imitative attitude displayed by many teachers in the selective sector to university-based subject definitions, be it deferential or strategic in origin.

An adequate summary of the above might be to state that, while the redefinition was achieved by the actions of various individuals and groups, acting as a social movement, this occurred in conditions which both partially determined the nature of the redefinition and made success possible. While, for example, Griffith and Mullins seem to be correct, in the light of this study, to stress the important role played by 'organizational leaders' in successful academic innovation, they have, in fact, presented no evidence to show that their presence is a sufficient, rather than a necessary, element of such processes. Here, specifically, had 'industry' not wanted more mathematicians, had 'government' not been concerned about science, had various factors — including the school/university discontinuity — not affected the supply of mathematicians, a major redefinition of school mathematics might not have occurred. But, it must be stressed again, these changed conditions need not have led to any redefinition and certainly not to any particular one. That a particular redefinition did occur depended on subject members and others perceiving opportunities for the promotion of their missions (and potential threats to their interests) in these conditions. It is, therefore, in the interplay between conditions, representing constraints and opportunities, and actions that the explanation of any given redefinition must be sought. (The fate of SMP's proposal for a single subject 'A' level serves as an illustration of this.) Furthermore, as can be seen from the particular case studied here, once a redefinition has been implemented at classroom level, various of the conditions for action change as a direct result. Here, for example, the nature of any problems of the school/university transition began to change. Other changes may well be described as unintended consequences. Here, for example, the spreading of elements of 'modern maths' into lower status schools might be seen in this light. Actions, therefore, change the conditions for future action — the process referred to by Archer, in a broader sense, as structural elaboration.[10] Taken together with other extra-subject changes in conditions, such as changes in beliefs concerning the economic efficacy of education, such changes motivate or make worthwhile new actions and projects, thus leading eventually to yet more redefinition. Such processes are, of course, just one example of the general social process captured by Bhaskar's transformational model of social activity.[11]

The Nature of the Redefinition

Davies has pointed to the tendency for debates on curriculum change to become all-embracing:

> In practice ... innovations operate on three fronts: at the level of the syllabus, at the level of the teaching methods employed, and at the level of theories of the whole purpose of education. Why this is so is an important subject for research.[12]

In relation to the redefinition of school mathematics discussed here, where this was certainly the case, one answer might be given in terms of the variety of interests whose missions articulated in some way with the nature of mathematics education. Industrial employers were concerned with content, pedagogy and the 'attitude' of their future graduate employees, university mathematicians shared these concerns in respect of their students and potential successors, and teachers, at all levels, were likely to find their practice legitimated or otherwise by the outcomes of any process of redefinition once begun in earnest. It was probably this wide range of occupational interests that grounded the breadth of a debate in which content, pedagogy, psychology and ultimate purpose all featured.

In spite of this breadth, however, certain key assumptions common to the major educational and subject subcultures of the time remained largely unchallenged. Young has argued that most innovations of the 1960s took for granted the reality of the divisions of 'ability' institutionalized in such practices as streaming.[13] In the case of mathematics, in spite of the concern of many (especially in the ATAM) to promote a non-arithmetic-based version of mathematics for the 'less able', his comments certainly seem to have applied. SMP, for example, having developed proposals for one 'type' of pupil, explicitly modified them for another. Such a lack of challenge to basic assumptions may, as Young implies, be a necessary condition for the 'success' of an innovation. More specifically, the lack, in the proposals of SMP and MME, of any challenge to the basic organizing principles of English educational life, together with their emphasis on bringing school mathematics 'up to date' (i.e., in line with developments in university mathematics), may partly account for their having so readily gained the cooperation of the university examination boards. Certainly, as was shown in chapter 10, where SMP did challenge even a subject-specific basic assumption (in the case of the double subject 'A' level requirement) the group met more resistance.

The case study material from the schools, as well as the more recent HMI survey,[14] suggests that the process of curricular differentiation, represented by SMP's having originally developed a numbered series of texts for 'O' level and a lettered series for CSE, was further continued in the schools. As Keddie has argued, ultimately, for pupils, 'subjects are what practitioners do with them'.[15] And, as did the humanities teachers she studied, so apparently do mathematics teachers in the comprehensive school differentiate the curriculum by 'type' of pupil. Such evidence as I presented in chapter 10 lends further support to Shipman's claims, already supported by a number of studies, that different types of schooling are being reproduced within these schools.[16] Although the evidence here only derives from two schools (but is partially supported by the HMI's findings[17]), it suggests that the categorical differentiation of the content of mathematics curricula by 'ability' that characterized the 1950s has, in fact, been reproduced in a new, if possibly less rigid, form in the 1970s.[18] (It may be that less differentiation now occurs by sex, but the nature of my evidence allows no adequate evaluation of this.) Other evidence also suggests that, pedagogically, little may have changed over the same period.[19]

At classroom level, therefore, the redefinition finally achieved by the actions of those involved in the social movement of the late 1950s and early 1960s has probably been primarily one of content. In Barnes' terms, mathematics teachers remain 'transmission' orientated,[20] but new content is, in many cases, being transmitted. (Ironically, however, it may be that the school/university transition has been made more difficult for some pupils as an unintended consequence of the activities of the reformers and their only partial success in achieving their aims. Bibby, in a recent study of university mathematics students,[21] has argued that, given the increasing rarity of Euclidean geometry as a part of 'O' level studies and the much lower take-up of SMP at 'A' level than at 'O' level, pupils may, in some cases, now find themselves less well-prepared for axiomatic approaches than they might have been before reform.)

The Control of Redefinition

Various contributors to *Knowledge And Control* argued that, in accounting for educational change, we should pay attention to the possible role of 'industry' as a definer of curricular reality. Esland, for example, argued:

> Industrial organizations are powerfully able to affirm or deny the validity of an epistemology and are, therefore, particularly important as plausibility structures.[22]

I argued in chapter 2 that the basis of this power had been left relatively unexamined in that collection. In the light of this study, at least in relation to the nature of secondary mathematics, it is perhaps possible to throw some more light on its basis, its partial nature and its partially conjunctural determination.

In the early twentieth century, the universities and independent schools had achieved a substantial degree of control over the definition of mathematics education (a control possibly reflecting the lack of industrial employment of graduate mathematicians, if not of mathematics, before the 1950s). It was seen that employers, in order to achieve new goals, had to enter the educational and political arenas, and work therein, to achieve their preferences. Their control of resources relevant to the achievement of the missions of various segments of the subject did ground some power over the mathematics curriculum, as did their ultimate control over entry to the labour market. However, especially in respect of graduate labour, they shared their interest in school and university mathematics with the universities, who could use their control over entry qualifications and the immediate supply of mathematics graduates as key resources in bargaining over any redefinition. The resultant redefinition of selective school mathematics therefore reflected the demands of actors from both extra-school arenas. When, as an unintended consequence of the employers' initial activities, the actual redefinition, which included as a result of intra-subject politics some modern algebraic emphases, became established 'lower down' the system, many employers of non-graduate labour reacted negatively. This demonstrates the temporary or conjunctural nature of the legitimacy of any particular definition of school knowledge.

The eventual spreading into school CSE courses, via SMP and other projects, of some elements of the redefinition — especially modern algebraic concepts — cannot easily, therefore, be seen as a direct response to the 'needs' of the economy, as a functionalist sociologist might argue, nor either to the demands of capital, as might be argued by some of the more simplistic versions of Marxist sociology. Rather, it was the result of the original demands of some powerful employers' representatives for redefinition and for an enhanced supply of mathematicians, coupled with the demands of some university mathematicians for change, having been mediated by other professional educators with some institutional autonomy and missions of their own.

It must be stressed, however, that the particular balance of power described in this study is likely, like any other, to have been socio-historically specific in its details. Furthermore, in subsequent years, employers and the state were to take a more explicit interest in the details of schools' work and to seek more direct means of control.[23] In such a changing context, or set of conditions for action, other strategies, processes and outcomes may have come to characterize subject definition. In this respect, a detailed study of the origins and fate of the more recent Cockcroft proposals for the reform of mathematics education might well be fruitful.

We might also hope to further our understanding of the development of school subjects through the comparative study of the processes of change in different subjects. These might usefully be chosen to vary on a number of dimensions. How, for example, did processes of change within subjects with no major university base, such as physical education and home economics, differ? Or in subjects with a well-developed university base but with no obvious industrial applications, such as history? In these cases, were different types of groups of actors involved? Was there more or less professional control? Was more or less industrial or other extra-subject support available (and on what conditions)? We now have a number of studies of redefinition which provide answers to some of these questions[24] and it would seem a potentially worthwhile project to develop, in the light of the evidence now available, a comparative analysis which would take us beyond the largely programmatic work of the early 1970s. It is also important that such theoretical work adequately grasps, in a way single studies usually can not, both extra- and intra-school processes of change. If this is achieved, the sociology of the school curriculum might begin, at last, to fulfil at least its explanatory promise.

Notes

1 BERNBAUM (1977), p. 64.
2 BERNSTEIN (1974), p. 155.
3 YOUNG (1972), p. 74.
4 ARCHER (1979). See also ARCHER and VAUGHAN (1971).
5 ARCHER (1979), p. 35.
6 GOODSON (1983); BALL and LACEY (1980); and GOULDNER (1971).
7 See, for example, HALSEY et al (1980).
8 DAVIES (1973), p. 324.
9 DAVIS and MOORE (1945), p. 243.
10 ARCHER (1979), p. 35.
11 BHASKAR (1979a), pp. 42–4 and passim.
12 DAVIES (1973), p. 324.
13 YOUNG (1972), p. 78.
14 DES (1979) and (1980).
15 KEDDIE (1971), p. 144.
16 SHIPMAN (1971). See also BALL (1981).
17 DES (1979) and (1980).
18 See COOPER (1985).
19 See COOPER (1976).
20 BARNES and SHEMILT (1974).
21 BIBBY (1985).
22 ESLAND (1971), p. 100.
23 See, for example, CENTRE FOR CONTEMPORARY CULTURAL STUDIES (1981) and LAWTON (1978).
24 See, for example, LAYTON (1973), GOODSON (1983), BALL (1982) and COOPER (1983).

Bibliography

Abbreviated Proceedings of the Oxford Mathematical Conference for School-teachers and Industrialists (1957), London, The Times.

ADVISORY COUNCIL ON SCIENTIFIC MANPOWER: COMMITTEE ON SCIENTIFIC MANPOWER (1959) *Scientific and Engineering Manpower in Great Britain*, Cmnd 902, HMSO.

ARCHER, M.S. (1979) *Social Origins of Educational Systems*, London, Sage.

ARCHER, M.S. and VAUGHAN, M. (1971), *Social Conflict and Educational Change in England and France, 1789–1848*, Cambridge University Press.

ASSISTANT MASTERS' ASSOCIATION (1957) *The Teaching of Mathematics*, Cambridge University Press.

ASSISTANT MASTERS' ASSOCIATION (1973) *The Teaching of Mathematics in Secondary Schools*, Cambridge University Press.

ASSOCIATION OF TEACHERS IN COLLEGES AND DEPARTMENTS OF EDUCATION (1956) *The Supply of Mathematics and Science Teachers*, London, Methuen.

BALL, S.J. (1981) *Beachside Comprehensive: A Case Study of Secondary Schooling*, Cambridge University Press.

BALL, S.J. (1982) 'Competition and conflict in the teaching of English: a socio-historical analysis', *Journal of Curriculum Studies*, 14, 1, pp. 1–28.

BALL, S.J. and LACEY, C. (1980) 'Subject disciplines as the opportunity for group action: a measured critique of subject subcultures', in WOODS, P.E. (Ed.) *Teacher Strategies*, London, Croom Helm, pp. 149–77.

BANKS, O. (1974) 'The "new" sociology of education', *Forum*, 17, Autumn, pp. 4–7.

BARNES, B. (1982) *T.S. Kuhn and Social Science*, London, Macmillan.

BARNES, D. and SHEMILT, D. (1974) 'Transmission and interpretation', *Educational Review*, 26, 3, pp. 213–28.

BECKER, H.S. (1963) 'Moral entrepreneurs', in his *The Outsiders: Studies in the Sociology of Deviance*, New York, The Free Press, pp. 147–63.

BELL, C. (1978) 'Studying the locally powerful', in BELL, C. and ENCEL, S. (Eds) *Inside the Whale*, Oxford, Pergamon, pp. 14–40.

BELL, E.T. (1945) *The Development of Mathematics*, New York, McGraw-Hill.

BELL, R. (1971) *Thinking about the Curriculum*, E283, Open University Press.

BEN-DAVID, J. and COLLINS, R. (1966) 'Social factors in the origins of a new science, the case of psychology', *American Sociological Review*, 31, 4, pp. 451–65.

BERGER, P. (1970) *A Rumour of Angels*, Harmondsworth, Penguin.

BERGER, P. and LUCKMANN, T. (1967) *The Social Construction of Reality*, London, Allen Lane.

BERNBAUM, G. (1977) *Knowledge and Ideology in the Sociology of Education*, London, Macmillan.

BERNSTEIN, B. (1967) 'Open schools, open society?', *New Society*, 14 September 1967.

BERNSTEIN, B. (1971) 'On the classification and framing of educational knowledge', in YOUNG, M.F.D. (Ed.) *Knowledge and Control*, London, Collier-Macmillan, pp. 47–69.

BERNSTEIN, B. (1974) 'Sociology and the sociology of education: a brief account', in REX, J. (Ed.) *Approaches to Sociology*, London, Routledge and Kegan Paul, pp. 145–59.

BERNSTEIN, B. (1975) 'Class and pedagogies: visible and invisible', *Educational Studies*, 1, 1, pp. 23–41.

BERNSTEIN, B. (1977) 'Aspects of the relations between education and production', in his *Class, Codes and Control*, Volume Three, London, Routledge and Kegan Paul.

BHASKAR, R. (1979a) *The Possibility of Naturalism*, Brighton, Sussex, Harvester.

BHASKAR, R. (1979b) 'On the possibility of social scientific knowledge and the limits of naturalism', in MEPHAM, J. and RUBEN, D-H. (Eds) *Issues in Marxist Philosophy*, Volume Three, Brighton, Sussex, Harvester, pp. 107–39.

BIBBY, N. (1985) *Curricular Discontinuity: A Study of the Transition in Mathematics from Sixth Form to University*, University of Sussex, Education Area, Occasional Paper No. 12.

BIRTWISTLE, C. (1959) 'Editorial', *Mathematics Teaching*, No. 10, July.

BIRTWISTLE, C. (1962) 'Editorial', *Mathematics Teaching*, No. 21, Winter.

BOARD OF EDUCATION (1934) *Senior School Mathematics*, HMSO.

BOARD OF EDUCATION (1937) *Handbook of Suggestions for Teachers*, HMSO.

BOARD OF EDUCATION (1938) *Report of the Consultative Committee on Secondary Education* (the Spens Report) HMSO.

BOARD OF EDUCATION (1943) *Report of the Committee of the Secondary Schools Examinations Council* (the Norwood Report) HMSO.

BOURDIEU, P. and PASSERON, J-C. (1977) *Reproduction in Education, Society and Culture*, London, Sage.

BRIGGS, B. (1957) Review of Hodson's *Introductory Comprehensive Mathematics, Mathematics Teaching*, No. 5, November.

BRITISH ASSOCIATION FOR THE ADVANCEMENT OF SCIENCE (1958) 'Contemporary problems in mathematical teaching and staffing', *Nature*, 182, pp. 1064–5.

BRITISH COMMITTEE ON CHEMICAL EDUCATION (1974) 'Mathematics and school chemistry', *Education in Science*, January, pp. 14–22.

BROOKES, W.M. (1957) Letter to the Editor, *Mathematics Teaching*, No. 5, November.

BROOKES, W.M. (1958) 'Childish topology', *Mathematics Teaching*, No. 6, April.

BUCHER, R. and STRAUSS, A. (1961) 'Professions in process', *American Journal of Sociology*, 66, January, pp. 325–334.

BURLEY, D.M. (1975) 'SMP: a disaster?', *Mathematics in School*, 4, 6, pp. 11–12.

CENTRAL ADVISORY COUNCIL FOR EDUCATION (1959) *Fifteen to Eighteen* (the Crowther Report) Volume One, HMSO.

CENTRAL ADVISORY COUNCIL FOR EDUCATION (1963) *Half Our Future* (the Newsom Report) HMSO.

CENTRAL ADVISORY COUNCIL FOR EDUCATION (1967) *Children and their Primary Schools* (the Plowden Report) HMSO.

CENTRE FOR CONTEMPORARY CULTURAL STUDIES (1981) *Unpopular Education*, London, Hutchinson.

CHAPMAN, J.V. (1959) *Your Secondary Modern Schools: An Account of their Work in the late 1950s*, London, College of Preceptors.

CHERKAOUI, M. (1977) 'Bernstein and Durkheim: two theories of change in educational systems', *Harvard Educational Review*, 47, 4, pp. 556–64.

CHOQUET, G. (1960) 'Modern mathematics and teaching', *Mathematics Teaching*, No. 14, November.

COCKCROFT, W.H. (1982) *Mathematics Counts: Report of the Committee of Inquiry into the Teaching of Mathematics in Schools under the Chairmanship of Dr. W.H. Cockcroft*, HMSO.

COHEN, S. (1972) *Folk Devils and Moral Panics*, London, MacGibbon and Kee.

COHN, P.M. (1958) *Linear Equations*, London, Routledge and Kegan Paul.

COLLINS, R.H. (1956) 'Mathematics in the secondary school curriculum', *Mathematics Teaching*, No. 3, November.

COLLINS, R.H. (1958) 'Mathematics in the secondary school curriculum — V', *Mathematics Teaching*, No. 7, July.

COOPER, B. (1976) *Bernstein's Codes: A Classroom Study*, University of Sussex, Education Area, Occasional Paper No. 6.

COOPER, B. (1982) *Innovation in English Secondary School Mathematics: A Sociological Account with Special Reference to SMP and MME*, DPhil thesis, University of Sussex.

COOPER, B. (1983) 'On explaining change in school subjects', *British Journal of Sociology of Education*, 4, 3, pp. 207–22.

COOPER, B. (1985) 'Secondary school mathematics since 1950: reconstructing differentiation' in Goodson, I.F. (Ed.) *Social Histories of the Secondary Curriculum*, Lewes, Falmer Press.

COTGROVE, S.F. and BOX, S. (1970) *Science, Industry and Society: Studies in the Sociology of Science*, London, Allen and Unwin.

CRANE, D. (1972) *Invisible Colleges: Diffusion of Knowledge in Scientific Communities*, University of Chicago.

CUNDY, H.M. (1960) Review of the work of Biggs and Dienes, *Mathematical Gazette*, 44, pp. 301–3.

CUNDY, H.M. and ROLLETT, A.P. (1961) *Mathematical Models*, 2nd ed., Oxford, Clarendon Press.

DAVID, T. (1963) 'Oxbridge entrance: the Caius meeting', *Universities Quarterly*, 17, pp. 360–76.

DAVIE, G.E. (1961) *The Democratic Intellect*, Edinburgh University Press.

DAVIES, I. (1973) 'Knowledge, education and power', in BROWN, R. (Ed.) *Knowledge, Education and Cultural Change*, London, Tavistock, pp. 317–37.

DAVIS, K. and MOORE, W.E. (1945) 'Some principles of stratification', *American Sociological Review*, 10, 2, pp. 242–9.

DAVIS, P.J. and HERSH, R. (1981) *The Mathematical Experience*, Brighton, Sussex, Harvester.

DEMPSTER, J.J.B. (1949) *Education in the Secondary Modern School*, London, Methuen.

DEPARTMENT OF EDUCATION AND SCIENCE (1973) *Statistics of Education*, Volume Two, HMSO.

DEPARTMENT OF EDUCATION AND SCIENCE (1979) *Aspects of Secondary Education in England*, HMSO.

DEPARTMENT OF EDUCATION AND SCIENCE (1980) *Aspects of Secondary Education in England: Supplementary Information on Mathematics*, HMSO.

DODWELL, P.C. (1957) 'The evolution of number concepts in the child', *Mathematics Teaching*, No. 5, November.

DURKHEIM, E. (1964) *The Division of Labour in Society*, New York, The Free Press.

EGGLESTON, J. (1977) *The Sociology of the School Curriculum*, London, Routledge and Kegan Paul.

ELLIS, J.F. (1960) 'Blackpool conference 1960: educating the educator', *Mathematics Teaching*, No. 13, July.

ESLAND, G.M. (1971) 'Teaching and learning as the organization of knowledge', in YOUNG M.F.D. (Ed.) *Knowledge and Control*, London, Collier-Macmillan, pp. 70–115.

FISHER, C.S. (1973) 'Some social characteristics of mathematicians and their work', *American Journal of Sociology*, 78, 5, pp. 1094–1118.

FLEMMING, W. (1980) 'The School Mathematics Project', in STENHOUSE, L. (Ed.) *Curriculum Research and Development in Action*, London, Heinemann, pp. 25–41.

FLETCHER, T.J. (1959) 'The new gamesmanship', *Mathematics Teaching*, No. 9, April.

FLETCHER, T.J. (1960a) 'Transition from school to university: international conference report', *Mathematics Teaching*, No. 12, March.

FLETCHER, T.J. (1960b) Review of Felix' *Exposé moderne des mathématiques élémentaires*, *Mathematics Teaching*, No. 13, July.

FLETCHER, T.J. (1961) 'The international commission at Krakow', *Mathematics Teaching*, No. 15, March.

FLETCHER, T.J. (1962) Letter to the Editor, *Mathematical Gazette*, 46, pp. 177–8.

FLETCHER, T.J. (Ed.) (1964) *Some Lessons in Mathematics*, Cambridge University Press.

FLOUD, J. and SCOTT, W. (1961) 'Recruitment to teaching in England and Wales', in HALSEY, A.H. et al (Eds) *Education, Economy and Society*, New York, The Free Press, pp. 527–44.

FORD, J. (1969) *Social Class and the Comprehensive School*, London, Routledge and Kegan Paul.

FYFE, R.M. (1957a) Report of a meeting on modern school mathematics, *Mathematics Teaching*, No. 5, November.

FYFE, R.M. (1957b) 'Operational algebra', *Mathematics Teaching*, No. 4, May.

FYFE, R.M. (1958) 'A teacher's questions', *Mathematics Teaching*, No. 6, April.

FYFE, R.M. (1959) 'Using aids in a grammar school', *Mathematics Teaching*, No. 9, April.

GIBSON, R. (1977) 'Bernstein's classification and framing: a critique', *Higher Education Review*, 9, Spring, pp. 23–45.

GOLDTHORPE, J.H. et al (1980) *Social Mobility and Class Structure in Modern Britain*, Oxford, Clarendon Press.

GOODSON, I.F. (1983) *School Subjects and Curriculum Change*, London, Croom Helm.

GOODSTEIN, R.L. (1957) Review of Piaget et al's *L'Enseignement des mathématiques, Mathematical Gazette*, 43, pp. 68–9.

GOODSTEIN, R.L. (1959) Review of Beberman's *An Emerging Programme of Secondary School Mathematics, Mathematical Gazette*, 43, p. 211.

GOODSTEIN, R.L. (1962) Reviews of *New Thinking in School Mathematics* and *Synopses for Modern Secondary School Mathematics, Mathematical Gazette*, 46, pp. 69–72.

GORBUTT, D.A. (1972) 'The new sociology of education', *Education for Teaching*, No. 89.

GOULDNER, A.W. (1971) *The Coming Crisis of Western Sociology*, London, Heinemann.

GRIFFITH, B.C. and MULLINS N.C. (1972) 'Coherent social groups in scientific change', *Science*, 177, pp. 959–64.

GRIFFITHS, H.B. and HOWSON, A.G. (1974) *Mathematics: Society and Curricula*, Cambridge University Press.

GUSTIN, B.H. (1973) 'Charisma, recognition, and the motivation of scientists', *American Journal of Sociology*, 78, 5, pp. 1119–34.

HAGSTROM, W.O. (1965) *The Scientific Community*, New York, Basic Books.

HALL, G.G. (1978) 'Applied mathematics', in WAIN, G.T. (Ed.) *Mathematical Education*, New York, Van Nostrand Reinhold, pp. 25–39.

HALL, H.S. (1955) *A School Algebra*, London, Macmillan.

HALL, S. et al (1978) *Policing the Crisis: Mugging, the State, and Law and Order*, London, Macmillan.

HALMOS, P.R. (1968) 'Nicolas Bourbaki', in KLINE, M. (Ed.) *Mathematics in the Modern World*, San Francisco, Freeman.

HALSEY, A.H. et al (1980) *Origins and Destinations*, Oxford, Clarendon Press.

HAMMERSLEY, J.M. (1968) 'On the enfeeblement of mathematical skills by "modern mathematics" and by similar soft intellectual trash in schools and universities', *Bulletin of the Institute of Mathematics and its Applications*, 4, pp. 66–85.

HARRIS, I. (1956) 'Wanted geometry, dead or alive', *Mathematics Teaching*, No. 3, November.

HARRIS, I. (1957) 'Computing and programming in schools', *Mathematics Teaching*, No. 5, November.

HAYMAN, M. (1975) 'To each according to his needs', *Mathematical Gazette*, 59, pp. 137–53.

HIRST, P.H. (1974) *Knowledge and the Curriculum*, London, Routledge and

Kegan Paul.

HODGE, W.V.D. (1955) 'Changing views of geometry', *Mathematical Gazette*, 39, pp. 177–83.

HOLT, B.W.G. (1970) 'Social aspects in the emergence of chemistry as an exact science: the British chemical profession', *British Journal of Sociology*, 21, pp. 181–99.

HOPE, C. (1957) 'Editorial', *Mathematics Teaching*, No. 5, November.

HOPE, C. (1958a) 'Filmstrip in mathematics', *Mathematics Teaching*, No. 6, April.

HOPE, C. (1958b) 'The printed word', *Mathematics Teaching*, No. 6, April.

HOPE, C. (1958c) Review of Anderson's *Arithmetic Tests for Fourth Year Juniors*, Mathematics Teaching, No. 8, November.

HOPE, C. (1959) Review of the Mathematical Association's *Mathematics in Secondary Modern Schools*, Mathematics Teaching, No. 11, November.

HOPE, C. (1961a) 'The teaching of statistics — Stage A', in *Mathematics Teaching*, No. 15, March.

HOPE, C. (1961b) Review of Halmos' *Naive Set Theory*, Mathematics Teaching, No. 15, March.

HOPE, C. (1961c) Review of Morgan's *The Teaching of Mathematics in the Secondary Modern School, Mathematics Teaching*, No. 15, March.

HUGHES, M.G. (1962) *Modernising School Mathematics*, London, Bell.

JAMES, E.J. (1958) *The Teaching of Modern School Mathematics*, Oxford University Press.

KEDDIE, N. (1971) 'Classroom knowledge', in YOUNG, M.F.D. (Ed.) *Knowledge and Control*, London, Collier-Macmillan, pp. 133–60.

KLINE, M. (1966) 'Intellectuals and the schools: a case history', *Harvard Educational Review*, 36, pp. 505–11.

KUHN, T.S. (1962) *The Structure of Scientific Revolutions*, University of Chicago.

KUHN, T.S. (1963) 'The essential tension: tradition and innovation in scientific research', in HUDSON, L. (Ed.) *The Ecology of Human Intelligence*, Harmondsworth, Penguin, pp. 342–56.

KUHN, T.S. (1970) *The Structure of Scientific Revolutions*, 2nd enlarged ed., University of Chicago.

LACEY, C. (1976) 'Problems of sociological fieldwork: a review of the methodology of "Hightown Grammar"', in SHIPMAN, M. (Ed.) *The Organization and Impact of Social Research*, London, Routledge and Kegan Paul, pp. 63–88.

LACEY, C. (1977) *The Socialisation of Teachers*, London, Methuen.

LANGFORD, W.J. (1958) 'Secondary school mathematics: an international survey', *Mathematical Gazette*, 42, pp. 177–93.

LAWTON, D. (1973) *Social Change, Educational Theory and Curriculum Planning*, London, Hodder and Stoughton.

LAWTON, D. (1978) *The End of the Secret Garden?*, Inaugural Lecture, University of London Institute of Education.

LAYTON, D. (1973) *Science for the People*, London, Allen and Unwin.

LEDERMANN, W. (1949) *Introduction to the Theory of Finite Groups*, London, Oliver and Boyd.

LIGHTHILL, J. (Ed.) (1978) *Newer Uses of Mathematics*, Harmondsworth,

Penguin.

LYNESS, R.C. (1969) 'Modern maths reconsidered', *Trends in Education*, No. 14, April, pp. 3–8.

MacDONALD, B. and WALKER, R. (1976) *Changing the Curriculum*, London, Open Books.

MACLURE, J.S. (1973) *Educational Documents*, London, Methuen.

MANSFIELD, D.E. and THOMPSON, D. (1962) *Mathematics: A New Approach*, London, Chatto and Windus.

MATHEMATICAL ASSOCIATION (1932) *The Teaching of Arithmetic in Schools*, London, Bell.

MATHEMATICAL ASSOCIATION (1934) *The Teaching of Algebra in Schools*, London, Bell.

MATHEMATICAL ASSOCIATION (1938) *A Second Report on the Teaching of Geometry in Schools*, London, Bell.

MATHEMATICAL ASSOCIATION (1950) *The Teaching of Trigonometry in Schools*, London, Bell.

MATHEMATICAL ASSOCIATION (1951) *The Teaching of Calculus in Schools*, London, Bell.

MATHEMATICAL ASSOCIATION (1953) *The Teaching of Higher Geometry in Schools*, London, Bell.

MATHEMATICAL ASSOCIATION (1957) *Analysis, Course I*, London, Bell.

MATHEMATICAL ASSOCIATION (1957a) *The Teaching of Algebra in Schools*, London, Bell.

MATHEMATICAL ASSOCIATION (1957b) *The Teaching of Algebra in Sixth Forms*, London, Bell.

MATHEMATICAL ASSOCIATION (1959) *Mathematics in Secondary Modern Schools*, London, Bell.

MATHEMATICAL ASSOCIATION (1968) *Mathematics Projects in British Secondary Schools*, London, Bell.

Mathematics, Education and Industry (1960), The Liverpool Conference, London, The Times.

Mathematics Today and Tomorrow (1961), Proceedings of the Schoolmasters' Conference held in November 1961 and sponsored by BP.

MAXWELL, E.A. (1961) 'Pastors and masters', *Mathematical Gazette*, 45, pp. 167–74.

MEETHAM, M.J. (1957) Review of Keith and Martindale's *Know Your Maths*, *Mathematics Teaching*, No. 5, November.

MERTON, R.K. (1957) 'The role set: problems in sociological theory', *British Journal of Sociology*, 8, pp. 110–20.

MESCHKOWSKI, H. (1968) *Introduction to Modern Mathematics*, London, Harrap.

MIDLANDS MATHEMATICAL EXPERIMENT (1963) *The Midlands Mathematical Experiment: O Level: Book 1–3*, London, Harrap.

MIDLANDS MATHEMATICAL EXPERIMENT (1964) *Report 1962–63*, London, Harrap.

MIDLANDS MATHEMATICAL EXPERIMENT (1967) *Report 1963–65*, London, Harrap.

MIDWINTER, E. (1977) 'Education', in WILLIAMS F. (Ed.) *Why the Poor Pay More*, London, Macmillan.

MINISTRY OF EDUCATION (1951) *The Road to the Sixth Form: Some Suggestions on the Curriculum of the Grammar School*, HMSO.

MINISTRY OF EDUCATION (1958) *Teaching Mathematics in Secondary Schools*, HMSO.

MINISTRY OF EDUCATION (1963) *Report of the Cambridge Conference*, Ministry of Education, Great Britain.

MONTGOMERY, R.J. (1965) *Examinations: An Account of their Evolution as Administrative Devices in England*, London, Longmans.

MOORE, D.T. (1959) 'Secondary modern mathematics — II', *Mathematics Teaching*, No. 11, November.

MORGAN, O.I. (1959) *The Teaching of Mathematics in the Modern School: A Practical Guide for the Non-Mathematician*, London, Harrap.

MULKAY, M.J. (1972) *The Social Process of Innovation*, London, Macmillan.

MULLINS, N.C. (1972) 'The development of a scientific speciality: the Phage group and the origins of molecular biology', *Minerva*, 10, pp. 51–82.

MULLINS, N.C. (1973) 'The development of specialities in social science: the case of ethnomethodology', *Science Studies*, 3, pp. 245–73.

MUSGROVE, F. (1968) 'The contribution of sociology to the study of the curriculum', in KERR, J.F. (Ed.) *Changing the Curriculum*, University of London, pp. 96–109.

NEWMAN, M.H.A. (1937) 'The unification of Algebra, the cause as seen from the university', *Mathematical Gazette*, 21, 325–9.

NEWMAN, M.H.A. (1959) 'What is mathematics?', *Mathematical Gazette*, 43, pp. 161–71.

NEWMAN, M.H.A. (1961) 'Modern mathematics and the school curriculum', *Mathematical Gazette*, 45, pp. 288–92.

ORGANIZATION FOR ECONOMIC COOPERATION AND DEVELOPMENT (1961a) *New Thinking in School Mathematics*, OECD.

ORGANIZATION FOR ECONOMIC COOPERATION AND DEVELOPMENT (1961b) *Synopses for Modern Secondary School Mathematics*, OECD.

PARKES, M.D. (1957) Report of the Oxford Conference, *Mathematical Gazette*, 41, pp. 199–201.

PARR, H.E. (1950) *School Mathematics*, London, Bell.

PARSONS, G.L. (1957) 'Teaching the teacher', *Mathematical Gazette*, 41, pp. 1–8.

PLANCK, M. (1950) *Scientific Autobiography*, London, Williams and Norgate.

PRING, R. (1972) 'Knowledge out of control', *Education for Teaching*, No. 89, pp. 19–28.

PRING, R. (1975) 'Bernstein's classification and framing of knowledge', *Scottish Educational Studies*, 7, 2, pp. 67–74.

RAYNOR, J. (1973) 'The curriculum, the teacher and the child', in SHIPMAN, M. and RAYNOR, J. *Perspectives on the Curriculum*, E283, Open University Press.

REEDER, D. (1979) 'A recurring debate: education and industry', in BERNBAUM, G. (Ed.) *Schooling in Decline*, London, Macmillan, pp. 115–48.

ROGERSON, A. (1975) 'The School Mathematics Project: a case study in the implementation of innovations', *Journal of Applied Educational Studies*, 3, pp. 9–11.

ROSENHEAD, L. (1961) 'The teaching of mathematics in schools: a criticism of the English educational system', *Mathematical Gazette*, 45, pp. 279–87.

RUBINSTEIN, D. and SIMON, B. (1969) *The Evolution of the Comprehensive School*, London, Routledge and Kegan Paul.

SCHOOL MATHEMATICS PROJECT (1974) *Manipulative Skills in School Mathematics*, London, SMP.

SCHOOLS COUNCIL (1971) *Report 1970/71*, London, Evans.

SCHUTZ, A. (1967) *The Phenomenology of the Social World*, Chicago, Northern University Press.

SERVAIS, W. (1956) 'Modèles logiques', in Ministère de l'Instruction Publique *Les modèles dans l'enseignement mathématique*, Belgium.

SHIPMAN, M. (1971) 'Curriculum for inequality', in HOOPER, R. (Ed.) *The Curriculum: Context, Design and Development*, Edinburgh, Oliver and Boyd.

SILLITTO, A.G. (1957) 'Dynamic geometry', *Mathematics Teaching*, No. 5, November.

SILLITTO, A.G. (1961) 'Movement and pattern in geometry', *Mathematics Teaching*, No. 15, March.

SMITH, D. (1971) 'Selection and knowledge management in educational systems', in HOPPER, E. (Ed.) *Readings in the Theory of Educational Systems*, London, Hutchinson.

SNELL, K.S. (1953) 'School mathematics today and tomorrow', *Mathematical Gazette*, 37, pp. 161–73.

STEADMAN, S.D. et al (1980) *Impact and Take-Up Project*, 2nd ed., London, Schools Council.

STEPHENSON, G. (1961) *Mathematical Methods for Science Students*, London, Longmans.

STEWART, I. (1975) *Concepts of Modern Mathematics*, Harmondsworth, Penguin.

STROUD, C.T. (1960) Letter to the Editor, *Mathematics Teaching*, No. 16, July.

SWINDEN, L.A. (1958) 'Some thoughts on the teaching of mathematics', *Mathematics Teaching*, No. 8, November.

TAYLOR, W. (1963) *The Secondary Modern School*, London, Faber.

THWAITES, B. (1961a) *Education: Divisible or Indivisible?*, Inaugural Lecture, University of Southampton.

THWAITES, B. (1961b) *On Teaching Mathematics*, Oxford, Pergamon.

THWAITES, B. (1969) 'Ways ahead in secondary school mathematics', *Bulletin of the Institute of Mathematics and its Applications*, 5, pp. 49–53.

THWAITES, B. (1972) *The School Mathematics Project: the First Ten Years*, Cambridge University Press.

THWAITES, B. (1975) 'Red herrings served in style', *The Times Educational Supplement*, 3 January.

VIG, J.N. (1968) *Science and Technology in British Politics*, Oxford, Pergamon.

WALKER, A.J. (1957) 'Numerical and practical methods of mathematics', *Mathematics Teaching*, No. 4, May.

WALKER, A.J. (1958) 'Statistics in school', *Mathematics Teaching*, No. 6, April.

WARING, M. (1975) *Aspects of the Dynamics of Reform in Secondary School Science*, PhD thesis, University of London, Chelsea College.

WHEELER, D.H. (1958) 'Middlesex and NW London Day Conference', *Mathematics Teaching*, No. 6, April.

WHEELER, D.H. (1960) 'Is sixth form teaching good enough?', *Mathematics Teaching*, No. 12, March.

WHEELER, D.H. (1961a) Letter to the Editor, *Mathematics Teaching*, No. 16, July.

WHEELER, D.H. (1961b) 'After the conference', *Mathematics Teaching*, No. 16, July.

WHEELER, D.H. (1961c) 'The new mathematics: case for reform unanswerable', *The Times Educational Supplement*, 4 August.

WHEELER, D.H. (1961d) 'The OEEC Reports' *Mathematics Teaching*, No. 17, Winter.

Who's Who 1974, Adam and Charles Black.

WILKES, M.V. (1966) *A Short Introduction to Numerical Analysis*, Cambridge University Press.

WILLIAMSON, W. (1974) 'Continuities and discontinuities in the sociology of education', in FLUDE, M. and AHIER, J. (Eds) *Educability, Schools and Ideology*, London, Croom Helm.

WOOTON, W. (1965) *SMSG: The Making of a Curriculum*, Yale University Press.

YOUNG, M.F.D. (1971) 'An approach to the study of curricula as socially organized knowledge', in his (Ed.) *Knowledge and Control*, London, Collier-Macmillan, pp. 19–46.

YOUNG, M.F.D. (Ed.) (1971) *Knowledge and Control*, London, Collier-Macmillan.

YOUNG, M.F.D. (1972) 'On the politics of educational knowledge: some preliminary considerations with particular reference to the Schools Council', in BELL, R. et al (Eds) *Education in Great Britain and Ireland*, London, Routledge and Kegan Paul, pp. 70–81.

YOUNG, M.F.D. (1973) 'Educational theorizing: a radical alternative', in *Education for Teaching*, No. 91.

Author Index

Abbreviated Proceedings of the Oxford Mathematical Conference for Schoolteachers and Industrialists, 123–5, 285
Advisory Council on Scientific Manpower, 123, 285
Ahier, J.
   see Flude and Ahier
Althusser, 32
AMA
   see Assistant Masters' Association
Archer, M.S., 26, 31, 33, 35, 65, 273, 279, 283, 285
Archer, M.S. and Vaughan, M., 283, 285
Assistant Masters' Association (AMA), 57, 61, 65, 68, 70, 88, 285
Association of Teachers in Colleges and Departments of Education (ATCDE), 92, 117, 122, 125, 285
ATCDE
   see Association of Teachers in Colleges and Departments of Education

Ball, S.J., 275, 283, 285
Ball, S.J. and Lacey, C., 283, 285
Banks, O., 32, 285
Barlow Report, 122
Barnes, B., 31, 281, 285
Barnes, D. and Shemilt, D., 269, 283, 285
Beatley
   see Birkhoff and Beatley

Becker, H.S., 122, 125, 210, 213, 229–30, 231, 233, 277, 285
Bell, C., 4, 285
Bell, E.T., 55–6, 67, 285
Bell, R., 87, 90, 247, 255, 267, 268, 285
Bell, R. *et al.*, 294
Ben-David, J., 29, 31
Ben-David, J. and Collins, R., 25, 33, 286
Berger, P., 33, 151, 155, 235, 272, 286
Berger, P. and Luckmann, T., 22, 33, 286
Bernbaum, G., 271, 283, 286, 292
Bernstein, B., 5, 6, 7, 13, 19–21, 22, 24, 31, 32, 33, 39, 65, 123, 138, 155, 272–3, 275, 283, 286
Bhaskar, R., 26, 31, 32, 33, 279, 283, 286
Bibby, N., 281, 283, 286
Birkhoff and Beatley, 165
Birtwistle, C., 81, 89, 242, 267, 286
Board of Education, 39, 46, 53, 66, 67, 286
Bourbaki [pseudonym], 56–7, 128, 151, 159, 163, 238, 254
Bourdieu, P., 19, 22
Bourdieu, P. and Passeron, J.-C., 33, 286
Box, S.
   see Cotgrove and Box
Briggs, B., 73, 88, 286
British Association for the Advancement of Science, 286
British Committee on Chemical

Education, 286
British Employers' Confederation, 168
Brookes, W.M., 75, 89, 286–7
Brown, R., 288
Bucher, R. and Strauss, A., 8, 24, 26–30, 31, 32, 33, 62, 64, 68, 69, 88, 159, 252, 274, 276, 287
Burley, D.M., 268, 287

Central Advisory Council for Education, 33, 65–6, 89, 123, 287
Centre for Contemporary Cultural Studies, 283, 287
Chapman, J.V., 43–7, 53, 66, 287
Cherkaoui, M., 33, 287
Choquet, G., 164, 165, 171, 222, 287
Cockcroft, W.H., 264, 266, 269, 282, 287
Cohen, S., 172, 287
Cohn, P.M., 67, 287
Collins, R.
   see Ben-David and Collins
Collins, R.H., 77–8, 89, 267, 287
Cooper, B., 4, 269, 283, 287
Cotgrove, S.F. and Box, S., 186–7, 206, 287
Crane, D., 9, 32, 287
Crowther Report, 40–1, 95, 122, 168, 169
Cundy, H.M., 165–6, 172, 237, 287
Cundy, H.M. and Rollett, A.P., 266, 287

Daily Telegraph, 121
Dainton Report, 40
David, T., 268, 287
Davie, G.E., 25, 33, 288
Davies, I., 13, 16, 32, 87, 90, 127, 154, 158–9, 171, 276, 279, 283, 288
Davis, K. and Moore, W.E., 277, 283, 288
Davis, P.J. and Hersh, R., 31, 288
Dempster, J.J.B., 43, 66, 288
Department of Education and Science (DES), 123, 269, 283, 288
Dodwell, P.C., 75, 89, 288
Durkheim, E., 20, 33, 288

Education in Science, 268
Eggleston, J., 150, 152, 153, 155, 209, 231, 233, 288
Ellis, J.F., 171, 288
Esland, G.M., 8, 13, 22–5, 27, 28, 30, 32, 33, 47, 48, 66, 73–4, 75, 89, 95, 123, 198, 207, 268, 275, 281, 283, 288

Fisher, C.S., 32, 288
Flemming, W., 145–6, 148, 166, 168, 265, 269, 288
Fletcher, T.J., 89, 163, 164, 171, 207, 227, 266, 288
Floud, J. and Scott, W., 33, 288
Flude, M. and Ahier, J., 294
Ford, J., 65, 288
Fyfe, R.M., 72, 74, 84, 88, 89, 90, 289

Gibson, R., 20, 33, 289
Goldthorpe, J.H. *et al.*, 206, 289
Goodson, I.F., 2, 4, 8–9, 32, 79, 89, 275, 283, 289
Goodstein, R.L., 162, 165, 171, 172, 289
Gorbutt, D.A., 32, 289
Gouldner, A.W., 283, 289
Griffith, B.C. and Mullins, N.C., 9, 32, 152, 155, 209, 231, 236, 248, 266, 267, 278, 289
Griffiths, H.B. and Howson, A.G., 57, 65, 67, 68, 70, 88, 289
Gulbenkian Report, 193, 195
Gustin, B.H., 32, 289

Hagstrom, W.O., 12, 32, 289
Halmos, P.R., 67, 155, 289
Hall, G.G., 67, 289
Hall H.S., 65, 289
Hall, S. *et al.*, 121–2, 125, 172, 214, 232, 233, 289
Halsey, A.H. *et al.*, 33, 283, 288, 289
Hammersley, J.M., 32, 96–100, 109, 113, 114, 117–19, 218, 252–4, 268, 289
Harris, I., 77–8, 81, 89, 289
Hayman, M., 259, 264, 269, 289
Her Majesty's Inspectorate (HMI), 39, 40, 46, 51–2, 54, 61–2, 127,

166, 263, 266, 280
Hersh, R.
  see Davis and Hersh
Hirst, P.H., 7, 32, 289–90
Hodge, W.V.D., 61, 64, 68, 142, 290
Hodson, J.D., 73
Holt, B.W.G., 29, 33, 290
Hooper, R., 293
Hope, C., 71, 73, 74, 77, 81–3, 88,
  89–90, 171, 200, 290
Hopper, E., 293
Howson, A.G.
  see Griffiths and Howson
Hudson, L., 290
Hughes, M.G., 62, 68, 154, 172, 206,
  232, 290

Inspectorate
  see Her Majesty's Inspectorate

James, E.J., 49–50, 52, 54, 66, 67, 80,
  82, 89, 290
Jeffery Report, 83

Keddie, N., 49, 66, 280, 283, 290
Keith and Martindale, 73
Kelsall Report, 145
Kerr, J.F., 141, 292
Kline, M., 154, 254, 268, 290
Kuhn, T.S., 7, 8, 10–12, 22, 31, 32, 33,
  114, 116, 128, 154, 161, 187–8, 205,
  252, 274, 275, 290

Lacey, C., 31, 202, 207, 275, 290
  see also Ball and Lacey
Langford, W.J., 129–30, 139, 148,
  166, 167, 172, 207, 217, 290
Lawton, D., 27, 33, 35, 63, 65, 273,
  283, 290
Layton, D., 283, 290
Ledermann, W., 60, 67, 290
Lesieur and Revuz, 164
Lighthill, J., 67, 290–1
Luckmann, T.
  see Berger and Luckman
Lyness, R.C., 254–5, 268, 291

MacDonald, B. and Walker, R., 33,
  291
Maclure, J.S., 65, 66, 122, 291

Mansfield, D.E. and Thompson, D.,
  155, 291
Martindale
  see Keith and Martindale
Mathematical Association, 4, 51, 54,
  57, 58–61, 65, 66, 67, 68, 80, 81, 89,
  123, 291
Mathematical Gazette, 172, 232, 267,
  268
*Mathematics, Education and
  Industry*, 154–5, 291
Mathematics Teaching, 88, 89, 90
Mathematics Today and Tomorrow,
  232–3, 291
Maxwell, E.A., 110, 111, 113, 114,
  115, 207, 291
Meetham, M.J., 73, 89, 291
Mepham, J. and Ruben, D.-H., 286
Merton, R.K., 27–8, 33, 291
Meschkowski, H., 67, 291
Midlands Mathematical Experiment
  (MME), 267, 268, 291
Midwinter, E., 33, 291
Ministry of Education, 40, 65, 66, 67,
  68, 124, 154, 155, 232, 292
MME
  see Midlands Mathematical
    Experiment
Montgomery, R.J., 94, 95, 123, 172,
  292
Moore, D.T., 80, 89, 292
Moore, W.E.
  see Davis and Moore
Morgan, O.I., 50–1, 52, 54–4, 66, 67,
  165, 292
Mulkay, M.J., 7, 31, 32, 292
Mullins, N.C., 7, 32, 292
  see also Griffith and Mullins
Musgrove, F., 10, 30, 32, 292

Nature, 130, 154
Newman, M.H.A., 60, 68, 166, 172,
  207, 217–18, 292
Newsom Report, 46–7, 53
Norwood Report, 39, 40, 48, 52, 74,
  75

OECD
  see Organization for Economic

Cooperation and Development
Organization for Economic
    Cooperation and Development
    (OECD), 67, 90, 171, 172, 222, 239,
    240, 253, 277, 292

Parkes, M.D., 172, 292
Parr, H.E., 65, 292
Parsons, G.L., 61, 68, 292
Passeron, J.-C.
    see Bourdieu and Passeron
Percy Report, 122
Planck, M., 12, 32, 292
Pring, R., 20, 32, 33, 292

Raynor, J., 2, 4, 292
    see also Shipman and Raynor
Reeder, D., 268, 292
Revuz
    see Lesieur and Revuz
Rex, J., 286
Rogerson, A., 265, 269, 292
Rollett, A.P.
    see Cundy and Rollett
Rosenhead, L., 134–5, 204, 207,
    292–3
Ruben, D.-H.
    see Mepham and Ruben
Rubinstein, D. and Simon, B., 66, 293

School Mathematics Project (SMP),
    269, 293
Schools Council, 267, 293
Schutz, A., 22, 33, 293
Scott, W.
    see Floud and Scott
Secondary Schools Examination
    Council (SSEC), 169–70
Servais, W., 87, 90, 293
Shaw, B., 254
Shemilt, D.
    see Barnes and Shemilt
Shipman, M., 280, 283, 290, 293
Shipman, M. and Raynor, J., 292
Sillitto, A.G., 89, 165, 171, 293
Simon, B.
    see Rubinstein and Simon
Smith, D., 32, 293
Smithie, 253–4

SMP
    see School Mathematics Project
Snell, K.S., 61, 68, 293
Spens Report, 39, 40, 48, 83
SSEC
    see Secondary Schools Examination
        Council
Steadman, S.D. *et al.*, 268, 293
Stenhouse, L., 288
Stephenson, G., 67, 293
Stewart, I., 67, 293
Strauss, A.
    see Bucher and Strauss
Stroud, C.T., 202–3, 207, 293
Swinden, L.A., 85, 90, 293

Taylor, W., 66, 79, 89, 293
Thompson, D.
    see Mansfield and Thompson
Thwaites, B., 68, 91, 107, 114, 115,
    122, 155, 171, 206–7, 231–2, 237–
    9, 255, 261–2, 266, 267, 268, 269,
    293
Times, The, 121, 122, 123, 125, 129,
    154, 157, 158, 167–71, 172, 207,
    210, 213–22, 231, 232, 245–6, 267
Times Educational Supplement, The,
    222, 256, 268

Vaughan, M.
    see Archer and Vaughan
Vig, J.N., 89, 92, 122, 293

Wain, G.T., 289
Walker, A.J., 81, 89, 293
Waring, M., 94, 123, 154, 224, 232,
    293
Wheeler, D.H., 72–3, 88, 162, 163,
    164, 171, 201, 202, 207, 222, 232,
    293–4
Who's Who, 206, 294
Wilkes, M.V., 67, 294
Williams, F., 291
Williamson, W., 32, 294
Woods, P.E., 285
Wooton, W., 154, 171, 294

Young, M.F.D., 13–19, 20, 22, 24, 28,
    32, 95, 104, 123, 271, 272–3, 275–
    6, 280, 283, 286, 288, 290, 294

Subject Index

AAM, 169, 226

ability
and curriculum differentiation, 43–7, 48–52, 54, 60, 63, 74, 78–85, 142, 196, 257–61, 264, 280

action
and curriculum change, 272–4

Adams, Ms, 168

agricultural research, 92

Air Transport Industry Training Board, 256

'A' level subjects, 7, 9, 37, 57, 94, 106, 107–8, 113, 116, 117, 118, 120, 129, 141, 145, 169, 189, 193, 195, 198, 212, 219, 220, 221, 222, 239, 245, 248–9, 251, 255, 279, 280, 281

algebras, 37, 38, 39, 42, 43, 52, 55–6, 57, 59–60, 62, 64, 72, 75, 76–7, 82, 87, 88, 100, 102, 103, 105, 113–14, 122, 128, 129, 136, 138, 142, 148, 151, 157–67, 171, 174, 183, 187, 191, 192, 193, 200, 201, 202, 203, 205, 238, 239, 240, 241, 251, 253, 258, 259, 261, 276, 277, 282

Allan, F.L., 216

American Mathematical Monthly, 129

Anderson, K., 74

arithmetic, 36–8, 39, 41, 42–3, 44, 46, 47, 52, 53, 81, 83, 100–1, 112, 136, 141, 162, 241, 256–61, 280

Armaments Research and Development Establishment, 103

Armstrong-Vickers, 105

Association of Education Committees, 201

Association of Education Officers, 201

Association for the Improvement of Geometrical Teaching, 37

Association of Public School Science Masters, 37

Association of Teachers in Colleges and Departments of Education (ATCDE), 139, 148, 223

Association for Teaching Aids in Mathematics (ATAM), 3, 48, 58, 62, 65, 69–90, 95, 121, 127, 132, 149, 151, 152, 157–8, 162, 165–7, 171, 173, 175–6, 189–93, 197, 200–5, 209, 222, 223–31, 237, 238, 239, 241–2, 249, 254, 274, 275, 276, 280
and ability, 83–5
activist members of, 69, 70–88
conferences of, 86, 87
and curriculum differentiation, 78–83
foundation of, 69, 70
journal of, *see Mathematics Teaching*
meetings of, 86, 87
membership of, 70, 85–6, 87–8
officials of, 71
perspectives on learning in, 70–8
perspectives on teaching in, 70–8
and teaching aids, 70, 71–2, 77, 79, 84–5

299

and views on school mathematics, 75–8
ATAM
  see Association for Teaching Aids in Mathematics
ATCDE
  see Association of Teachers in Colleges and Departments of Education
ATM, 223
  see also Association for Teaching Aids in Mathematics

Barwell, 120
Beard, R., 200, 201
Beardwood, 226–7
Beberman, 129, 165, 166
Becher, R.A., 243, 267
Beeching, 136, 148
Begle, Prof., 183, 184, 192, 198
Belgium
  work on topology in, 163
biology, 9
Birmingham, University of, 129
Birtwistle, 70, 86, 246, 254
Blackpool conference (1958), 79
Blakey, 108, 116
Bolyai, 59
Bondi, H., 267
Boolean algebra, 87
  see also algebras
Boothby, Lord, 218–19
Bosanquet, 136, 137
boys
  and mathematics, 40–1, 43–7, 53–4, 104
  see also gender
BP
  see British Petroleum
Brierly, 144
Bristol Aeroplane Co. Ltd., 134
Britain, *passim*
  economic aspects of, 92, 98, 157, 256, 277
British Association, 37, 130, 167, 168, 221
British Iron and Steel Federation, 100, 134
British Petroleum (BP), 158, 223–9, 270

British Thomson-Houston Co. Ltd., 101, 134
Brookes, W.M., 78, 149, 176, 189, 225, 227
Brown, 261
Bryan, 243
Burnham arrangements, 79
Busbridge, 110

calculus, 38, 39, 55, 57, 61, 82, 102, 162, 241
California, 245
Cambridge, University of, 37, 40, 56, 94–5, 106, 107, 108, 109, 116, 119, 120–1, 148, 150–1, 188, 196, 229, 248
Cambridge Board, 39
Camier, 142
Cartesian geometry, 59
  see also geometry
CBI
  see Confederation of British Industry
Certificate of Secondary Education (CSE), 255, 257, 258, 261, 262, 264, 268, 280, 282
China
  technology in, 98
Choquet, G., 87, 88, 162
Churchill College (Cambridge), 170, 211
Clarendon Report, 36–7
Clarkson, 86
Coaker, 224
Cobb, 107, 112–13, 114, 115
College Entrance Examination Board, 128
colleges of technology, 218, 221
Collins, R.H., 70, 78, 79, 86, 132, 149, 164, 203, 222, 239–40, 241, 244, 265
Combridge, 224, 225, 226, 227, 228
commerce
  and curriculum change, 13
Commission on Mathematics, 128–9
Commons
  see House of Commons
comprehensive schools, 1, 226–7, 255–7, 259–60, 262–4, 266, 280
  see also mathematics, and non-

selective schools
computer programming, 137, 138
computers, 7, 57, 93, 98, 99, 100–1,
    103, 104–5, 115, 118, 136, 137, 138,
    140–1, 148, 174, 187, 219, 238, 260
computing
    see computers; computer
        programming
Confederation of British Industry
    (CBI), 256, 260
Conference of Professors of
    Mathematics, 222, 223
Conference on Training and Research
    Potential in Mathematics (1958),
    159
conferences of mathematicians
    see entries for particular
        conferences, especially Liverpool
        conference; Oxford conference;
        Southampton conference
Conservative party, 221
Contemporary School Mathematics
    project, 269
Continuation Committee, 222–3
Cooke, Miss, 116, 117
Cooper, J.L.B., 214–15
Costain, 219
Courtaulds, 94, 134
Cundy, H.M., 62–3, 152, 244, 245
curriculum
    and commerce, 13
    content of, 13–25
    and examinations, *see*
        examinations
    and industry, 13, 24–5; *see also*
        industry
    innovation in, 2
    'intended', 2
    mathematics, *passim*
    and pedagogy, 13–25, 35–65; *see*
        also pedagogy
    and social class, 19
    sociology and the, *passim*
    'transactional', 2
'curriculum entrepreneurs', 210

Daniels, Prof., 129
Dartford Grammar School, 78
Davison, 119
Descartes, 67

    see also Cartesian geometry
deviance, 210, 229–30
Dick Shephard School, 84
Dienes, 165
Dieudonné, J., 159, 161, 165
direct grant schools, 176, 184, 246
dominance
    in society, 15–18
Donnellan, 166
Dorrington, 228
Durran, 96, 132

Eccles, 168, 199, 219, 221
Education Act (1944), 42
Edwards, 224
Egner, 143–4, 148, 170
elementary schools, 27, 35–6, 42, 52,
    53, 63, 273
employment
    see industry, and mathematics
Engineering Industry Training Board,
    256
English Electric Co. Ltd., 102, 134
Environmental Studies, 9
Euclidean geometry, 36–7, 56, 58, 61,
    112, 138, 142, 164, 188, 239, 260,
    281
    see also geometry
Evans, P., 215–16
examinations, 3, 4, 37, 39, 40–1, 42,
    72, 79–80, 87, 93–4, 99, 106–12,
    119, 120, 138, 142–3, 148, 149,
    188–9, 203, 239, 248, 254, 263–4
    see also 'A' level subjects; 'O' level
        subjects

Fehr, H., 159
Felix, 164–5
Ferranti Ltd., 100, 134
Fielker, 201
Fletcher, T.J., 70, 71, 77, 87, 162, 192,
    201, 225
fluid flow, 105
France
    mathematics in, 158–67, 215, 252
    see also Bourbaki [Author Index];
        Royaumont seminar
Frankl, 224
Fryer, 227, 229
Fyfe, R.M., 77, 78, 84, 86, 149

Gagarin, U., 220
games
  theory of, 205
Gattegno, 70, 71, 74, 77, 86
Gauss, 55, 59
Geary, Dr, 55, 59, 113, 114, 226
gender
  and computing, 104–5
  and curriculum differentiation, 40–
    1, 43–7, 48, 52–4, 63, 146
  and industry, 104–5
  and mathematics, 40–1, 43–7, 52–
    4, 63, 104–5, 116–17, 275, 280
General Certificate of Education
  (GCE), 7, 39, 42, 44, 46, 47, 63,
    79–80, 81, 83, 112, 119, 151, 164,
    198, 202–3, 219, 237, 247, 263, 276
geography, 9
geometry, 36–7, 38, 39, 42, 43, 50, 52,
    54, 55, 56, 58–9, 61, 62, 72, 73, 81,
    82, 107, 108, 109, 112, 114, 119,
    128, 136, 138, 141, 142, 159, 161–2,
    164, 165, 187, 188, 200, 201, 239,
    240, 241, 251, 259, 260, 281
  see also Cartesian geometry);
    Euclidean geometry
girls
  and mathematics, 40–1, 43–7, 53–
    4, 105, 106, 116–17, 129, 131,
    147, 169, 216, 222
  see also gender
Goddard, 170
Godfrey, 37
grammar schools, 27, 36–41, 42, 44,
    50–2, 80, 81, 84, 87, 122, 131, 138,
    139–40, 142, 147, 176, 184–5,
    189, 190, 211, 246–7, 258, 260
Griffiths, H.B., 101, 103, 249
groups
  and knowledge definition, 14–16,
    18, 19, 21, 31
Guiseppi, 77, 86
Gulbenkian Enquiry into 'A' level
  syllabuses, 129

Hailsham, Viscount, 219, 221
Hammersley, J.M., 91, 96–100, 102,
    105, 112, 116, 120, 121, 122, 151,
    152–3, 167, 173, 174, 184, 193, 197,
199, 218, 237, 239, 276
Handbook of Suggestions for Teachers
  (1937), 42
Hardy, 56
Harris, I., 70, 86, 87
Harrow [school], 37
Hastie, 136
Headmasters' Conference, 168–9,
  242
Her Majesty's Inspectorate (HMI),
  48, 52, 57, 106, 131, 148, 149, 152,
  167, 169, 170, 177
Herbert, 108–9
Herne, 101, 105
Hilbert, 56, 59
Hilton, 194, 197
Hinshelwood, 115
Hirst, 105
HMI
  see Her Majesty's Inspectorate
HMSO [Her Majesty's Stationery
  Office], 184
Hoare, Mrs, 105
Hodge, Sir W., 222
Holman, 120
Hope, C., 77, 86, 88, 128, 152, 159,
  161, 162, 164, 165, 166, 192, 200–3,
  205, 221, 222, 239–40, 242, 243–4,
  248, 249, 265
Hopkins, 103
House of Commons, 218–19, 220–1
House of Lords, 218–19
Howson, A.G., 207, 238–9, 243, 244,
  245, 255, 262, 267
Huddersfield Technical College, 256

IAAM, 141, 166
IAH, 185, 211
IAHM
  see Incorporated Association of
    Headmasters
ICI, 94, 102, 103, 134
ICSITM
  see International Commission for
    the Study and Improvement of
    the Teaching of Mathematics
Illinois, University of, 129
image-manipulation, 25
Impact and Take-up Project, 250

Incorporated Association of
  Headmasters (IAH), 144, 170
Incorporated Association of
  Headmasters and Headmistresses,
  222
independent schools, 27, 36–41, 109,
  120–1, 131, 150–1, 153, 175–81,
  184, 185, 189–94, 205, 246, 250,
  281
  see also mathematics, and selective
    schools; public schools
India
technology in, 98
individuals
  and subjects, 29, 31
Industrial Fund for the Advancement
  of Scientific Education in Schools,
  94, 134, 243
industry
  and contacts with teachers, 117, 141
  and curriculum change, 13, 24–5,
    281–2
  and education, 45, 98–100
  employment in, 91–4, 100–5, 118–
    19, 136, 145–7, 150
  and mathematics, 24, 28, 30, 45, 77,
    91, 98–105, 115, 116, 118–19,
    120, 122, 130–8, 141, 145–71,
    148, 149–50, 176–83, 184, 186–
    7, 192, 194, 197, 198, 199, 212–
    13, 214–15, 218, 219, 224–6,
    230–1, 250, 253, 255, 256, 269–
    70, 273–4, 277, 278, 279
Institute of Mathematics
  proposal for an, 130, 170
Institute of Mathematics and its
  Applications (IMA), 248, 252
integrated studies, 22
International Commission for the
  Study and Improvement of the
  Teaching of Mathematics
  (ICSITM), 70, 77, 86, 87, 151,
  162–7, 183, 191, 200, 230
International Congress of
  Mathematicians (1962), 166, 203
International Union of
  Mathematicians, 159

Jackson, 138

Jeffery, G.B., 39, 40, 61
JMB
  see Joint Matriculation Board
Joint Mathematical Council (JMC),
  223, 248
Joint Matriculation Board (JMB), 107,
  108, 112
Jones, T.A. 96, 117, 118–19, 120, 151,
  170, 237, 245

Kerruish, 101–2, 104–5
Klein, 56, 59
knowledge
  definition, 5–31
Knowledge and Control, 13, 22, 281

Labour Party, 259–60
Land, 116, 117, 120, 139–40, 159
Langdale, 136, 148, 256
Langford, W.J., 205, 228, 246, 248
Laybourn, 167
Lee, Sir Desmond, 245
Leverhulme Trust, 243
Lewis, K., 102, 103–4, 268
Lightfoot, Dr, 108, 112
Lighthill, J., 217
linear programming, 105, 136, 141,
  160
Liverpool conference (1959), 69, 78,
  91, 127–55, 163, 165, 167, 168, 169,
  170, 171, 174, 181, 183, 196, 204,
  205, 224, 254, 256
  issues discussed at the, 134–47
  participation in the, 130–4, 177–8,
    180–1
Lloyd, 191
Lobachewsky, 59
local education authorities (LEAs),
  244, 249–50
Lockwood, E.H., 169, 215
London Board, 141
London Institute, 74
London Mathematical Society, 146,
  223
London Study Group, 163–4
Longbottom, 256
Loveday, 141

Macro, 113

Manipulative Skills in School Mathematics, 262

Mansfield, 151

Marlborough College, 134

Marxism, 14–15, 282

Mathematical Association, 3, 37–41, 48–9, 52, 57, 58–61, 62–3, 64–5, 69, 70, 75, 76, 78, 83, 85, 86, 87, 96, 105, 106, 110, 111, 117, 119, 121, 127, 129, 140, 146, 149, 151–2, 157–8, 165–7, 168, 173, 174, 175–6, 185, 188, 200–5, 209, 217, 223–31, 237, 246, 248, 250, 259, 265, 276, 278

Mathematical Association of America, 129

Mathematical Gazette, 62–3, 119, 162, 165, 226, 237, 245, 253

mathematical modelling
see modelling

mathematics
applied, 17, 37, 43–6, 57, 62, 77–8, 92, 96–105, 112, 113, 116, 120, 122, 127, 134, 138, 148, 149, 150, 151, 167, 168, 174, 183, 184, 187, 188, 190, 193, 194, 195–6, 197, 205, 210, 230–1, 238–9, 242, 251, 252, 254, 272, 275, 276
arithmetic-based, *see* arithmetic
attitudes to, 102–3
'crisis' in, 209–23, 230–1
curriculum of 1950s, 35–68
and differentiation, 36–65
and examinations, *see* examinations
and gender, *see* gender
'hard', 253
and industry, *see* industry
and modelling, *see* modelling
'modern', 1, 2, 75–8, 80–3, 85, 87–8, 102, 112, 128–9, 148, 157–67, 173–207, 217–18, 221, 222–3, 224–5, 229, 230, 239, 240–2, 249–50, 252–62, 279
and non-selective schools, 36, 41–8, 52, 63, 64, 78, 265–6
pure, 17, 55, 63, 87, 99, 112, 128–9, 159–67, 183, 184, 187, 188, 193, 194, 195, 201, 205, 210, 231, 242, 251–4, 265–6, 272, 275

and resources, *see* resources
in secondary school curricula, *passim*
and selective schools, 36–41, 48, 54–63, 64, 91–125, 127–55, 175, 186, 187–9, 204, 211, 214, 218, 222, 230, 237–8, 242, 247, 252, 255, 258, 272, 274, 275–6, 278, 282
and sexual differentiation, *see* gender
as social phenomenon, 7–31
and sociology, *passim*
'soft', 253–4
as subject, 274–6
'traditional', 1
in universities, *see* universities
X courses in, 195–7, 198
Y courses in, 195–7
Z courses in 195–7

Mathematics in Education and Industry project, 269

Mathematics Teaching, 71–7, 78, 84, 85, 87, 162, 163, 164, 165, 201, 202

Mathews, G., 269

Mauldon, 110–11

Maxwell, E.A., 159, 166, 176, 194, 204, 267

medical research, 92

Metropolitan-Vickers Electrical Co. Ltd., 102, 104, 117, 134

Midlands Mathematical Experiment (MME), 2, 3, 13, 16, 69, 71, 76, 77, 78, 95, 132, 152, 203, 235–70, 275, 276, 280
compared with SMP, 242–50, 265
funds of, 243–4, 265
meetings attended by members of, 244
personnel of, 239–40
proposals by, 240–2
schools associated with, 246–7

Ministry of Education, 48, 140, 145, 147, 148, 199, 211, 222

'missions', 26–31, 62, 75–6, 86–8, 151–2, 197, 198–9, 209, 221, 223, 230, 235, 272, 274, 277, 279, 281–2

MME
  see Midlands Mathematical
    Experiment
modelling
  and mathematics, 57, 103–4, 105,
    116, 122, 134–5, 136–8, 144,
    148, 181, 187, 192, 193, 197,
    205, 224, 230, 239
Monte Carlo methods, 105
'moral entrepreneurs', 210, 213, 277
Morris, R., 46, 176, 189, 191, 267
Morris, T.D., 237, 238–9

National Coal Board, 101, 105
National Science Foundation (of
  USA), 147, 181, 198, 213, 218
National Service, 145
Newman, M.H.A., 129, 203–4, 205,
  217–18
non-selective schools
  see mathematics, and non-selective
    schools
Northern Universities Board, 141
NSF
  see National Science Foundation
Nuffield Foundation, 18, 243
numerical analysis, 112, 114, 119, 136,
  137, 140–1, 148, 160, 187 230, 241

OEEC, 86, 128, 157–67, 225, 229,
  239, 252
Office for Scientific and Technical
  Personnel (of OEEC), 128, 157
'O' level subjects, 73, 117, 137, 139,
  141, 191, 221, 222, 239, 240, 242,
  245, 247, 249, 255, 259, 262, 268,
  280, 281
Ollerenshaw, 214, 232
oscillations
  non-linear, 105
Owen, 100–1, 116
Oxbridge
  see Cambridge, University of;
    Oxford, University of
Oxford, University of, 37, 40, 94–5,
  106, 107, 108, 109, 116, 119, 120–1,
  148, 150–1, 188–9, 196, 229, 248
Oxford and Cambridge Board, 177
Oxford conference (1957), 69, 77, 88,

91–125, 127, 130–4, 148–54, 165,
  167, 168, 169, 170, 171, 173, 174,
  181, 183, 205, 224, 226, 237, 253,
  254
debates of the, 96–120
participation in the, 96–7, 130–4,
  177–9, 181

Papy, 164, 183, 192, 200, 201, 202
paradigms
  in science, 8, 11–12
Parkes, 228
Parliament, 19, 158
  see also House of Commons;
    House of Lords
Peart, 220–1
pedagogy
  and Association for Teaching Aids
    in Mathematics, 70–88, 242
  and curriculum, 13–25
  and mathematics curricula, 35–65,
    280
  and MME, 241
  and non-selective school
    mathematics curricula, 41–8
  and selective school mathematics
    curricula, 36–41
  and SMP, 262–3, 266
  views on, at Liverpool conference,
    136–8, 144, 147, 148–9, 151
  views on, at Oxford conference,
    99–100, 102–5, 115
  views on, at Royaumont seminar,
    162
Peel, R.F., 218
Penfold, 228
Peskett, J., 70, 71
Peterson, A.D.C., 95, 123, 169, 218
Physical Science Study Committee,
  128
Piaget, J., 75, 76, 88, 165, 200, 201,
  230
Poland
  ICSITM meeting in (1960), 164
Powell, Dr, 107, 109–11, 113, 114,
  115
power
  and resources, 26–31
  see also resources

primary schools, 119, 122
probability theory, 112–13, 136, 138, 161, 162, 188, 239, 241, 263
professions, 8, 22, 24, 26–30, 31, 276
public schools, 27, 35–6, 63, 111, 251, 254, 273, 276
  see also independent schools; mathematics, and selective schools
Pugsley, Sir A., 168

Quadling, D.A., 62, 96, 108, 109, 110, 111, 120, 149, 151, 237, 244

raising of the school leaving age, 168
Rankin, 216
redefinition
  and curriculum, 277–83
resources, 26–31, 75–6, 79–81, 94, 144, 150, 153, 157, 167, 171, 184, 197, 209–33, 235–70, 272–4, 277–8, 281–2
Reuter, 120
Revised Code (1862), 36, 41
Robins, M.F., 215
Rollett, A.P., 61–2, 106, 127, 145–7, 148–9, 155, 168, 169, 176–7, 201, 237
Rolls Royce, 101, 103
Rosenhead, L., 131, 134–5, 137, 174, 184, 185
Royal Society, 106, 146, 223
Royaumont seminar (1959), 86, 158–67, 169, 171, 191, 192, 194, 200, 204, 230, 240, 277
rural studies, 2
Russia
  see Union of Soviet Socialist Republics

St. Dunstan's project
  see Contemporary School Mathematics project
School Certificate, 39
School Mathematics Project (SMP), 1, 2, 3, 4, 13, 16, 18, 19, 62, 63, 76, 91, 94, 95, 96, 107, 108, 118, 132, 134, 151, 153, 165, 166, 173, 176, 189, 191, 193, 223, 235–70, 274, 275,

276, 278, 279, 280, 281, 282
  compared with MME, 242–50, 265
  critical reactions to, 250–66
  funds of, 242–4, 249, 265
  meetings attended by members of, 244
  personnel of, 237, 249
  proposals of, 237–9
  schools associated with, 246–7
  teacher training conferences of, 249
School Mathematics Study Group (SMSG), 128, 181, 183, 189, 191, 197, 198–9, 245
Schools Council, 17–19, 243, 250, 273
science, 22, 107, 108, 209–10, 221, 236, 248
Science Masters' Association, 94, 221
Scott, 102–3, 120, 136, 144, 149
secondary modern schools, 27, 42–7, 50–1, 63, 78–83, 87, 119, 131, 140, 142, 151, 200, 201, 202–3, 242, 256–8, 275–6
Secondary Schools Examination Council (SSEC), 39
selective schools
  see mathematics, and selective schools
Sellers, 224
Servais, W., 162
Shell Petroleum Ltd, 94, 134
Shipbuilding Industry Training Board, 256
Siddons, 37
Smith, 170
SMP
  see School Mathematics Project
SMSG
  see School Mathematics Study Group
social class, 15, 19, 27, 36
social conflict, 20
social structure, 14–15, 20, 26–31
sociology
  of education, 2, 7,9
  functionalist, 14–15
  Marxist, 14–15
  and mathematics, *passim*
  of the professions, 2, 7, 8
  of science, 2, 7–13

Weberian, 14–15
Southampton, University of, 173, 174
Southampton conference (1961), 96,
  122, 167, 173–99, 200, 203, 209,
  210, 212, 215, 217, 218, 220, 222,
  224, 225, 229, 231, 237, 238, 239,
  243
  Central Committee of the, 197–9
  Concluding Chapter Committee of
    the, 197–9
  finance for the, 182
  Industrial Committee of the, 197–9
  finance for the, 182
  Industrial Committee of the, 186–7
  Introductory Chapter Committee
    of the, 184–6
  'Mathematics in Schools'
    Committee of the, 189–94
  participation in the, 175–81
  'School to University' Committee
    of the, 187–9
  University Mathematics
    Committee of the, 194–7
Sputnik satellite, 128
statistics, 57, 61, 81, 99, 100–1, 103,
  112–13, 119, 136, 137, 138, 141–2,
  148, 160, 161, 162, 187, 239
Stewart, W.A.C., 218
Stockholm, 203–4
Stoker, 244
Stone, M.H., 159
structure
  and curriculum change, 272–4
subjects
  'careers' of, 22–5
  changes within, 13–25
  concept of, 10, 13–25
  and individuals, 29
  mathematics as, *see* mathematics
  and resources, 26–31; *see also*
    resources
  as social systems, 10, 26–31
Swain, 183, 189, 192
symbolic interactionism, 8, 22

Tammadge, 78, 132, 149, 176, 189,
  193, 218, 232
Taunton Report, 36, 41
Taylor, 102, 104, 117–18, 120

Teacher Advisory Council, 219
teachers
  and change, 64
  and educational subcultures, 27–8
  and mathematics curriculum,
    passim
  and Oxford conference, 96–7, 105–
    22
  and Liverpool conference, 130–4,
    142–4, 148–54
  shortage of, *see* teachers, supply of
  supply of, 92–3, 106, 117, 127, 129,
    139–40, 143–4, 145, 147, 148–9,
    166, 167, 168, 170, 174, 183–6,
    195, 198, 210–11, 213, 217, 218–
    19, 220, 222, 230, 246, 277
  training of, 63, 116, 129–30, 139,
    185, 199
Teaching Mathematics, On, 175, 181,
  183, 194, 197, 204, 211
technical colleges, 106, 131–3, 140–2,
  148, 214, 218
technical schools, 247
Technical School Headmasters'
  Association (Midland Region), 240
textbooks
  functions of, 31
  and mathematics, 31, 69, 72–3, 86,
    129, 141, 143–4, 151, 161, 163,
    167, 192, 194, 198, 199, 235–70,
    275, 280
  in schools, 12–13, *see also*
    textbooks, and mathematics
  and science education, 10–12
Theron, P., 159
Thwaites, B., 2, 4, 96, 108, 153, 158,
  167, 173–99, 209–23, 231, 237–9,
  242–5, 248–9, 255, 261–2, 265, 269
  278
Tomkys, 143–4, 148
Tory party
  see Conservative party
Trends, 254
trigonometry, 37, 38, 39, 52, 136, 161,
  259, 263
Trivett, 86, 164
TUC Conference (1960), 168
Tucker, Prof., 162
Tumau, 164

UGC
  see University Grants Committee
Union of Soviet Socialist Republics
  (USSR)
  mathematics education in, 145
  space programme of, 128
  technology in, 98
  threat from, 93
United States of America (USA)
  mathematics in, 127, 128–30, 141,
    146, 147, 159, 161, 162, 165, 166,
    167, 181, 198–9, 205, 213, 215,
    218, 245, 252, 254, 276
  science education in, 10–11
  technology in, 98
University Grants Committee
  (UGC), 139
universities
  entrance requirements for, 94–5,
    148, 170, 189, 194, 212, 221, 229,
    248–9
  and knowledge definition, 15, 16
  and mathematics, 3, 10, 12–13, 18,
    30, 31, 35, 37, 41, 54–63, 64,
    75–6, 77, 81, 88, 91–125, 127–
    55, 159–67, 175–81, 183, 184–6,
    187–97, 198, 199, 201, 204, 205,
    209, 211–23, 224, 225, 229, 230,

    235, 237, 238, 246, 248–9, 250,
    251, 252–4, 266, 272, 273–4,
    275–6, 278–9, 280, 281–2
  and professional issues, 28
Unwin, 108, 109, 111, 119

Varlow, 140–1
vector analysis, 112, 113, 138, 148,
  160, 162
Vice-Chancellors' Committee, 219–
  20, 222
Vickers [Company], 94
Victorian period, 36

Waddams, 109, 110, 111, 121
Wall, 159
Waltham, 228–9
Weberian sociology, 14–15
Wheeler, D.H., 225, 229
Wilmore, 138, 148
Wilson, 169
Winchester [school], 111
Woodford, T.E.C., 168
Wooldridge, 115
Worcester, 249
World of Mathematics, 259

Young, 137–8